JUNG'S HERMENEUTIC OF DOCTRINE

American Academy of Religion
Dissertation Series

edited by
H. Ganse Little, Jr.

Number 32

JUNG'S HERMENEUTIC OF DOCTRINE
Its Theological Significance
by
Clifford A. Brown

Clifford A. Brown
Jung's Hermeneutic of Doctrine

Its Theological
Significance

=Scholars Press=

Distributed by
Scholars Press
101 Salem Street
Chico, California 95926

JUNG'S HERMENEUTIC OF DOCTRINE
Its Theological Significance

Clifford A. Brown
Ph.D., 1977, University of Chicago
Chicago, Illinois

Library of Congress Cataloging in Publication Data

Brown, Clifford Alan
    Jung's hermeneutic of doctrine.

    (American Academy of Religion dissertation series ;
no. 32)
    Bibliography: p.
    Includes index.
    1. Psychoanalysis and religion. 2. Theology,
Doctrinal—History—20th century. 3. Jung, Carl
Gustav, 1875–1961. I. Title. II. Series: American
Academy of Religion. Dissertation series—American
Academy of Religion ; no. 32.
BF175.B69   230'.01'9   80-20795
ISBN 0-89130-437-1 (pbk.)

Printed in the United States of America
1 2 3 4 5
Edwards Brothers, Inc.
Ann Arbor, Michigan 48106

TABLE OF CONTENTS

ACKNOWLEDGEMENTS

I wish to express my indebtedness to those members of the Analytical Psychology Club of Chicago whose friendship sustained me during the most difficult and intensive years of research that went into this dissertation and whose keen interest in the practical ramifications of Jung's psychology catalyzed and enriched my efforts to come to terms with Jung. I also want to thank David Tracy and Peter Homans, not only for the substantive contributions they have made to the dissertation's shape and design, but also for the steadying guidance they have offered me throughout its writing.

I am grateful to my father, the Divinity School of the University of Chicago, and the University of Winnipeg for having extended to me financial assistance. Thanks also are due to Langdon Gilkey for his penetrating comments on Chapters IV and V of the dissertation, and to Barry Robinson and Andris Taskans for their editorial assistance.

Finally, allow me to offer a word of thanks to my friends and family for patiently enduring my own impatience and frustrations with what so often seemed to be an interminable task.

INTRODUCTION

C. G. Jung's interpretation of Christian doctrine has held
a certain fascination for theologians for several decades now.
This is evident in the abundance of commentary on Jung's
thought that has appeared in recent theological literature.
Despite this widespread interest in Jung, however, there has
yet to emerge a consensus on the nature and extent of the
theological significance of his doctrinal studies.

This is not surprising for a number of reasons. For one,
the range of viewpoints expressed in this commentary is as broad
and varied as is the diversity of interests, styles and stances
that characterizes theological inquiry in the contemporary
period. Because there is no single dominant style, tradition
or method that shapes and gives homogeneity to the discipline
of theology today, it can hardly be expected that theological
interpretations of Jung will display a uniformity of viewpoint.

Secondly, the very nature of Jung's style of thinking poses
difficulties for those who would come to terms with him. His
thought moves in many directions and on many levels. He jumps
from clinical to cultural materials and then back again,
bridging between personal and collective worlds of imagery and
meaning, between modern and ancient times, between West and
East, etc. In so doing he digresses, amplifies, and "free
associates" to the point where it is exhausting to follow him.
To compound these difficulties, the terminology he employs is
oftentimes fluid and at many points ambiguous. For these
reasons, Jung's thought has invited misunderstanding, confusion
and even consternation.

Thirdly, Jung's personal ties and close collaboration with
Sigmund Freud, during the years 1906-1912, have served to
further complicate the efforts of theologians to enter into
conversation with him. His much publicized break with Freud
was perceived by many to have been intimately bound up with the
two's divergent interpretations of religion. Because the
theological community had discerned in Freud's psychologization

1

of religion an extreme antipathy towards it, they expected and
hoped all the more to find in Jung someone who would set forth
an explicitly positive evaluation of the religious dimension
of human life.

To a certain extent these expectations were met, but not
entirely, for the acrimony of the debate between Freud and
Jung could not long disguise the indebtedness of the latter to
the work of the former.[1] The lines of filiation between the
two were eventually to awaken in some theologians the same kind
of wariness with Jung that Freud's "psychologism" had elicited
earlier. Theology's initial interest in and indeed enthusiasm
for Jung's positive regard for religion did not succeed, then,
in dispelling an uneasiness vis-à-vis his attempts to psycholo-
gize religious forms of expression. It was to prove as difficult
in Jung's case as it had proved in Freud's to gauge the extent
to which his personal religious predilections influenced and
colored the psychological workings of his method when applied
to religion. The fact that these predilections contrasted
sharply with those of Freud only served in the long run to
render more problematic, not less, the efforts of some theologians to come to terms with Jung.

All of these factors have considerably dimmed the once
lively prospects for an on-going dialogue and even collaboration
between Jungian psychology and Christian theology. We concur
with James Heisig when he writes:

> It would, I think, be fair to characterize the
> present state of scholarly relations between Jungian
> psychology and theology as chaotic. If one takes the
> trouble to study the shelves of books and reams of
> articles that have appeared on the subject, one is
> consistently left with the impression of an adventure-
> some, potentially fruitful and perhaps even revolutionary
> inter-disciplinary project that has somehow failed to
> make a presentable case for itself. The initial
> skirmishes between uninformed critics and uncritical
> devotees have gone on unabated and the few flashes of
> brilliance have done little to enlighten matters.
> Darkness continues to hover over the waters. Perhaps
> every human process of creativity requires such a
> period of chaos; but until we can acknowledge this
> state for the *rudis indigestaque moles* that it is,
> we can have no hope of moving through it.[2]

This "chaotic" state of affairs would seem to counsel us
to adopt one of two courses: either resignation to an opportunity

now lost or the fashioning of a new line of approach. We have
chosen the latter course. We do so full well cognizant of the
problems and pitfalls that have bedevilled many a theological
commentator on Jung. This recent history notwithstanding, we
shall not be dissuaded from our own efforts to come to terms
with him. It is incumbent upon us, especially given the limited
success of previous efforts in this regard, to set forth in
these introductory remarks what it is that impels us to take
up this task anew.

The principal factor that leads us to do so is our strong
suspicion that Jung's psychology and in particular his psychology of *doctrine* may well prove to serve theology well as a
resource with which to resolve a number of issues contemporary
theologians are presently confronted with. Chief among these
is the issue of what we shall call the communicative power of
Christianity's central doctrinal expressions. Of what does
this power consist? How can one account for its apparent wane
in the modern period? Why is it that Christianity's central
doctrinal expressions no longer seem capable of conveying
meaning with the power and freshness and compellingness that
they once did? In what ways might their communicative power
be rediscovered and take on new life?

We shall attempt to demonstrate in the course of our study
that Jung's psychology of doctrine goes considerable lengths
towards resolving the issues these questions raise. Because
the Christian theologian is inevitably confronted with them
today, because they are *his* questions as well as Jung's, it
seems to us that he can only benefit from giving serious
consideration to the way Jung deals with them. And so we
propose in what follows to make of doctrine and its interpretation the common meeting-ground between Jungian psychology and
Christian theology.

But it is not only this shared set of concerns and
questions that has led us to conceive of our study of Jung as
a study of his psychology of doctrine. A number of strategic
considerations have also suggested to us the advisability of
doing so. First and foremost of these is the fact that it was
above all else to doctrine that Jung turned when he addressed
himself to specifically Christian themes, to the Christian

faith and tradition. Because he accorded to doctrine a
privileged place in the whole sweep of his interpretive
studies of religious materials,[3] we are persuaded that an
examination of his work in this particular domain will be
instrumental in shedding light on the purposes, method and
results of his psychology of religion in general.

Secondly, the fact that Jung's interpretation of doctrine,
perhaps more than any other facet of his work, has provoked
heated controversy counsels us to take careful heed of it.
For it is only by scrutinizing anew those elements of his
thinking that have given rise to controversy that we can reason-
ably expect to resolve the issues underlying it. These issues
have posed serious obstacles to the kind of theological collaboration with Jung we are here envisioning. Clearly, then, we
will need to address ourselves to Jung's psychology of doctrine
explicitly if we are to hope to contribute to improving the
prospects for this collaboration.

For these reasons Jung's doctrinal studies invite the
attention of those theologians who wish to enter into conversation with him. For these reasons we will make this area of
his work the central object of our inquiry.

If our remarks thus far have indicated where it is that
we will engage in theological conversation with Jung, we have
yet to explain how we propose to do so. How will we approach
our topic? How do we intend to organize and structure our
inquiry? We will begin our study by taking stock of previous
attempts on theology's part to come to terms with Jung. We
shall do so in order to highlight the problems and possibilities
inherent in the most frequently employed ways of reading him.

The three chapters to follow will comprise the main body,
the heart, of the dissertation. They will hinge on Chapter III--
an attempt to reconstruct the manner in which Jung's psychological method of interpretation emerged and took shape in the
course of his efforts to interpret a broad range of what we
shall term *fantasy* materials.[4] We will attempt to show that
the inner workings of this method were originally devised in a
domain (fantasy) quite distinct from the domain of our more
immediate interests (doctrine), and only subsequently applied to
the latter.

Focusing first on Jung's interpretive work with fantasy and only then--in Chapter IV--moving to his psychology of doctrine will enable us to bring to light the nature of the integral relationship between the latter and the whole of Jung's psychological work and thought. It will help assure that we do not excise the one from the other, that we approach our topic with the clinical and therapeutic aims and concerns of his psychology clearly in mind. And it will serve as a means by which we will be able to familiarize ourselves with the most distinctive features of Jung's version of depth psychology without having at the same time to survey the whole sweep of it.

And so in Chapters III and IV of our study, we will differentiate these two domains of his interpretive work, analyze them each in turn, and then juxtapose and compare our findings in each of them. Our immediate purpose in so doing will be to reconstruct the methodological underpinnings that give unity to the whole of this interpretive work, and thereby to bring to light the singular nature of Jung's method and its achievement. Our ultimate purpose will be to demonstrate how theology stands to benefit from an appropriation of specific features of this method.

We will argue that Jung's is a method whose principal aim is to unearth and elucidate dimensions of meaning that are not immediately self-evident and apparent. It seeks above all else to disclose these hidden and elusive reaches of meaning--what we shall call with Jung the *symbolic* reaches of meaning inherent in that which is undergoing interpretation, whether it be fantasy or doctrine. To our mind this is precisely what *hermeneutical* modes of reflection are specifically designed and uniquely suited to do.[5] It is for this reason that we have deemed it fitting and clarifying to term Jung's method a hermeneutical one.

The central importance that the symbolic assumes in all of Jung's interpretive work has dictated that we abstract therefrom and set forth his understanding of it at the outset of our exposition of his method. We shall do so in Chapter II below. Our findings here will be foundational for everything that follows; they will enable us to anticipate in a provisional way how we shall ultimately envision the unity of method and

purpose that undergirds Jung's studies of fantasy and doctrinal
materials.

This long search for the methodological underpinnings of
Jung's work will comprise the middle three chapters of our
study. They will be framed by two chapters--the one, a survey
and evaluation of Jung's theological interpreters; the other,
an attempt, by way of conclusion, to appraise the theological
value of his hermeneutic in the light of our findings in the
intervening chapters. Both chapters will serve to situate our
study of this hermeneutic in relationship to what we have here
envisioned to be an on-going and far-reaching dialogue with
Jung. The former will focus on how others have perceived the
challenges and opportunities of such a dialogue; the latter,
on how we perceive them.

We have in the foregoing outlined in skeletal form how we
intend to organize our account of Jung's hermeneutic of
Christian doctrine. We need now to clarify what it is that
leads us to expect that the particular line of approach to Jung
we are proposing here will improve the prospects for a fruitful
collaboration between Jungian psychology and Christian theology.
It is incumbent on us to do so, especially in view of the fact
that theology's previous efforts to come to terms with Jung
have met with only limited success.

We have reason to believe that our own efforts in this
regard will contribute to the dialogue between Jung and theology
if they prove to clarify the nature of the method underlying
Jung's interpretive work and in particular his doctrinal studies.
For it is our view that theology cannot hope to benefit from
the results of this work if the method that yielded these
results is not first taken account of. And we have found, for
reasons that will become clear in Chapter I, that it is precisely
at this critical juncture--viz. the methodological foundations
of his psychology--that theological interpreters of Jung have
been most prone to misconstrue him. It is these considerations
that have led us to conceive of our study of Jung's interpretation of Christian doctrine as an examination of the *method*
operative therein.

We would hope, moreover, that calling attention to the *hermeneutical* nature of this method and correlatively to its deep respect for the inherently *symbolic* nature of Christian doctrine will increase the likelihood that theology will stand to benefit from it. For heretofore commentators on Jung have neglected to explicate what we will argue is the distinctive mode of hermeneutical reflection at work in Jung's psychology.[6] Our efforts to do so are undertaken with this neglect in mind. Approaching our subject in this way, in a way that others have not attempted, may well prove to cast fresh light on it.

More importantly, this line of approach has been fashioned in order ultimately to facilitate a consideration on theology's part of the possible uses it might make of Jung's hermeneutic in the light of its current efforts to draw upon a whole range of hermeneutical modes of reflection and to explicate the symbolic dimensions of meaning inherent in religious language and phenomena.

To be sure, his hermeneutic is but one among many that have emerged in the last one hundred odd years; and his understanding of the nature of symbolism constitutes but one of many theories that presently elicit the theologian's attention. Ideally theology should aim to take account of the whole plethora of these methods and theories. It would be premature on our part to attempt to articulate here why it is that theology, confronted as it is by this impressive array of methods, should give particular consideration to Jung's. We will not do so until we have examined at close hand the various components of this method and the ways in which Jung has put it to use. We may anticipate, however, from the very manner in which we have framed our inquiry, that when we turn in its concluding chapter to a delineation of those aspects of his psychology of doctrine that theology stands most to benefit from, many will have direct bearing on the issues of symbol and hermeneutics and their role in theological reflection. The fact that these issues are vital ones in contemporary theological discussion gives us all the more reason to hope that the line of approach to Jung we have fashioned here will pave the way for a fruitful collaboration between his psychology and Christian theology.

It is this hope that motivates us to undertake the study
we have here been readying ourselves to undertake; it is this
hope that will animate our study from beginning to end. We
cannot now know, however, whether or not this hope will be
fulfilled, not at least pending completion of the inquiry we
have here mapped out.

Having outlined some of the factors that have complicated
and hampered theology's efforts to "converse" with Jung, having
explained what it is that impels us to enter into these
conversations and where we propose to do so, having outlined
how we intend to structure and organize our discussion, and
finally, having stated why we feel that the way we will do so
stands a fair chance of yielding significant results, we are
now prepared to take up the tasks that we have set for ourselves.

CHAPTER I

THEOLOGICAL INTERPRETERS OF JUNG

We begin our study with a survey of the variety of
responses Jung's religious thought has met with in recent
theological literature. We make this our starting point in
order 1) to clarify the nature of the options available to
theologians who would wish to come to terms with Jung, 2) to
shed some light on the range of methodological stances and
styles presupposed by these responses, 3) to evaluate the
limitations and achievements of each of them, and 4) to better
assure that our own approach to Jung will be viewed as just
that, as one approach among many, and at the same time as one
that has taken shape with the values and limits of other approaches clearly in mind.

Before proceeding, we will specify some of the parameters
within which this chapter is conceived. First of all, we do
not purport to offer here an exhaustive survey; the sheer
number of commentaries that have appeared in the last three or
four decades would not make such an undertaking feasible.
Rather we will limit ourselves to a representative sampling of
a selected number of resources. Nor will we attempt to address
ourselves to all manner of commentary on Jung's religious
thought; it is the *theological* commentary and literature that
is our particular concern. Accordingly, we have singled out
for examination here those writings which address themselves to
explicitly theological issues and to the ways Jung entertains
and raises such issues. All of them have been authored either
by theologians by vocation, or by those who, coming at Jung
from related fields, are sufficiently interested in theological
questions and in the theological significance of Jung's work,
to have entered into, for the purposes of their study, an
explicitly theological line of inquiry. This means that we
will exclude from our purview those readings of Jung's religious
thought undertaken from the vantage point of many other disciplines, e.g., literary criticism, anthropology, history of
religions, etc.[1]

Finally, it is our purpose here to survey theological
readings of Jung, not the many subtle, scarcely detectable ways
Jung has influenced and permeated the twentieth century
theological mind. Hence in what follows we will address ourselves to those works which explicitly and self-consciously
advance a thoroughgoing interpretation of Jung's religious ideas
and of their bearing on manifestly theological concerns. To be
sure, we will encounter among them some readings of Jung which
do not limit themselves to commentary and analysis per se, but
instead move in synthetic and constructive directions, and
show themselves to be grounded in a personal appropriation of
Jung that makes of him a creative resource for theologizing
proper. We shall see, however, that only certain styles of
reading him ready theology for such an appropriation, and we do
not wish to confine our attention to these alone. Rather we
wish to illumine the complex of reasons, methodological and
otherwise, that lead some to deny the very possibility of such
an appropriation, while leading others to unhesitatingly
undertake it.

One further preliminary is in order--we have adopted an
order of exposition that will allow recurring and contrasting
features of various readings of Jung to come to light as we
proceed. We will not attempt to characterize and differentiate
these features ahead of time, but only as we encounter them in
the course of what follows.

We begin with Father Raymond Hostie's *Religion and the
Psychology of C. G. Jung*.[2] We do so because it is one of the
most extensive studies of the totality of Jung's religious
thought, and because it epitomizes a style of reading Jung that
is very pervasive in theological literature. We will not
attempt to take the whole of the work into our purview; rather
we wish to confine our comments to those aspects of it which
attempt to delineate and come to terms with the method Jung
employs in addressing himself to specifically religious themes
and questions.

Hostie divides the development of Jung's religious ideas
into three periods: 1) 1905-1912, when he was most under the
influence of Freud; 2) 1912-1937, when his more "pscyhological"

or clinically oriented works were written; and 3) 1937-   ,
when he became more interested in religion for its own sake.[3]
In the first two periods, i.e., until late into his life and
work, we are told that Jung remained almost exclusively identified with "Kant's theoretical agnosticism."[4] This methodological stance is construed as "the postulate of the unknowability of the object in itself," which held for Jung the
"advantage of freeing his investigations from any sort of
supervision by philosophy or theology."[5]

Hostie shows himself to be uncertain as to how to come to
terms with this earlier stage in Jung's development. On the
one hand Jung's Kantian "agnosticism" frees him to approach
religion in a way commensurate with his professedly "empirical"
standpoint;[6] on the other hand it militates against his being
able to shed any light on the nature of the relationship
between religious phenomena and "objective" reality: "How is
it possible to regard religion as an irreducible function if it
does not bear any relation to any objective reality?"[7]

But if he finds questionable Jung's adoption of a scientific
empirical standpoint, he is even more troubled by the fact that
in his later period Jung appears to move beyond this standpoint
altogether:

>...he went right outside the field of psychology
>and plunged head foremost into the error committed
>by so many scientists: dazzled by the effectiveness
>of their empirical method within their own science,
>they have no eyes for any methods of an ontological
>kind.[8]

It is evident that Hostie sees Jung to be encroaching upon
ground not properly his own, upon terrain that ought to be
occupied by theology, and theology alone.

Nowhere does this viewpoint come more clearly to the fore
than in his critique of Jung's forays into the field of doctrinal
interpretation:

>Jung's comparative researches have not put theology
>in his debt; on the contrary, they have only increased
>the danger, not only that the absolute transcendence
>of the mystery will be lost sight of, but, even more,
>that people will give themselves a pat on the back
>for having come to such a vast comprehension and
>understanding of the dogma that faith itself is no
>longer necessary.

> ...When he comes to the end of his investigation
> he is further away from the dogma of the Trinity than
> ever, despite having begun with the actual words used
> by the Church Councils.
>   Jung's attempts to make the dogma of the Trinity
> acceptable are rotten at the root.[9]

It is this deep concern to safeguard the "absolute transcendence
of the mystery" that leads Hostie to reject any and all attempts
to offer a psychological interpretation of dogma.[10] It is not
simply psychology per se, however, that endangers dogma, but
rather any attempt on the part of reason to penetrate "the
mystery": "*Nothing* drawn from *any* idea of God can help to
throw *any* light on God's being."[11] In view of this seemingly
unbridgeable gap between man's ideas of God and God himself,
one wonders what positive role is left for theology to play, if
it cannot employ images, conceptions, and/or constructs of the
divine.

     In concluding his study, Hostie sets forth what he believes
to be some of the values and limits of psychological studies of
religious phenomena:

> ...I accept the validity of a psychological study
> "of the religious person" and "of religion proper,
> i.e., of religious contents." In itself such a study
> can add nothing to our intellectual understanding of
> dogma, nor does it help us to practice any religious
> ideal; it can however help us indirectly towards a
> better appreciation of anything non-genuine in
> religious attitudes and of the repercussions that
> psychic dispositions can have in symbolic represen-
> tations of revealed truths.[12]

What is of particular interest to us in this statement is that
it is dogma and dogma alone that Hostie claims to be immune
from psychological interpretation, and this despite the fact
that he fails to explain why dogmatic expressions are not to be
included among "religious contents" in general or "symbolic
representations of revealed truths" in particular. For, as we
shall see in Chapter IV below, it is dogma that Jung's psychology of religion is most manifestly concerned with. In view of
the central place his interpretation of dogma occupies therein,
it is not surprising that Hostie tends to regard the whole of
it as a transgression into a seemingly sacrosanct realm.

     In summary, we have seen that Hostie finds wanting Jung's
earlier as well as his later approaches to the study of religion--

the former because the "determination to remain absolutely faithful to the proven methods of his own science"[13] that it is based upon renders him impotent to discourse on the "objective realities" that underlie religious phenomena, and the latter because he transcends these "proven methods" and attempts to discourse on matters he is not competent to pass judgment on. In assessing these criticisms, we should underscore the obvious--they are based on the presupposition that psychological and theological methods, modes of discourse and interpretation, and realms of subject-matter are distinct; the distinction and differentiation is not to be eroded or mitigated in any way. In evidence implicitly throughout the work, this standpoint becomes explicit in its concluding section:

> ...psychology can tell us nothing about metaphysics or theology in themselves or anything about their specific object....
>   ...The religious function is rooted in man, but revealed truths have their source in God; and whenever these two realities come together, any confusion of them is fatal.[14]

Hostie's work is to be valued for recognizing some of the ways Jung undercuts this differentiation, especially in his later work. For this reason, his is a useful study, which reveals that Jung is a religious thinker who cannot be contained or confined in any one sphere, who moves across and subverts the most carefully constructed of methodological boundaries.[15] And yet the very recognition of this fact constitutes sufficient grounds, given Hostie's axiomatic starting-point, for discounting the theological relevance of his psychological interpretation of Christian doctrine. The result, given the central importance of the latter in Jung's work, is a severe constriction of the possibilities for collaboration between theology and Jungian psychology.

To recapitulate, we have found in Hostie's work a clear expression of a theological style of reading Jung, a style which does not hesitate to recognize that his psychology does in fact impinge at critical junctures upon Christian theology, but which at the same time is sharply critical of it precisely at those points where it does so.

We have encountered elements of this style--epitomized
perhaps better than anyone else by Hostie--in a goodly number
of other works, the most important of which we wish to refer to
here, even if we may not submit them to detailed textual scrutiny.

Howard L. Philp's *Jung and the Problem of Evil*[16] is a
personal response to Jung's religious views, the outcome of an
extended correspondence with him. Philp begins his study by
avowing:

> My interest in psychology was stimulated because
> I believed that with the writings of Freud, Jung and
> other workers on the psychology of the unconscious,
> new knowledge of the utmost importance for theology
> and pastoral work was becoming available....If modern
> man were in search of a soul I felt that the Church
> was the place where he should be helped to find it,
> and no study which might contribute to this end should
> be neglected.[17]

He goes on to acknowledge that he turned critic of Jung only
after many years of sincere seeking after psychology's truth,
adding: "If I have become a critic it is not that I like this
role but because I have been disappointed in my search, expect-
ing too much, promised too much, and disbelieving many of the
answers to my questions."[18]

There then follows a critique of the consistency with
which Jung adheres to an empirical standpoint and method:

> ...instead of sometimes insisting, as Freud did,
> on being an empiricist, whatever that might mean or
> however short a distance that will carry you, I
> believe that it would be more accurate to acknowledge
> that you have been driven to deal with subjects where
> you have either to become a metaphysician or a
> theologian with the equipment which these must have,
> or to pass the subjects over to those who have this.[19]

Here Philp is attempting to call Jung to a response, to a
clarification of the seeming discrepancies between his professions and his performance. And although in so doing he appears,
like Hostie, to find fault with Jung for having disregarded
certain methodological constraints, he shows himself less
certain than does Hostie as to which of the two--profession or
performance--needs to be brought into conformity with the other.
On the one hand he calls Jung to recognize that he has assumed
many of the theologian's tasks; on the other hand, he appeals
to him to stop short of undertaking them:

> Surely you must admit, if your approach is purely
> empirical, that you are dealing with nothing more
> than psychological phenomena, and that any theological
> and metaphysical implications attached to them should
> be left to theologians and metaphysicians. No one
> could be more honest in intention than you are, but
> you do not, I think, realize how far you have moved
> into theological and metaphysical realms in much
> of your later work, such as *Answer to Job* and *Aion*.[20]

This statement serves well as an illustration of what we
would term a "minimalist" reading of the meaning of *psychological*, i.e., one that makes of psychic meanings and expressions
"nothing more than" what they ostensibly are. But, as we shall
argue when we turn to this question in the chapter to follow, it
is Jung's recognition of and respect for the symbolic dimension
of meaning inherent in all psychic life that is the most
distinctive feature of his understanding of the human psyche.
And it is nowhere more evident than here, than in his reliance
on the symbolic, that for Jung the psyche is irreducible and
unfathomable in its reaches and depths. A "minimalist" reading
of psychic meaning and the human psyche, then, is simply not
reconcilable with his intentions, professions and with the
whole thrust of his psychology.

If we are right in so arguing, if Philp is mis-reading Jung
here at this most fundamental of points, then we cannot but
conclude that the whole of his interpretation of Jung's religious
thought is handicapped from the very beginning. It is one thing
to set over against Jung's an alternative view of the nature of
the psyche; it is another to attribute to him a view that is not
his own and then to fault him for not remaining true to it.

Joseph Goldbrunner, a German Catholic priest-theologian,
is yet another of the proponents of this way of reading Jung.
His work, *Individuation: A Study of the Depth Psychology of Carl
Gustav Jung*,[21] is important, because more forthrightly than any
other work we have encountered, it interprets Jung's religious
thought as "psychologism," which is defined by Goldbrunner as
"the levelling down of supra-psychic realities to the level of
purely psychic reality."[22] No attempt is made, however, to
elaborate on the meaning of either "supra-psychic" or "purely
psychic" here; and so the reader is left with scant indication

of why Goldbrunner wishes to differentiate them, nor with any
inkling of whether he conceives of them as inter-related
realities.

We see in this notion of psychologism the same minimalist
understanding of psychic reality that appears in Philp. This
recurring theme alerts us to its central importance in the whole
style of reading Jung we have been examining. For the principal
concern of this style is to maintain a differentiation between
psychological and theological areas and modes of inquiry that
is sufficiently clear-cut to enable one to identify without
ambiguity those psychological inquiries into matters religious
which are encroachments or infringements upon a clearly demar-
cated theological sphere of discourse. Now any minimalization
of the breadth and depth of psychic reality will constitute a
corresponding restriction in the range of questions and scope
of subject-matter a psychologist will feel competent to entertain and include in his purview. And such a restriction no
doubt serves well those who wish to decrease the likelihood of
an overlapping of psychological and theological terrains.

But before evaluating this way of reading Jung, we wish
first to include brief mention of the interpretation Martin
Buber presents in his *Eclipse of God*.[23] Here we encounter a
less wide-ranging, but nonetheless more penetrating critique of
Jung than any of those surveyed thus far.

It is Jung's passing utterances on revelation and faith,
and his more extensive discussions of the God-question that
most disturb Buber. If it is the human subject that hears and
sees in "the depths of the human soul" what is disclosed to it
with the power of a revelation, then the content of such a
revelation is presumed to emanate from the soul, to be derived
from it, to have been "produced" by it.[24] Similarly if an image
of deity is experienced by recourse to the soul, then, Buber
tells us, it is really a question of the soul experiencing
itself.[25] And so, to his mind, Jung's psychology of religion is
at its heart a religious psychology, a "religion of pure psychic
immanence,"[26] in which no distinction is possible between the
subject and object of religious experience.

Such a religion is no more than a "pseudo-religion," for it fails to "bear witness to an essential personal relation to One who is experienced or believed in as being absolutely over against one."[27] Jung is consequently made to resemble Feuerbach: "The Godhead no longer takes the place of the human self as it did in mankind up till now. Man now draws back the projection of his self on a God outside of him....In His place he knows the soul or rather the self."[28]

The thrust of Buber's critique, then, centers on his contention that Jung moves so far in the direction of a collapse of the distinction between God and the soul or self as to render an inter-personal relationship between the two inconceivable. And in so doing he undercuts the very ground of Judaeo-Christian theism.[29] Moreover, and this is what is of particular interest to us here, Buber traces this inadequate differentiation between the human soul's experience of itself and of the divine, between its self-images and its God-images, back to Jung's failure to differentiate psychological from religious concerns and questions:

> What Jung is to be criticized for...is that he over-
> steps with sovereign license the boundaries of
> psychology in its more essential point....
>   ...he makes assertions about religious subjects
> which overstep the realms of the psychiatric and the
> psychological--contrary to his assurance that he
> remains strictly inside them.[30]

We see, then, that Buber gives voice to his criticisms in ways strikingly similar to Hostie, Philp, et al.

It should by now be sufficiently apparent that a wide range of theologians of varied religious backgrounds and from differ-ing theological vantage-points share deep misgivings over the extent to which Jung oversteps his professedly empirical approach to religion. The frequency with which these misgivings are voiced counsels us to give careful heed to them.

On the one hand we recognize that Jung has brought upon himself much of these criticisms. Here we are in agreement with those who, like Philp, point out the disparities between his methodological professions and his performance. Surely it is these disparities that have invited the consternation and misunderstanding Jung's work has so often met with in the

theological community. We have found, in fact, that the
professions most noted by the theological commentators surveyed
above--Jung's appeal to such terms as "empirical," "phenomenological,"[31] and even "metaphysical" neutrality[32]--are vague and
misleading attempts to describe the stance and method at work
in his psychology of religion.

But does this dearth of terminological clarity constitute
sufficient reason for dismissing the theological import of
Jung's work? We would argue that it does not. For one, these
are not the only methodological designations Jung has recourse
to; he also calls his a "constructive" method, or, as we shall
see, a "symbolic" as distinct from a semiotic method, and even
refers to it on one occasion as a "hermeneutic" one.[33] To our
mind these designations merit closer attention than they have
heretofore received, and certainly more scrutiny than the terms
which have so often preoccupied Jung's theological interpreters.[34]

Secondly, however, and even more importantly, the very
evidence of this terminological ambiguity in Jung's writings
provides all the more reason to look beyond it, to examine his
method in act, to attend to his performance, as distinct from
his professions. For we suspect that his performance outstripped
his conceptualizations of it, that the method he relied upon
came to be devised only in the course of his interpretive work.
If we are correct in this surmise, we can reconstruct the nature
of the method only by examining closely the content of this work.

But if Jung has brought upon himself many of these misgivings, we feel that the way in which the theologians surveyed
above give voice to them further confuses the real nature of the
issues at stake in theology's encounter with Jungian psychology.
For it strikes us that too often the apparent issue--the need to
maintain intact the distinction between psychological and
theological methods--is but a guise for a more troubling and
vital concern--the need to differentiate and keep intact two
distinct realms of subject-matter. Whether it is the very
legitimacy of a psychological interpretation of Christian dogma
that is in question (Hostie), or the attempt to discern the
presence of God in the soul of man (Buber), Jung is seen to
address himself to motifs and realities that theology and
theology alone is presumed capable of dealing with.

It is our view, however, that theology is ill-advised to
attempt to immunize particular religious subjects from psychological scrutiny. A psychologist of religion cannot be
expected in principle to limit his investigations to a particular range of religious phenomena, to particular genres and
forms of religious expression. We seriously doubt whether
divisions of subject-matter will resolve the question of the
nature of psychology's and theology's respective tasks. It will
not do to assert that psychology is equipped only to speak of
the soul or psyche of man, and should accordingly leave to
theology and theology alone the task of speaking of God.
Neither Jung nor Buber would isolate the one from the other;
both envision the two to be in intimate relationship, and both
attempt, from their respective vantage-points and with their
own methods, to illumine the nature of this relationship.

Buber understands this, but cannot reconcile himself with
it. And it is at this point that he utters his methodological
caveats--Jung *qua* psychologist is simply not equipped to speak
of the soul/psyche in relation to anything "super-psychic";[35]
he should properly speak only of psychic reality. Jung pro-
tests that all religious statements are inherently psychic,
because it is the human psyche which gives expression to them.[36]
Buber counters that this does not say much. And so the dialogue
degenerates into the theologian denying the psychologist what
he sees to be his rightful prerogative--full license to submit
to psychological scrutiny whichever facets of the religious
life of man he deems of interest to him. We think it futile,
however, for theologians to attempt to delimit retrospectively
what Jung himself refused to delimit--the range of subject-
matter he took into his purview in the course of his interpretive work.

To recapitulate, we have found that too often those commentators who raise the methodological question of Jung's work
allow their interest in it to be diverted into an attempt to
divide realms of subject-matter in such a way as to isolate a
psychological from a well-nigh self-enclosed theological realm.
That they are side-tracked in this way from the question of
method frustrates their desire to clarify it, and thereby
greatly decreases the likelihood that their own way of reading

Jung will eventuate in a theological appropriation of what is
determined to be of value in his work.

We ourselves do not feel that the question of method--
i.e., of Jung's method and of the uses theology might make of
it--can be adequately clarified by recourse either a) to his
most frequently used designations for it, or b) to a strategy
that would differentiate psychological and theological methods
more in the interests of isolating and separating the one from
the other than with the aim of inter-relating the two. For
these reasons, then, even if we welcome the fact that Hostie,
Buber and others have raised the question of method, we are led
to conclude that the manner in which they raise it hinders far
more than it helps the prospects for an extensive collaboration
between theology and Jungian psychology.

Perhaps the best-known Catholic theologian who has commented
in depth on Jung, in the English-speaking world at least, is
Victor White. He is known for his several articles on Jung,[37]
as well as his two books, *God and the Unconscious*[38] and *Soul and
Psyche: An Enquiry into the Relationship of Psychotherapy and
Religion*.[39] White's work is significant inasmuch as he was one
of the very few theologians to have won Jung's personal trust
and friendship, although as personal correspondence between them
reveals,[40] this friendship became strained and frayed as a
result of the fact that ultimately they could not see eye to eye
with each other on religious matters of profound personal importance to both of them.

White's writings show him to be predisposed to find in
Jungian psychology much that is of value for Christian theology.
His aim is to initiate and sustain a wide-ranging dialogue with
Jung. It is with this aim in mind that White in his *Soul and
Psyche* articulates in a systematic way what he holds to be the
common ground between psychological and theological studies:
viz. the human soul, which, he says, cannot be distinguished
from the psyche.[41] In so doing, he stands opposed to those who
would maintain that the two disciplines have little to say to
each other, that the subject-matter of one has little to do with
the subject-matter of the other. To White's mind, theology and
psychology cannot but talk to each other, for they both must
address themselves to the nature and workings of the soul/

psyche of man. *How* they do so, what language, methods,
assumptions and insights they will rely upon in their discourse
about the soul will differ in important respects, but *that* they
both do so and must do so is what it is essential for both
disciplines to recognize at the outset of any conversation
between them.

But if this mutual recognition impels the two disciplines
towards conversation, it does not insure that extensive collaboration or agreement will result. In fact White recognizes that
it is the very existence of this common ground that can bring
them into conflict with each other.[42] He perceives and is
disturbed by a number of such points of conflict, most of which
come to the fore as a result of Jung's later works, especially
"Answer to Job."[43] His predisposition to find in Jung a useful
theological resource does not lead him to skirt or downplay
these difficulties. Quite to the contrary; much of his work is
an attempt to wrestle with them, and where possible to resolve
them. For White the most troubling of these are Jung's critique
of the Christian understanding of evil and his interpretation
of the image of God in man.[44] We will not attempt to untangle
the tangled web of controverted issues that White's conversations
with Jung involved him in. We do wish, however, to highlight
some of the points he raises with Jung on the question of God-
imagery, because our own reading of Jung will pivot on his
re-interpretation of the trinitarian God-image of the Christian
tradition.

The difficulty centers on what White perceives to be Jung's
inability or unwillingness to maintain intact his distinction
between the image of God and the reality of God.[45] Images of
God are a matter of "psychic" or "human" experience which may
or may not pertain to the reality of God, and certainly may not
be confused with or equated with God Himself: "No Christian,...
can allow for a moment that any psychic experience,...can
possibly *be* God....To do so would for us be idolatry."[46] But
Jung, in ostensibly speaking of *God* as such, does not make it
sufficiently clear that he is in actuality speaking of a
particular kind of God-experience and God-imagery. White argues,
then, that Jung the psychologist is not to lose sight of the fact
that *as* a psychologist he must not entertain the question of the

reality of that to which this imagery refers. To do so would
be inconsistent with the canons of his professedly empirical
method.[47] However, the problem is that Jung, particularly in
"Answer to Job," speaks as if this question were very well
decided for him, as if the reality underlying the imagery were
well-nigh indubitable.[48] This is as disturbing to White as
was Jung's earlier "Kantianism," which seemed to entail the
belief "that God is in no way rationally knowable or even
approachable."[49]

At this point we need to underscore the obvious--that we
encounter here several of the elements prominent in Hostie's
and Buber's critiques of Jung--the inconsistent adherence to
his empirical standpoint, the tendency to blur the distinction
between man's images of God and the reality of God, which
transcends all human representation, etc. The recurrence of
these same themes in White is all the more noteworthy in view of
the fact that it is his intention, unlike Hostie and Buber, to
draw upon and appropriate Jungian insights wherever possible in
his theological work.

What is it, then, that leads all of these theologians,
despite their differences of background, orientation and style,
to share the same misgivings over Jung's use of God-language?
We suspect that the root cause of their uneasiness is the fact
that the particular kinds of God-images he unearthed in the
psyche of modern man can only with the greatest difficulty be
assimilated into the dominant currents of biblical and classical
Christian imagery of God. The *content* of this imagery is clearly
dissonant with the content of the Judaeo-Christian tradition's
ways of imaging God.[50] Perhaps the crux of the issue, then, is
not so much that Jung loses sight of the distinction between
images of God and the reality of God, but rather that he inter-
relates two sets of images which White for one does not wish to
see melded together.

That Jung construes the meaning of doctrinally shaped and
formalized God-imagery in terms of images seemingly unrelated
to it is, to be sure, a bold undertaking, which has perplexed
and befuddled many of his commentators. But we will attempt to
demonstrate in subsequent chapters that the logic and plausi-
bility of this undertaking can only be appreciated when the

method underlying it is appreciated. For, as we shall see, it
is a method that relies above all else on the symbolic as an
interpretive principle. Only when this is taken into account
can it be understood how and why Jung amplifies one set of
images in terms of another, how and why he can systematically
view images of God in man as images of man himself, how and
why he can construe God-language as inherently anthropological
language without thereby reducing or losing sight of its
ostensive meaning and reference to the divine.

But we do not wish to anticipate further the line of
argumentation we will pursue below. We only wish to indicate
how White's uneasiness about the content of the God-imagery
Jung chose to interpret, together with the methodological
constraints he attempts to impose on Jung, lead him to misconstrue the achievement of Jung's psychological reading of the
Christian God as well as the nature of the challenge it poses
for Christian theology.[51]

In summation, we have found in White a stance vis-à-vis
Jung that we would liken to that of Philp, who in all earnestness wishes to arrive at a meeting of minds with Jung but
cannot. In this respect they both differ from commentators such
as Buber or Hostie, who show themselves to be ill-disposed from
the very outset of their commentaries to find in Jung someone
with whom they can ally themselves. But from whatever predis-
positions these theologians begin, their "conversations" with
Jung all run aground on strikingly similar points--perceived
points of incompatibility between the Jungian and the theological
enterprises. And thus, despite their differences of predisposition, of theological style and background, we have chosen to
group them together in our survey, for they all single out
these incompatibilities and they all regard them as serious if
not prohibitive obstacles to a theological appropriation of
Jung's brand of psychology.

In turning to Hans Schaer's *Religion and the Cure of Souls
in Jung's Psychology*,[52] we encounter a study whose standpoint
vis-à-vis Jung is markedly different from any of those surveyed
heretofore. For Schaer, a Swiss Protestant pastor-theologian,
shows himself to be decidedly sanguine about the prospects for

fruitful collaboration between Jungian psychology and Christian
theology. The dominant concerns of his work are 1) to bring
the reader to a recognition that this psychology is rooted in a
positive regard for and evaluation of the whole of the religious
life of man, and 2) to draw out the implications of this positive
regard, to point out the ways it leads Jung to illumine certain
aspects of religion which would otherwise escape one's attention. These aspects comprise religion's psychic roots and
functions.[53] Because Jung uncovers the fact that religion is
rooted in the unconscious, he is able to show how it cuts
across the whole of man's psychic life, and not just his mind
or consciousness.[54] Moreover, he shows how it functions in
such a way as to guide the individual forward to the realization
of his psychic wholeness:

> Religious experience can be defined by saying that
> it tends towards psychic integration. Religion is
> the acknowledgement of the things that consciousness
> fails to realize;...religion contributes substantially
> to a man's total structure, and a living religion is
> needed for the full development of personality.[55]

Schaer's account of Jung tends to approximate the religious
life of man to the personal process of self-realization, to
what Jung terms "individuation."[56] Such an interpretation is
of value, inasmuch as it serves to lay bare the religious intent
and thrust of the whole of Jung's psychology, which is, as
Schaer himself states, a "religious psychology" as much as, or
even more than a psychology of religion.[57] But the concomitant
danger of this emphasis is an over-emphasis on the personal and
the experiential nature of religion at the expense of or neglect
of the collective and formal dimensions of religious life. Jung
extends considerable attention to both of these dimensions;
Schaer, however, tends to dichotomize the two, and in so doing
underestimates Jung's respect for the power of the mediating
structures of religion, for its ecclesiastical elements and
forms.[58] He attributes to Jung a vision of a fully de-eccles-
iasticized religiosity:

> Our task now, says Jung, is...stripping off the last
> vestiges of ecclesiasticism that cling to the Protes-
> tant Church--which means that the individual must
> himself be the bearer of further changes and new
> religious experiences....This new pattern of religious

> experience will be individual. It will, in
> Jung's view, be Christian, but not ecclesiast-
> ical....there can only be personal solutions and
> salvation, and this demands a *personal* stake.[59]

Implicit throughout the work is the expectation that the
dialogue it has undertaken will eventuate in an appropriation
of Jung's understanding of religion, of the religious dimension
of man, of *homo religiosus*. Inasmuch as theology today seems
more determined than ever to articulate the nature of this
dimension, it will be indebted to Schaer for making available
to it a comprehensive account of Jung's thought in this regard.[60]

Schaer's study serves us well as an illustration of a
sympathetic reading of Jung's religious thought. It is significant, if only because it points up the fact that not all those
theologians who are eager to enter into dialogue with Jung run
aground, as do White and Philp, of what are felt to be points of
conflict or incompatibility between psychological and theological
methods, concerns and priorities.

We need to be circumspect, however, with regard to the kind
of reconstruction of Jung provided us here, not only because
Schaer too readily attributes to him a reduction of religion to
its personal and individual components and experiences, but more
importantly, because it seems to us that his adoption of Jung's
frame of reference as his own undercuts the very dialogue he
is so eager to pursue and contribute to. The conversation is
carried out so much on Jung's terms that one wonders, when all
is said and done, whether Schaer's can really be termed a
dialogical discussion, one in which two mutually contributing
participants are involved. To be sure, he seeks in his concluding chapter to find corroboration for Jung's views in such
liberal Protestant theologians as Hermann Lüdemann and Friedrich
Schleiermacher.[61] These are passing remarks, however, that stop
short of a concerted effort to spell out the points of conver-
gence between liberal theology and Jungian psychology. The
standpoints of each are never sufficiently differentiated and
juxtaposed to enable the reader to gauge whether or not a dialogue
is in fact taking place.

Although there are few proponents of Schaer's style of
reading Jung in the theological community, we do find in a

recent work, Charles B. Hanna's *The Face of the Deep: The Religious Ideas of C. G. Jung*[62] many of the same emphases and assumptions. Hanna's professed aim is to delineate the challenge Jung poses to the contemporary Christian's self-understanding.[63] His desire, however, to gain for Jung as sympathetic a hearing as possible in the Christian community has led him to fashion a commentary on Jung that is little more than a catalogue of his principal religious ideas. His is a reading of Jung that stops short of an evaluation and critical assessment of the challenge that underlies these ideas. Hanna is worthy of mention here, then, if only because we see in him another instance of a theologian having thoroughly identified with and adopted as his own Jung's religious standpoint.

     In our study of Jung we do not contemplate the kind of marriage or assimilation that Schaer and Hanna envision. Nor, on the other hand, do we intend to permit what are sources of conflict or tension for some to deter us or distract us from an evaluation of Jung which, it is hoped, will lead us to a discovery of specific features of his work which, if appropriated by theology, will be of benefit to it. We are suggesting, then, that neither of the styles of reading Jung epitomized by Hostie and Schaer can serve us as models in the kind of endeavor we wish to undertake. The former makes of the dialogue a debate, a debate that eventuates in the two participants talking over each other; the latter reduces dialogue to something approaching a monologue.

     On the other hand, we stand indebted to both of these contrasting approaches, however wanting we have found them to be. For the former succeeds in bringing to light the need that the standpoints and methods of the two disciplines be clarified, differentiated, and only then inter-related. And the latter leads us to recognize that no theological appropriation can be a meaningful and fruitful one, apart from a willingess on theology's part to seek Jungian thought out on its own terms, to engage in a process of attentive and creative listening.

     The foregoing survey has focused on works which address the full scope of Jung's psychological and religious thought. We

also wish, however, to take into our purview a representative
sampling of those theologians who have addressed themselves
to particular facets of Jung's work, and who have done so in
such a way as to draw upon Jung and to make use of him as a
creative resource for their own theologizing. We will do so
because we deem it imperative to take stock of the fact that the
many difficulties which have beset theologians' efforts to
converse with Jung have not prevented some of them from appro-
priating specific features and insights of his work.

We will consider here three works in particular: Frank
Bockus' "The Self and Christ: A Study of Carl Jung's Psychology
of the Self and Its Bearing on Christology,"[64] John S. Dunne's
A Search for God in Time and Memory,[65] and a short statement
by Paul Tillich at a memorial meeting following Jung's death.[66]

Bockus' principal theological interests center on the
Christian doctrines of man and of Christ. He begins his study
with a clear recognition of the anthropological thrust of
Jung's thought:

> The work of C. G. Jung is characterized by an explicit
> concern for the question of essential human nature....
> To be sure, he remained throughout his lifetime an
> avowed empiricist and phenomenologist, but his
> psychiatric practice and his psychological investiga-
> tions always proceeded beyond the phenomenological
> manifestations of personality to the normative substrate
> of human nature.[67]

With this recognition as a touchstone, he goes on to make of
Jung's notions of the self and self-realization the foundation
for his own constructive Christological work: "The original
hypothesis of the present inquiry was that Jung's psychology of
the self has direct bearing on the contemporary constructive
task in Christological thought."[68]

Bockus' use of "essential human nature" as the pivotal
notion in his Christology is reminiscent of Schleiermacher's
doctrine of Christ, the influence of which is particularly felt
in his assertion that, "The thesis which draws together the
study in the constructive formulation is: The archetype of the
God-Man, decisively disclosed in Jesus Christ, is the original
fact in every man."[69] Jesus Christ is taken as the full disclosure of "essential man," and thus as the ground of human
personality.

But we need not enter into the specifics of Bockus'
development of this thesis in order to appreciate the underlying
form his argument takes. He simply follows the natural and
logical movement in Jung's psychology of the self from its
concern with the particularities of personal life and development, as encountered in clinical experience, to an interest in
the "essential man," in human nature as such. In so doing, he
finds in Jung a resource with which to lay the philosophical
and anthropological foundation for a theological exposition of
the doctrine of Christ: "We have appropriated his concept of
the self, especially the archetype of the God-Man....In so doing
we have had to go beyond the methodological limits of his own
views."[70] Bockus contends, then, that this area of Jung's
psychology carries with it implications which Jung was unwilling
or unable to spell out, that philosophy and theology can come
to his aid, meeting him precisely at his limits, and carrying
his insights beyond the framework in which they were originally
propounded.

In summation, here we clearly encounter a theologian who
presumes and argues that Jung's psychology can be effectively
employed as a resource with which to deal with specific theological problems. In what follows we will reaffirm in our own
way what Bockus has affirmed--that the (religious) anthropology
implicit in Jung's psychology of the self and its realization
constitutes one of the areas of his thought that theology stands
most to benefit from.[71]

In turning to Paul Tillich and the ways he finds in Jung a
creative resource for his theology, we are handicapped by the
fact that he has not left us with a systematic statement of his
stance vis-à-vis Jung. He has, however, addressed himself
explicitly to depth psychology as a whole and its influence on
contemporary theology[72] as well as to the importance of Jung's
understanding of religious symbolism.

In the latter instance, Tillich argues that Jung has
articulated

> ...the basic elements of a meaningful doctrine of
> symbols: ...the distinction of symbol from sign as
> well as from allegory,...the necessity of using
> symbols in order to grasp dimensions which cannot

> be grasped in any other way,...the mediating,
> opening-up, healing power of symbols,...their
> arising from a union of the collective unconscious
> with the individual consciousness, and so on.[73]

Moreover, he sees in Jung's theory of the archetype a means by
which the Protestant discovery of the dynamics of the life and
death of particular symbols can be integrated with the Catholic
concern for the enduring elements of symbolic meaning.[74] For
these reasons Tillich finds Jung's understanding of symbolism
helpful for "inter-theological discussion."[75]

He does not in this cursory statement, however, focus on
the specifics of Jung's notion of symbol, nor does he attempt
to bring to light Jung's account of the role symbols play in
personal development. And yet, that Tillich acknowledges the
value of his views at all is, given our purposes, noteworthy,
inasmuch as we will attempt to demonstrate the central place
symbol occupies in the whole sweep of Jung's thinking and
interpretive work.

This is but one of the many ways Tillich testifies that the
insights of modern psychology have contributed to the theologian's tasks. Even more important for him is depth psychology's
understanding of man. Its "description of man's existential
predicament--in time and space, in finitude and estrangement--
in contrast to man's essential nature," its capacity to
illumine "the characteristics and symptoms of this estrangement"
and its relation to disease, are all "of infinite value for
theology."[76] For they succeed in raising "the question that is
implied in man's very existence," a question that systematic
theology cannot be expected to address or answer unless it has
first heard and felt and understood it in all its painful force.[77]

Tillich argues, then, that theology needs to listen atten-
tively to what depth psychology is saying of man in his existential state, in his state of fallenness, of brokenness, of
sickness. For all the pathologies of human life are pathologies
of the spirit; it makes no sense for theology to speak of
salvation, of healing, if it does not correlate what it says of
it with what it understands of sickness in all its forms.[78] And
so for Tillich the theological categories sin and redemption are
intimately inter-connected with the psychological categories
sickness and health, even if not wholly reducible to them.

In short, the doctrine of salvation, the Christian
affirmation of "the participation of the whole being in
unambiguous or eternal life," can be meaningfully explicated
only if it is shown to impinge on all facets of the human
predicament:

> ...the theologian must show how the creation of a
> centered self by the experience of ultimate concern
> spreads healing forces over a personality in *all*
> dimensions of his being. He must show this in the
> dimensions of the spirit, of psychological self-
> awareness, of bodily functions, of social relations
> and of historical self-realization.[79]

Because theology must strive to put in perspective the whole
person "in all dimensions of his being," and because depth
psychology is uniquely suited to illumine the nature of
personality and the pathologies and possibilities of its
development, Tillich sees in it an indispensible resource for
theology. Hence, it is evident that he discerns the need for
an extensive and systematic theological appropriation of depth
psychology's understanding of man, and in particular of his
lived "estrangement." And so he delineates many of the specific
ways this view of man has had and will continue to have a
decisive impact on Christian theology.

But it is not simply that the one discipline needs to heed,
rely upon and borrow particular insights and findings of the
other. The relationship he envisions is much more extensive
even than that:

> ...it is possible to reject the attempts of some
> theologians and some psychologists to divide these
> two realms carefully and give to each of them a
> special sphere. It is...possible to disregard those
> people who tell us to stay in this or that field:
> here a system of theological doctrines and there
> congeries of psychological insights. This is not
> so. The relationship is not one of existing along-
> side each other; it is a relationship of mutual
> interpenetration.[80]

Tillich's own theological method of correlation, then, prevents
him from demarcating the terrain of the two disciplines in any
way that would isolate and insulate the one from the other. In
this significant respect, his style of approach to psychology
is in sharp contrast with those whose chief concern is to keep
the lines of demarcation clear and distinct.

In summation, Tillich is one theologian whose reading of
Jung and the whole movement of depth psychology not only
demonstrates a marked readiness to listen to and appropriate
his/its discoveries; more importantly, he goes to considerable
pains to clarify the particular junctures where this appropriation can best take place. As our concluding chapter will
testify, we concur with Tillich that what depth psychology and
in particular Jung have said of the nature of symbolism and the
nature of man represents an achievement that contemporary
theology can ill afford to disregard.

Dunne's work, *A Search for God in Time and Memory*, is not
a detailed, analytical commentary on Jung, but rather a
synthetic and constructive theological work which draws on him
as well as on many other religious, literary and philosophical
figures. Dunne does not deem it necessary or appropriate to
advance a rationale for his recourse to Jung; nor does he
attempt to make of his interpretation a means of calling the
whole theological community to the kind of appropriation of
Jung he himself has achieved. In these respects his style of
reading him is unlike Tillich's and Bockus'. He simply goes
about the business of putting Jung to work for his own theological purposes without elaborate justification.

The major aim of his work is to make of the phenomenon of
life-story a principal resource for theological reflection.[81]
Accordingly, it proceeds by submitting a rich variety of life-
stories, ancient and modern, to careful and comparative
investigation. The study culminates with the attempt to relate
these stories of man to man's "stories of God," and ends with a
critique of the primacy of the self in the modern life-story:

> ...our express purpose was to unravel the story of
> the self and to reach its boundaries. We have looked
> for a greater story, a story of God, of which the
> story of the self would be a part. We have found
> that there is a story of the soul which is left
> untold in the story of the self, that man does not
> live by self alone.[82]

It is not surprising, given these purposes and concerns,
that Dunne, in turning to Jung, focuses on his own life-story.
He thus confines his dealing with him for the most part to his

autobiographical work, *Memories, Dreams, Reflections*, which,
because of its relatively recent (and posthumous) date of
publication (1963), was unknown to most of the interpreters of
Jung we have studied. The autobiography recounts vividly
Jung's lifelong efforts to fathom the dark recesses of his at
times decidedly peculiar "God-experience" and God-imagery. It
is these memories, dreams and reflections that Dunne is concerned
to interpret. He sees in them something paradigmatic of modern
man's experience of God, which he calls "an experience of
unmediated existence," one "in which there is nothing human
between man and God to put man in touch with God or to shield
him from God," in which there are no spiritual or temporal forms
of mediation between man and God.[83] This unmediated encounter
with the divine brings Jung close to disintegration, to madness;
it is his confrontation with the depths, with the unconscious,
which in his case carried with it an encounter with the dark
face of the divine turned demonic.[84]

This kind of experience poses what for Dunne is a most
troubling question: how is modern man to cope, apart from
mediation, with the sheer immediacies of his encounter with the
demonic, with the "dark forces" of life, with evil? Jung
testifies that he was delivered from his demons, from imminent
madness, through the titanic effort to understand and "differentiate" the dark forces that lurked within him.[85] Dunne, however,
shows himself to be less than satisfied with this response, and
counters that it stops short of the Christian response to evil,
which affirms that redemption issues from sympathetic suffering,
from com-passion, which transforms the pervasive darkness of
life in ways that insight in and of itself can never do.[86]

And so, having entered into and unravelled Jung's own life-
story and personal *mythos*, Dunne finds that at this significant
juncture he must distance himself from it. That he does so,
however, is less relevant to our purposes than the fact that he
discerns in Jung's articulation of this *mythos* a paradigmatic
expression of modern man's life-story, and that he chooses to
make of this as well as other life-stories integral components
of his own mode of theological reflection.

We have discerned in Dunne's work, then, a distinctive and
creative way of using Jung which we feel could prove fruitful to

theology in two important respects. The first pertains ·to what
we would call a theology of culture--to theology's efforts ⁄to
reflect upon the cultural and religious consciousness of modern
man. It seems to us that all Dunne says of Jung has a direct
bearing on this task, because he succeeds in highlighting the
ways Jung's life-experience and religious thought give dramatic
voice to modern man's cultural and religious *mythos*. Secondly,
the very fact that Dunne sees fit to rely upon the category of
life-story in interpreting Jung, that he casts Jung's religious
thought in the form of a personal and cultural story and as a
result is better able to illumine the nature of his thought, we
feel can only add impetus to the efforts of other theologians
to make of the category story a central one in their own
theologies; to relate it to its kindred terms myth, history,
narrative discourse, etc.; and to reflect upon the realities to
which these terms refer.[87] We would add that in what follows
below our own reliance on the term *story* is greatly indebted to
Dunne, for it is a self-conscious attempt to follow up on and
extend his use of the term by applying it to Jung's psychology
of fantasy and doctrine.[88]

     In grouping together Bockus, Tillich and Dunne, we do not
mean to imply that they interpret Jung in the same, or even
similar ways. Their readings of him are different, because
their theological purposes, methods and interests are different.
     But if the content of their interpretations differs, there
are nonetheless certain formal features all three of them share
in common. First, they all display a marked readiness to find
in Jung insights and views of theological value. In this
respect their approach to Jung can be likened to Schaer's and
Hanna's.
     They do not, however, attempt to address themselves to and
come to terms with the full gamut of Jung's psychological and
religious thought, nor do they see fit to incorporate it in its
totality into their own theological perspective and work. And
in these respects they differ significantly from Schaer and
Hanna. Theirs is a nuanced, not a wholesale appropriation of
Jung, one that draws upon him only at particular points. This,
for us, is the second and most distinctive feature of their

way of reading him--the discrimination they exhibit in singling
out and delineating only those facets of his thought that they
judge to be of value for their own theological work.

Thirdly, and this point follows naturally from the second,
their readings of Jung extend beyond commentary and interpretation per se, into a constructive process of theologizing that
draws upon him as a needed and creative resource. They do not
simply propose how Jung might be of use to theology; they
actually go about the business of using him.[89] It is one thing
to envision an appropriation of Jung that has yet to take place,
and another to attempt to achieve what is envisioned. Theirs,
clearly, is an approach to Jung in which interpretation opens
into appropriation.

This is what makes Bockus, Tillich and Dunne worthy of
inclusion here--their work testifies to the fact that a theological appropriation of Jung, in delimited areas, can take
place and indeed, to some degree, has already taken place.
Moreover, we have seen fit to single them out for an additional
reason: they each draw upon areas of Jung's work--life-story,
religious symbolism, and what we shall call *religious anthropology*[90]--which, given the purposes of this study, will be of
particular interest to us throughout all that follows.

We have passed in review a variety of theological literature on Jung. We have distilled from this literature three of
its major approaches and styles. And we have identified the
significant achievements and/or limitations of each of them.
We have felt it essential to introduce our study in this way in
order to situate what we will undertake to do with Jung in
relationship with what others have done with him. This chapter
is intended, then, to serve as a backdrop against which the
values and limits of our reading of Jung will be the more
readily discernible.

In conclusion and in anticipation of the line of inquiry
we will pursue in subsequent chapters, we wish to call attention
to the ways our findings above will have a direct bearing on
the strategy we will adopt in approaching Jung below.

As regards the style of reading him that Schaer epitomizes,
not only has it served to remind us of the obvious--that

pre-requisite to any conversation with and appropriation of
Jung is a readiness to listen to him and hear him out on his
own terms. More importantly, it has led us to be wary of the
desire to attempt a wholesale appropriation of Jung. Such a
desire tempts one to see in him a finished theology in its own
right, which, we feel, is to make of him what he is not. And
so Schaer has taught us, despite himself, that we need not and
indeed should not read Jung *as* a theologian in order to make
theological use of him.

From Tillich, Bockus and Dunne we have learned that a
theological appropriation of Jung succeeds best when it is
nuanced and discriminating, when it self-consciously attempts
to set clearly for itself the parameters within which it proceeds. Such a strategy stops short of the tendency to identify
with and make wholly one's own Jung's standpoint, while at the
same time circumventing the pitfalls of the style of reading
him which runs aground whenever any one of his at times idiosyncratic religious ideas and beliefs is felt to be unpalatable.

Although we have noted these pitfalls in our accounts of
Hostie, Buber, White, etc., we wish to stress that we nonetheless remain indebted to them, not only for drawing attention to
the many sources of tension between Jungian psychology and
Christian theology, but also for raising pointedly the methodological question that underlies and undercuts all of these
points of conflicts. For in so doing they alert us to the fact
that its resolution will do much to overcome the misunderstand-
ings and tension which have accompanied and hampered so much of
the dialogue between theologians and Jung.

That they address the question and *how* they do so are two
different matters, however. We have already discussed at
length the problems inherent in the way they attempt to differentiate Jung's psychological from a properly theological method:
the tendency to rely on his methodological professions rather
than his performance, and to differentiate in order to distan-
tiate, etc. The very pervasiveness of these problems in
theological commentary on Jung dictates that we take careful
heed of them in all that follows. This is, in fact, why we will
make of our study of Jung a study of his *method*--in order to
respond to and hopefully rectify some of these problems. For

until the distinctive features of this method are clarified,
theologians will be unable to even begin to determine the
nature of the relationship that ought to exist between their
own methods and Jung's.

Accordingly, in the three chapters to follow, it is our
principal aim to cast fresh light on the methodological underpinnings of Jung's work. We will argue that the nature of the
method underlying the whole of his psychology and in particular
his psychology of doctrine can best be clarified by construing
it as a hermeneutical one. Approaching Jung in this way will
carry with it the advantage of better enabling theology to
bridge the methodological gap between Jungian psychology and
itself (a gap which Hostie and others would wish to maintain).
For the whole field of hermeneutics is one that more and more
detains theology's attention today; and the methodological
scrutiny theology is currently subjecting itself to is leading
many to take stock of the points at which it ought to conceive
of itself and reconstitute itself as an inherently hermeneutical
discipline.[91] Now if the methods of Jungian psychology and
Christian theology can both be rightfully termed hermeneutical,
each in its own distinct ways (and in senses and at points that
need still to be specified), then we cannot but surmise that
the disciplines will have far more to say to each other than
Hostie, Buber, Philp and even White have led us to believe. And
so, our efforts in the chapters to follow to explicate the
hermeneutical nature of the method at work in Jung's psychology
are designed to counter those who, in their desire to differentiate psychological and theological methods of inquiry--a
desire we full well share--do so in such a way as to severely
curtail the points of contiguity between the two.

Let this suffice to indicate the principal ways we will
attempt in what follows to avoid the problems and capitalize on
the possibilities inherent in each of the styles of reading Jung
surveyed above. With these problems and possibilities clearly
in mind, we may now begin our own exposition of Jung's psychology
and its bearing on Christian theology.

CHAPTER II

SYMBOL AND PSYCHE IN JUNG'S PSYCHOLOGY

It is our intention in this chapter to set forth the
central features of Jung's understanding of symbol. First we
will examine the meaning he ascribes to the term. This will
require that we abstract from the dense and often convoluted
world of his thought the central features of his many attempts
to formulate a clearly defined notion of symbol. Then we will
examine how Jung makes use of this notion in his psychology,
with particular reference to the way he employs it in his
account of the dynamics of psychic conflict and growth.

In allowing *symbol* to serve as the point of entry into our
study of Jung, we will avail ourselves of a fixed point from
which to view the two areas of his thought we will focus on
below--viz. personal fantasy and Christian doctrine.[1] We would
hope that this will better enable us to envisage his wide-
ranging interpretive enterprise as a whole, and thereby to come
to discern the unity of method upon which it is based. We
propose, then, to make of Jung's understanding of symbol the
guiding thread in our study, an unravelling of which will lead
us to enter more fully and deeply into the inner workings of his
hermeneutic method.

Jung's Notion of Symbol

It is evident from even a cursory review of Jung's writings
that *symbol* is one of the most frequently employed terms in
his thought. It is so central to his psychology that he feels
compelled again and again, in a variety of different contexts,
to define as precisely as he can its meaning. And he does so
with what for him is a surprising degree of consistency. Note,
for example, his statements that

> ...a symbol is the best possible expression for an
> unconscious content whose nature can only be guessed,
> because it is still unknown.[2]

> ...symbols are the best possible formulation of an
> idea whose referent is not clearly known.[3]

> ...the symbolic expression... [is] the best possible
> formulation of a relatively unknown factor which
> cannot conceivably be more clearly or characterist-
> ically represented.[4]

> The true symbol...should be understood as an
> expression of an intuitive idea that cannot yet
> be formulated in any other or better way....true
> symbols,...[are] attempts to express something for
> which no verbal concept yet exists.[5]

The key elements in all of these formulations can best be summed
up as "the best possible expression for something relatively
unknown."[6] It will be well to keep this abbreviated formula
clearly in mind throughout our study of Jung, for it is the
lowest common denominator of meaning that he assigns to the
term symbol, and represents one of the few instances in his
writings where his terminology is clear-cut.

Its Component Parts

It is evident then that Jung fashioned for himself a
readily identifiable *notion* of symbol. But before examining
the ways his psychology relies on and makes use of this notion,
we need first to break it down into its component parts. We
will do so in the hope that we will thereby be better able to
discern what for Jung is the peculiar and enigmatic nature of
symbolic expressions.

To view a symbol as "the best possible expression for
something relatively unknown" is first and most obviously to
view it as an *expression* (for something). We will construe
expression in its broadest sense, as a cover-word for all
human representations, acts, words, events, creations, images.
This breadth in the range of what, potentially at least, can
take on a symbolic dimension, raises the question of whether or
not there are any limits at all to this range.[7]

Secondly, a symbol is viewed not merely as *any* expression
(for something), but as the *best possible* one. *Best* implies
that there is a certain appropriateness about the given means
of expression, that it is peculiarly apt and well suited to
evoke and convey the reality symbolized. The word *possible*,

however, connotes a certain limit, a certain finitude in the means of expression employed, which in turns calls into question the adequacy and effectiveness with which the symbol communicates that which is symbolized. Taken together, the qualifiers *best possible* serve to point out that there is no more adequate means of expression available than that actually employed.

Third is the preposition *for*, which makes evident the representational function of the expression. The symbol *stands* for something, i.e., something is expressed and conveyed by virtue of something else. The *for* serves as a bridge between the expression and the reality expressed; it is the link, indelible in the symbol itself, between *signifier* and *signified*.[8]

Next is the word *something*, i.e., that which is symbolized, the reality expressed and designated by the symbol. The main point to be made here is the simple fact that for Jung there is *some*thing for which the symbol stands. In other words, the expression does not exist in a vacuum; it is not its own reality. Rather it designates something other than itself.

Lastly, the reality expressed is not just anything, but something *relatively unknown*. Because this brings us to the most elusive element of Jung's notion of symbol, we would do well to take stock of the variants in his way of formulating it. Note, for example, that he refers to that which is symbolized as "something that still belongs entirely to the domain of the unknown or something that is yet to be,"[9] something which is "not clearly known,"[10] "something that is little known or completely unknown,"[11] "something suprahuman and only partly conceivable,"[12] "something not easily defined, and therefore not fully known,"[13] or as "a meaning that for the time being is unknown."[14] These variations in his wording only serve to clarify the single-mindedness of his intent, which is to stress the unspecifiable and mysterious nature of that which is symbolized, without at the same time consigning it to unknowability, to the realm of the unintelligible. We cannot fail to note that to every claim that the reality symbolized eludes man's "full," "clear" or "complete" knowledge Jung adds a corresponding qualification--it is not *yet* known, it is *still* unknown, or *relatively* unknown. The consistency with which he reiterates this qualification cannot be passed over lightly,

for it carries with it the clear implication that the opacity,
the mystery, the obscurity of that which is symbolized is not to
be taken as total, as final, as absolute; but rather as something
that is *provisional* in nature.

We would maintain, then, that this qualification constitutes an essential element in Jung's understanding of symbol;
it serves to call attention to the tension that is built-in to
the very structure of symbols, a tension which, from the point
of view of that which is symbolized, exists between its actual
status as a relatively unknown and its potential status as a
more fully known; or, from the point of view of the human
subject, between not knowing and coming to know.[15]

The Distinction between Symbol and Sign

Jung repeatedly warns against temptations that would lead
one to evade this tension by collapsing too quickly the "relatively unknown" into something presumed fully and perspicuously
known.[16] In his view such temptations eventuate in a disregard
for and erosion of the distinction between *symbol* and *sign*:

> A symbol is an indefinite expression with many
> meanings, pointing to something not easily defined
> and therefore not fully known. But the sign always
> has a fixed meaning, because it is a conventional
> abbreviation for, or a commonly accepted indication
> of, something known.[17]

Jung returns again and again to this distinction;[18] he
relies upon it as a means of clarifying the inner constitution
of symbolic expressions. As he conceives of it, this constitution is based upon the intrinsic link that exists between
signifier and signified.[19] To state that an expression assumes
symbolic status when there is no better way of signifying the
reality in question than that actually employed--when that which
is signified is done so in an "unsurpassable way"[20]--is to maintain that the signified is accessible only in and through the
signifier. Apart from the signifier the signified will remain
unknown. In the case of a sign, however, it is known *indepen-
dently* of the signifier, which is a more or less arbitrary
convention used to designate and *re*-present a reality previously
known. In short, signs are not constituted by the interdepen-
dence between the expression itself and the reality for which

it stands, whereas in the case of symbols there is a necessary
relationship between the two.

The Communicative Power of Symbol

But the assertion that symbols express a reality other than
themselves in an "unsurpassable" way, in a way that "cannot
conceivably,...be more clearly or characteristically represented,"[21] in and of itself does not account for how they do so.
How is it that *this* particular concrete, figurative means of
expression and not another is the *best possible* one? How do
symbols make known what they represent, especially in view of
the fact that the realities represented are "relatively unknown"?
These questions bring us face to face with what surely is the
symbol's most enigmatic and mysterious trait--its uncanny power
to express the seemingly inexpressible.

Throughout all that follows in the course of this chapter
we will concern ourselves with the way Jung's psychology
clarifies the nature of this communicative power. We shall take
as our immediate point of departure his contention that symbols
"mean more than they say."[22] This suggests that symbols serve
as carriers of hidden or unspecified meanings which "have an
effect even though they cannot be grasped intellectually."[23]

Jung's claim that "the emotional effect of symbols does
not depend on conscious understanding"[24] accords with his propensity to trace the origin of symbolism to an unconscious
ground: "...symbolization comes about firstly because every
human being has unconscious contents, and secondly because
every object has an unknown side."[25] It is not surprising that
a symbol means more than it says if it emanates from the unconscious, if it is an "expression for an unconscious content."[26]
For in Jung's view a vast reservoir, an inexhaustible multipli-
city of meaning inheres in the unconscious reaches of psychic
life.[27] Symbols not only emerge from this depth and breadth of
meaning, but in so doing they also mirror and transmit particular
aspects of it. They thereby serve to carry unconscious contents
to the threshold of consciousness. And yet it is a dim and
fleeting level of consciousness that is attained; the meanings
conveyed remain shrouded in the obscurity of the unconscious
background from which they emerge.

It is apparent then that the communicative power of
symbols depends upon their capacity to act as bridges between
the unconscious and conscious polarities of psychic life. But
to come to a deeper understanding of how symbols act in this
way requires that we set forth in general outline Jung's understanding of the dynamics of psychic life. And so we must now
turn to a whole range of issues and themes that lie at the very
heart of his psychology: What, according to Jung, is the nature
of the human psyche? What are the most significant features of
his account of psychic activity? of psychic conflict? of
psychic transformation?

In providing summations of Jung's views on these questions,
we will be extending considerably the scope of our inquiry,
which heretofore has abstracted Jung's understanding of symbol
from his psychological thought in order to achieve a measure of
clarity on the meaning he ascribes to the term. Now, however,
we must abrogate the limits we have imposed on our inquiry in
order to examine how Jung makes use of this term in his understanding of the life and development of the psyche.

The Nature of the Psyche

Psyche is one of those elusive terms in Jung's writings
that befuddles his interpreters and resists any clear definition. In fact Jung often forswears any attempt to define psyche
in deference to what he claims is its mysterious and unknowable
nature:

> ...no one knows what "psyche" is, and one knows just
> as little how far into nature "psyche" extends.[28]

> The only thing that can be established with certainty,
> in the present state of our knowledge, is our ignorance
> of the nature of the psyche.[29]

> If the human psyche is anything, it must be of
> unimaginable complexity and diversity....I can only
> gaze with wonder and awe at the depths and heights of
> our psychic nature.[30]

> The psyche is part of the inmost mystery of life.[31]

> Our psyche...remains an insoluble puzzle and an
> incomprehensible wonder, an object of abiding
> perplexity--a feature it shares with all Nature's
> secrets.[32]

However, despite this emphasis on its inscrutability, we can
ill afford to beg the question of the meaning of psychic
reality for Jung, inasmuch as it is the central reality with
which he is concerned throughout his writings. Moreover, to
our mind a study of the varied contexts and ways in which he
employs the term reveals that he assigns to it an identifiable
nexus of meaning, notwithstanding the fact that he never
explicates this meaning in a systematic manner.

Before attempting to delineate this meaning, however, we
need to take note of an important terminological ambiguity.
In Jung's German *die Psyche* or *das Psychische* and *die Seele*
are fully interchangeable terms.[33] As the editors of Jung's
Collected Works point out, this poses a difficult problem for
the English reader.[34] But inasmuch as *die Psyche* tends to
supplant *die Seele* in Jung's later works,[35] and inasmuch as
his original works in English employ the term *psyche*, rather
than soul,[36] we will hold to the view that the translation of
both *die Psyche* and *die Seele* by the English word *psyche* (the
procedure actually adopted by the translator of *The Collected
Works*, R. F. C. Hull) is the most reasonable way to resolve
the ambiguity in question.

A further source of confusion arises from the fact that
Jung shows himself less concerned to delimit the range of psychic
reality than he is to leave open his conception of it to the
widest and fullest possible scope of interpretation. In *Civilization in Transition*, for example, he feels free to speak of
the psyche as "the God-given essence of man."[37] This expansive
tendency that Jung's writings are wont to exhibit is designed
to counter those who would explain the psyche in terms of something other than itself in order to minimize its reality:

> There is...no ground at all for regarding the psyche
> as something secondary or as an epiphenomenon; on
> the contrary, there is every reason to regard it, at
> least hypothetically, as a factor *sui generis*.[38]

> The psyche has a peculiar nature that cannot be reduced
> to anything else.[39]

> ...we must really ask: How do we know so much about
> the psyche that we can say "only" psychic?[40]

These complicating factors notwithstanding, let us attempt
to extrapolate from his varied usage of the term the salient
features in his understanding of the nature of the human psyche.
We need first to consider his assertion that "the psyche is a
conscious-unconscious whole";[41] it embraces "the totality of
all the psychic processes, both conscious as well as unconscious."[42] If we can allow for the tautology of this statement,
it can be seen to demonstrate Jung's intention not only to
point to the bipolar character of psychic reality, but also to
lay stress on its all-inclusive, comprehensive nature. It
becomes evident, then, that for Jung the full range of conscious
and unconscious contents and processes constitutes the human
psyche.[43] And if this is the case, we are better able to see
why he regards it as ultimately unfathomable and unknowable;
for intrinsic to it is an unconscious dimension, and the
reaches and contents of the unconscious are unspecifiable and
unknowable pending their emergence into consciousness.

If, then, we can conceive of Jung's view of psychic
reality in its broadest sense as the totality of man's mental
and affective processes, both conscious and unconscious, we
arrive at a rudimentary notion of psyche, one, moreover, that
approximates to the human subject per se. In what follows in
this and subsequent chapters, we will thereby interpret the
embodied human psyche of any given individual as the personal,
empirical *self*.[44] We should emphasize, however, that by
empirical self we mean to designate neither the archetypal
Self, which for Jung is a technical term that refers to the as
yet to be realized goal of personal development;[45] nor the *ego*,
which Jung takes to be the "centre of the field of consciousness";[46] but rather the individual personality, which is always
a composite of the two, which is an ego *on the way to* the more
fully integrated and "individuated" form of personal being
represented by the archetypal Self.

Psychic Activity

But this skeletal notion of the human psyche sheds little
light on the actual content and processes of its life and
development. Accordingly, we will now outline some of the
major characteristics of psychic activity, as Jung understands

them, in an attempt to bring to light the depth and breadth of
his view of the psyche.

We will begin by emphasizing the fact that Jung interprets
the activity of the psyche in highly dynamic terms. An incessant dynamism characterizes all psychic processes, not only
because the psyche's unconscious ground generates an unending
stream of fantasy-processes and images, but also because these
fantasies impinge upon one's consciousness, thereby facilitating
an on-going interaction between the two poles or dimensions of
psychic life. In fact Jung suggests that psychic activity would
not even be possible apart from the tension catalyzed by the
bipolar opposition of conscious and unconscious forces: "...all
consciousness, perhaps without being aware of it, seeks its
unconscious opposite, lacking which it is doomed to stagnation,
congestion, and ossification. Life is born only of the spark
of opposites."[47]

To his mind the vitality of the psyche depends upon the
uninterrupted interplay of these forces. We would add that for
Jung the opposition between conscious and unconscious represents
but one instance, albeit the most paradigmatic one, of a wide
range of opposing forces that manifest themselves in the life of
the psyche, whether they be masculine/feminine, matter/spirit,
light/dark, introversion/extraversion, regression/progression,
etc. Moreover, all these forms of polar opposition generate
tension, conflict and ultimately, as we shall see, personal
becoming.

In his account of psychic activity, Jung makes extended
use of the term *psychic energy*, which he conceives of as "an
inclusive term for psychic intensities."[48] His intention in
relying upon this conception was to offer it as an alternative
to the Freudian notion of libido, an idea Jung felt was too
exclusively captive to Freud's sexual theories.[49] For Jung it
was imperative that a more "neutral" term be found, one which
would embody the total range of human desires and drives--whether
instinctive, emotional, spiritual, etc.--without elevating any
one of them to a pre-eminent position in the life of the psyche.
We shall have occasion in what follows below to probe more
deeply into the uses Jung makes of this term. Here we wish
simply to point out in general terms the first and most

significant of the qualities Jung attributes to psychic
activity--viz. its incessant dynamism and his penchant to
articulate this dynamism in terms of his notion of psychic
energy and the interplay of psychic opposites. Note, for
example, his statement that "the psyche appears as a dynamic
process which rests on a foundation of antithesis, on a flow
of energy between two poles."[50]

And yet it is an orderly flow; that is to say, there is a
capacity inherent in the psyche to order its activity, to direct
it along meaningful paths. And this brings us to a second
characteristic: viz. the "self-regulating"[51] and *purposive*
nature of psychic activity: "...it is a hypothesis of the
greatest heuristic value that the psyche is essentially purposive and directed."[52]

The importance Jung accords to this purposiveness is well
illustrated by his notion of *compensation*. He refers again and
again to the compensatory function of dreams and other forms of
psychic life for the most part generated by the unconscious.[53]
By this he means that the unconscious is activated in such a way
as to correct unadapted attitudes of consciousness: "The unconscious compensation of a neurotic conscious attitude contains all
those elements that could effectively and healthily correct the
one-sidedness of the conscious mind."[54]

A third characteristic we will mention is the propensity
of psychic processes to seek their own representation:

> We would expect that all psychic activities would
> produce images of themselves and that this would be
> their essential nature without which they could not
> be called "psychic."...
>   ...the psyche consists essentially of images.
> It is a series of images in the truest sense,...a
> structure that is throughout full of meaning and
> purpose; it is a "picturing" of vital activities.[55]

On the one hand, then, Jung speaks of the psyche ener-
gistically, vitalistically, i.e., in highly dynamic terms, while
on the other hand he implies one can speak of it only in terms
of the particular forms and images this energy assumes:

> Energy in itself is neither good nor bad, neither
> useful nor harmful, but neutral, since everything
> depends on the *form* into which energy passes. Form
> gives energy its quality. On the other hand, mere
> form without energy is equally neutral.[56]

And so it would seem that Jung understands the relationship
between the energy and the imagery of the human psyche to be an
interdependent one.[57]

Psychic Conflict

     To attribute this vitality, this purposiveness and this
"image-making" capacity to the human psyche is not to presume
that its life unfolds without hindrances and at times crippling
conflicts. Jung's writings, in fact, reveal a keen awareness
of the inevitability and severity of these conflicts. His
essay "On Psychic Energy" represents his clearest attempt to
offer an explanation of their origin.[58] It is the relationship
between self and world that provides the framework in which he
situates his account of conflict. Up to a point the psyche
shows itself capable of reconciling the many at times competing
demands of self and world. When this process of regulation and
adaptation is working well, the "flow" of one's psychic energy
will be capable of mediating between the opposites, between
self and world, or one might say, between self and other.
"During the progression of libido the pairs of opposites are
united in the co-ordinated flow of psychic processes."[59]

     However, the process becomes problematic, because inevitably
at some point the psyche cannot keep up with the complexity and
rapidity of the changing circumstances of life: "...it may
easily happen that an attitude can no longer satisfy the demands
of adaptation because changes have occurred in the environmental
conditions which require a different attitude."[60] Because
conscious attitudes tend to persist, one's manner of adaptation
begins to suffer from what Jung calls "consciously willed one-
sidedness."[61] The progression of libido ceases, gets frozen
in its tracks, and then dams up within the psyche.

     This "stoppage" in the easy flow of energy increases the
intensity of certain psychic forces or images, giving rise to
what Jung terms *complexes*, which he defines as "certain constella-
tions of psychic elements grouped round feeling-toned contents."[62]
The fact that these elements are "feeling-toned" or "strongly
accentuated emotionally" serves to indicate that they are
"incompatible with the habitual attitude of consciousness."[63]

Jung links complexes to "the inherent tendency of the
psyche to split," to what he calls *dissociation*.[64] For
accompanying the emergence of the complex is a heightened
tension between the opposites that ensues as a result of the
damming up of psychic energy: "...the stoppage is always marked
by the breaking up of the pairs of opposites....The longer the
stoppage lasts, the more the value of the opposed positions
increases."[65]

The theoretical basis then of Jung's understanding of
conflict is shaped from the notions of psychic energy, complex
and dissociation: "The tension leads to conflict, the conflict
leads to attempts at mutual repression, and if one of the
opposing forces is successfully repressed, a dissociation
ensues, a splitting of the personality, or disunion with oneself."[66]

And so it is clear that Jung views psychic conflict as
a form of disrelation between psychic opposites, a state
originally set in motion by a disrelation between self and world.
When the tension between opposites reaches a point of actual
dissociation,the psyche's capacities for self-regulation are
severely jeopardized. This is because the existence of the
repressed opposite in the unconscious acutely disturbs the
psyche, thereby throwing out of balance the interaction between
conscious and unconscious: "...the repressed opposite...,
instead of working as an equilibrating force, has an obstructive
effect, thus hindering the possibility of further progress."[67]
Unconscious tendencies and impulses can no longer compensate
for one's conscious orientation; on the contrary, they only
exacerbate the difficulties one experiences in adaptation.

Regression

Having set forth the general outlines of Jung's account of
psychic conflict, we need now to raise the question: how are
such conflicts resolved? It is at this point that we come to
a pivotal notion in Jung's explanation of psychic processes:
"The struggle between the opposites would persist in this
fruitless way if the process of regression, the backward movement of libido, did not set in with the outbreak of the
conflict."[68] *Regression* denotes a turning in, an involution of

psychic energy into the depths of the person, as well as a
withdrawal from the world. It is a necessary step backward
that will later pave the way for a dramatic shift in the flow
of energy forward.

With regression the flow of energy that is blocked by the
disrelation between the self and its environment is diverted
away from the environment to a deeper ground in the unconscious,
where fantasy contents and processes are activated by virtue
of the influx of energy. And these contents, once awakened,
constitute "germs of new life and vital possibilities for the
future."[69] The regressive turn of one's energies inward, then,
leads provisionally to adaptation to one's "inner world," which
in turn frees one ultimately to new forms of adaptation to
one's wider social and natural world.[70] This accords with
Jung's understanding of psychic development as a dialectical
process of regressive and progressive movements of adaptation,
a process that pivots on shifting currents of energy inward and
outward. "Libido moves not only forwards and backwards, but
also outwards and inwards."[71]

The Transformation of Psychic Energy

But however much regression paves the way for new life, it
cannot in and of itself effect it. The problem of rechannelling
the energy that has built up in the psyche, or as Jung has stated
it, of finding the "right gradient" remains:

>...it does not lie in our power to transfer
>"disposable" energy at will to a rationally chosen
>object....Psychic energy is a very fastidious thing
>which insists on fulfilment of its own conditions.
>However much energy may be present, we cannot make
>it serviceable until we have succeeded in finding
>the right gradient.[72]

Jung conceives of the dynamics of energy-flow in terms of
the analogy of a water-course;[73] normally, water follows the
gradient of least resistance--i.e., downward. But if the path
is blocked, the water dams up and has nowhere to go but backwards until a point is reached where it can flow around the
obstacle. Similarly, in a conflictual situation the flow of
psychic energy is reversed; it follows the path inwards, into
the hinterlands of the psyche, or backwards into the psychic

past, reactivating at first fantasies and longings of early
childhood, and then the pre-infantile, collective contents of
the unconscious.

It is during this process of reactivation that energy is
canalized into new paths. By *canalization* Jung means "a
transfer of psychic intensities or values from one content to
another."[74] Energy is converted or "transformed" from one form
into another: "The transformation of instinctual energy is
achieved by its canalization into an *analogue of the object of
instinct.*"[75]

Jung regards the symbol as the primary means by which this
transformation is effected.[76] Because it provides the necessary
"analogue" to the instinct, it serves to re-shape the gradient
one's psychic energy follows.[77] The symbol is able to do this
because man possesses more energy than his instincts could ever
possibly consume; there is a surplus of energy in the human
psyche that exceeds what is needed "to sustain the regular flow
of life."[78] The symbol "taps" and draws upon this surplus,
attracting energy to itself, and in so doing guides it along a
steeper gradient: "Only where a symbol offers a steeper gradient
than nature is it possible to canalize libido into other forms."[79]
Once the regressive direction of the flow of energy is reversed,
new "avenues for the self-realization of libido"[80] are found.
Adaptation between self and world can proceed anew.

Symbols and the Development of the Psyche

And so we have come to that point in Jung's psychology
where he calls upon his notion of symbol and puts it to use in
his account of the life and development of the psyche. It is
the symbol that, in its capacity to effect transformations of
psychic energy, paves the way for the resolution of psychic
conflicts:

> ...the conflict can only be resolved through the
> symbol.[81]
> ...there is an ever growing danger of a flooding
> and disintegration by unconscious contents; but all
> the time the symbol is developing which is fitted to
> resolve the conflict.[82]

We are proposing, then, that the role Jung sees symbols to
play in the development of the psyche centers on their ability
to resolve such conflicts.

Symbols as Mediators between Conscious and Unconscious

But in order to understand how symbols function in this
way we need to take up anew all that we have said above about
their communicative power, and specifically our finding that
symbols act as bridges between the conscious and unconscious
polarities of the psyche, thereby rendering more permeable the
wall or threshold that divides the one from the other: "The
saving factor is the symbol, which is able to reconcile the
conscious with the unconscious and embrace them both."[83] In
acting as mediators between conscious and unconscious worlds,
they fulfill an indispensable psychic need--they facilitate
the movement of energy within the psyche and thereby quicken
the interplay between all of its forces. And so symbols mediate
not simply between unconscious and conscious, but precisely by
so doing, between the whole gamut of contending forces and
factors in the human psyche.

Jung's writings return again and again to the symbol's
capacity to mediate between and thereby bring about what he
terms a *conjunction* or union of psychic opposites:

> ...symbols [which] have the character of "wholeness"
> and therefore presumably *mean* wholeness...are
> "uniting" symbols, representing the conjunction of
> a single or double pair of opposites,...They arise
> from the collision between the conscious and the
> unconscious and from the confusion which this
> causes.[84]

> The symbol is the *middle way*, upon which the
> opposites unite towards a new movement.[85]

> ...symbols...make the irrational union of opposites
> possible.[86]

We should not forget that when he invokes this theme, he is not,
as it might appear, speaking abstractly, but is referring to
the actual ingredients of lived conflicts which have a very
painful and oftentimes debilitating impact on the lives of those
who experience them. Jung, after all, was first and foremost a
psychologist whose theoretical work emerged from and was made to

serve his practical, clinical, therapeutic concerns.[87] To our
mind his understanding of symbol was born of these concerns,
and thus can be fittingly designated a *psychology* of symbol in
a pre-eminent sense, the chief purpose of which is to provide
an account of the ways symbols serve to facilitate psychic
development.

We have seen then that for Jung the role symbols play in
the resolution of psychic conflicts depends on their capacity
to mediate between the contending forces in the human psyche
that generate these conflicts. We would add that to view
symbols as mediators is ultimately to view them as *healers* and
reconcilers of all the inner divisions and splits that beset
psychic life:

> ...the ego rent between thesis and antithesis finds
> in the uniting middle territory its counterpart, its
> reconciling and unique expression, and eagerly seizes
> upon it, in order to be delivered from its division.
> Hence, the energy created by the tension of the
> opposites flows into the mediatory expression.[88]

Perhaps we can clarify the nature of the mediating,
reconciling and healing capacity Jung attributes to symbols if
we reflect once again on his *notion* of symbol. In returning to
this notion here, we shall attempt to integrate the distinction
we have drawn between its most important constituent elements--
viz. *best possible expression* and *something relatively unknown*--
with our finding that for Jung symbols represent in a paradigmatic way points of conjunction between unconscious and conscious
factors in the psyche. Let us designate that which is symbolized
by a given symbol, i.e., the "something relatively unknown," as
its (provisionally) *unconscious* content and meaning; and the
concrete figure, i.e., the "best possible expression," as the
symbol's *conscious* and ostensive component and meaning.[89] We
are then able to perceive more clearly that the conjunction
between conscious and unconscious that takes place in every
symbol and that every symbol embodies and represents (and that
Jung contends is indispensable to the development of the human
psyche) is central to the symbol's very constitution. It would
thus seem that the effectiveness with which symbols mediate
between unconscious and conscious can be best explained in
terms of their nature, for it is of the very essence of symbols,

in Jung's view, to be a marriage, a point of conjunction between
unconscious and conscious elements. In other words, because
they emerge from and are fashioned out of both conscious and
unconscious factors in the human psyche, they are pre-eminently
suited to forge indissoluble points of linkage between the two.[90]

The Prospective Meaning of Symbols

But we have not yet delineated all the consequences that
follow from the mediation and transformation of energy symbols
effect. We have seen that every emergence of a symbol into
one's awareness can be taken as a specific moment of transforming significance, which gives evidence of a freeing of energy
from the fissures and pains of one's past and present experience.
But the mediating, transforming and healing power of symbols not
only mends these wounds, but also opens one to a new range of
possibilities to be lived out in an as yet to be realized
future:

> ...the symbol contains possibilities for new energic
> deliveries, i.e., the release of libido unconsciously
> bound. The symbol always says: in some such form as
> this will a new manifestation of life, a deliverance
> from the bondage and weariness of life, be found.[91]

In other words, symbols serve at one and the same time to
release energy from its bonds and to guide it forward along
specific paths. Note, for example, Jung's references to symbols
as "stepping stones to new activities"[92] and as "the directive
signs we need in order to carry on our lives."[93]

It is apparent, then, that for Jung symbols are capable of
bringing persons to a heightened awareness of the lines of
their future development. Herein lies what he calls their
prospective meaning:

> The value of the symbol...lies in the fact that
> it has a meaning for the actual present and for the
> future, in their psychological aspects. For the
> Zurich school the symbol is not merely a sign of
> something repressed and concealed, but is at the
> same time an attempt to comprehend and to point the
> way to the further psychological development of
> the individual. Thus we add a prospective meaning
> to the retrospective value of the symbol.[94]

In short, symbols make possible intimations of one's "future conscious achievements."[95] That Jung attributed this capacity to symbols testifies to the highly privileged position his notion of symbol assumed in his account of the development of the human psyche.

This theme in his psychology of symbol, however, raises a dilemma for the interpreter of Jung: do symbols merely point one ahead to possibilities for new life, or do they actualize here and now a measure of this new life? To our mind they function in both ways for Jung; their emergence into consciousness not only presages an as yet unrealized change in persons, but also bears witness to a realignment of forces that has already occurred in the psyche. In other words, the power of symbols is *actual*, as well as virtual. Their very emergence in and of itself effects a new attitude, and this attitude, if taken sufficiently seriously, if put to the test of life, will accelerate the process of growth, will bring to fruition those "seeds of incalculable possibilities"[96] that forever germinate in the wellsprings of man's imagination.

To assign a prospective meaning to symbols, then, is not to deny the life-giving power they may bring in the present moment of one's life, but rather to maintain that concomitant with this gift of new life here and now is a revelation of an even greater newness that is yet to be attained.

Recapitulation

We have reviewed the salient features in Jung's account of the way symbols serve the needs and purposes of the developing self. Framing our discussion in terms of his understanding of psychic activity has permitted us to see that what for Jung is the remarkable vitality and dynamism of man's psychic life as well as its apparently limitless capacity to form images of itself--its energy and its imagery--work together to make possible the realization of a fuller and more integrated form of selfhood. Moreover, we have found that these self-regulating capacities owe their efficacy primarily to the symbol. Because it surfaces as just the right image at just the right time, it succeeds in re-shaping (i.e., transforming) and re-channelling (i.e., canalizing) the disposable energy of the psyche. Herein

constitutes what Jung terms the "saving" significance of
symbolic images[97]--the mysterious way they emerge at the most
critical junctures in a person's life and overcome the warring
strife of contending, indeed disintegrating, forces in the
psyche. Nowhere more clearly than here, than in the realm of
symbol-formation, does psychic activity show itself to be
innately self-ordering, i.e., inherently purposive.

     We are therefore led to the conclusion that for Jung the
psyche's capacity to form symbolic images of its own processes
is *indispensable* to its well-being and continued development.
To our mind this is one of the axiomatic tenets of Jung's
psychology. For Jung every symbol embodies a range of meanings
that have a direct bearing on the developing psyche or self,
precisely because every symbol emerges from this psyche or self
and carries with it an image, in however obscure a form, of
that from which it has emerged.

     But how then do these findings pertain to the communicative
power of symbols? What light does Jung's psychological account
of symbols shed on their strange propensity to mean more than
they say? This is a question that has remained with us throughout our inquiry, but which we have been unable to deal with
decisively pending our exposition of the role symbols play in
mediating between conscious and unconscious and thereby facilitating psychic development. In retrospect we can now discern
more clearly than before that in Jung's view this communicative
power centers on the fact that symbols shape and guide the whole
of man's psychic life and hence speak to him of his developing
psyche or self:

> ...authentic symbols...provide the directive signs
> we need in order to carry on our lives in harmony
> with ourselves.
>   The symbol...represents an attempt to elucidate,
> by means of analogy, something that still belongs
> entirely to the domain of the unknown or something
> that is yet to be. Imagination reveals to us, in the
> form of a more or less striking analogy, what is in
> the process of becoming.[98]

These directive signs, however, are but inklings and intimations
of an unrealized future; nevertheless, they still serve to disclose, even if in an obscure and veiled fashion, what one has
yet to become.[99]

We would draw attention here to the implicit correlation
Jung's account of the prospective meaning of symbols makes
between the inherently "unfinished" nature of personal becoming
and the "as yet unknown" nature of that which is symbolized.
For the fact that he relates the one to the other serves to
bring to light the *not yet* quality that underlies both symbolic
knowing and personal becoming, and that imparts to each a
similar tension. We have already noted how the relationship
between a symbol's manifest and latent meanings evokes a peculiar
tension; we will now extend this point one step further by
adding that Jung, precisely because he construes symbolic
expressions as veiled representations of the psyche or self,
approximates the tension with which they are imbued to the
tension that pervades all personal becoming--i.e., to the tension
between my actual and potential, real and ideal, present and
future selves.

It would seem then that the "something relatively unknown"
that lurks within the symbol mirrors my as yet unknown and
unrealized future. Perhaps it is the futility of attempting
to come to any "full" and "clear"[100] knowledge of this future
that necessitates reliance upon symbolic modes of knowing, lest
the path one is to follow into its mystery and obscurities not
be lit "ahead of time" at all. If this is the case, it becomes
all the more evident that personal becoming is so intimately
bound up with and rooted in symbolic knowing that the one
cannot but proceed in conjunction with the other. And so to our
mind Jung's psychology of symbol, in setting forth the view that
symbols convey, however obscurely and enigmatically, what one is
yet to be, illumines in a significant and telling way the nature
of their communicative power.

In the foregoing we have argued that Jung's psychology
demonstrates how and why symbols are indispensable to psychic
development, and concomitantly, to what we are now calling
personal becoming. But we have only intimated thus far what,
in his view, this becoming comprises. In order to provide an
adequate account of it we need to take into our purview the
clinical and cultural context in which Jung worked and thought.
To whom is Jung's psychology directed? What kind of materials

does he work with and deem symbolic? And what does he hope,
practically, to accomplish in so doing? It is these questions
that we will make our point of departure in the chapter to
follow. Our discussion of them will serve not only to familiarize ourselves with what we have found to be the most fundamental
concerns and aims of Jung's psychology, but also to bring to
light the interpretive method Jung devised in the course of his
clinical work. As we shall see, this method was specifically
designed to enable persons to discover and draw upon the
symbolic power and meaning inherent in their psychic life, to
appropriate and live out the "lines of advance that are symbolically indicated"[101] therein--in short, to facilitate symbolic
knowing and personal becoming. Because this is the case, it
would seem that we cannot expect to understand in depth the one
or the other, or for that matter the integral relationship
between the two, until we have explicated the various components
of this method and laid bare the pivotal role it plays in Jung's
psychology. Our findings thus far, then, must remain provisional
pending completion of these larger tasks.

CHAPTER III

JUNG'S SYMBOLICS OF FANTASY

In this chapter we intend to undertake an in-depth examination of Jung's interpretation of fantasy. Here we take *fantasy*
to be the most suitable term by which to designate the whole
range of imaginative contents and processes that Jung encountered
and dealt with in the course of his clinical and therapeutic
work. It is imperative that we turn to this area of his psychology, if we are to succeed in bringing to light the distinctive
features of the hermeneutical method he relied upon in his life-
long efforts to elucidate the symbolic depth of meaning underlying man's psychic life. For, as we shall see, it is Jung's
fascination with fantasy and the critical importance he accords
to it in the developmental processes of his patients that leads
him to devise this method. And so, in order to insure that our
explication of Jung's interpretation of Christian doctrine will
be firmly anchored in the dominant underpinnings of his psychology, we shall first address ourselves in depth and at length to
his interpretation of fantasy and only then will we turn to his
doctrinal studies. It is our hope that proceeding in this way
will enable us to uncover the central nucleus of the hermeneutical method that in-forms all of Jung's interpretive work.

The Interpretive Context

We will begin with a series of preliminary questions, a
discussion of which is designed to delineate what we will call
the *interpretive context*. First we shall seek to clarify what
Jung means by fantasy. What exactly is being interpreted here?
i.e., what does the field of interpretation encompass for Jung?
Secondly we shall ask: what is the range of human subjects
actually and/or potentially involved in the fantasy-processes
and their interpretation that are described in his writings?
Lastly we will ask: what value does Jung place on the part
played by an interpretive approach to one's fantasy-life in

fulfilling the needs of the developing psyche? i.e., what is
his view of the psychological utility of interpretation?

The Field of Interpretation

No doubt what we have learned in Chapter II of the pre-
eminent place the category *symbol* assumes in Jung's psychology
would lead us to believe that, in turning here to his interpretive method, we would concern ourselves first and foremost with
how he applies this method to explicitly symbolic expressions.
But the difficulty of determining, apart from an act or process
of interpretation, which expressions are symbolic and which are
not, has led us to adopt another course--inwhat follows we will
view *fantasy* as that which is to be interpreted, and *symbol*, not
as an object of interpretation, but as an interpretive device.
To understand the propriety of so doing, we need to specify
what Jung means by fantasy in relation to what we have previously
said of his notion of symbol.

We have already suggested that he conceives of fantasy in
very broad terms. In *Psychological Types*, for example, Jung
advances a composite notion of fantasy, one that embraces

> ...two different things: 1. a *fantasm*, and
> 2. *imaginative activity*....By fantasy in the sense
> of *fantasm* I mean...merely the output of creative
> psychic activity, a manifestation or product of
> a combination of energized psychic elements.[1]

> Fantasy as *imaginative activity* is, in my view,
> simply the direct expression of psychic life, of
> psychic energy which cannot appear in consciousness
> except in the form of images or contents,... [it]
> is identical with the flow of psychic energy.[2]

It is clear, then, that in Jung's view fantasy encompasses all
of the imaginative life of the human psyche, and that he intends
the term to refer to the specific contents or images of this
life as well as to its energic processes. In order to be faithful to the composite nature of this notion, our own language
will attempt to maintain intact the distinction between fantasy
images and fantasy *processes*, while at the same time employing
the word *fantasy* as a general term that is inclusive of both
these aspects.

Juxtaposing this skeletal notion of fantasy and the notion
of symbol presented in Chapter II, we see that the former lacks

the specificity of meaning that Jung assigns to the latter.
Symbolic images are symbolic by virtue of their peculiar
capacity to express in the best possible way realities that
would otherwise elude one's understanding. Fantasy-images,
on the other hand, may or may not have this power; they may or
may not be symbolic.

But if this is the case, which fantasy images take on this
symbolic power? We will find an answer to this question in what
Jung calls *the symbolic attitude*, by which he means "a definite
view of life endowing the occurrence, whether great or small,
with a meaning to which a certain deeper value is given than to
pure actuality."[3] In Jung's view, one is able to discover the
symbolic depth of meaning that underlies one's fantasy-life
only if one first approaches it with this attitude well in mind:

> Whether a thing is a symbol or not depends
> chiefly upon the attitude of the consciousness
> considering it; as for instance, a mind that regards
> the given fact not merely as such but also as an
> expression of the yet unknown....
> ...This assumption is absolutely possible to
> every consciousness which is orientated to the deeper
> meaning of things, and to the possibilities such an
> attitude enfolds.[4]

In other words, one is free to read fantasy in a symbolic or
non-symbolic manner; whether or not a particular fantasy image
takes on a symbolic range of meaning depends entirely upon the
interpretive stance one assumes vis-à-vis one's imaginative life.
We may infer, then, that to Jung's mind intrinsic to all fantasy
contents or images is a *potentially* symbolic dimension, yet one
whose actualization awaits the assumption of this interpretive
stance.

We have therefore chosen to construe *fantasy* as a neutral
term, i.e., as a term that designates a wide range of psychic
phenomena *qua* phenomena, while viewing *symbol* as a more evalua-
tive term, i.e., as one that accords to these phenomena a
special significance. To our mind this way of differentiating
the two terms is true to the manner in which Jung employs them:
"...we must remember the working hypothesis we have used for
the interpretation of dreams: the images in dreams and spontaneous fantasies are symbols, that is, the best possible
formulation for still unknown or unconscious facts."[5] Note here

that while it may seem as if Jung is equating the meaning of
fantasy and symbol, it would be more precise to say that he is
proposing to view a more general and less defined word (fantasy)
in terms of a more specific and differentiated term (symbol);
the logic of his juxtaposition is more subtle than a matter of
simple equation.

It would seem more appropriate, then, to construe the
latter as an interpretive device, rather than as a word intended
to refer to a readily recognizable class of human expressions.
For in Jung's view there are no available criteria with which to
determine, apart from the interpretive process itself, which
particular words, acts, gestures, objects and images are
symbolic and which are not. Hence throughout all that follows
we will not speak of *symbols* as such, but rather of the *symbolic*
as an interpretive principle, i.e., as a means by which Jung
attempts to call attention to and elucidate the depth of meaning
underlying man's psychic life.

In short, in shifting our focus in this chapter from symbol
to fantasy, we are not leaving all that we have said of Jung's
understanding of symbol behind; rather we are subsuming it into
what we shall say below of his interpretation of fantasy materials. Jung's interpretive method is designed above all else
with these materials in mind; and so the field of interpretation
is made up not of symbolic expressions as such, but rather of the
imaginative processes and contents these materials record. For
economy of treatment's sake, we will limit this field to the two
principal types of fantasy materials Jung's writings deal with--
fantasies of sleep, i.e., dreams,[6] and those of one's waking
life. These writings give ample evidence of the great extent
to which Jung's clinical work centered on the interpretation of
these two forms of fantasy;[7] they provide numerous transcriptions
of the accounts given of these fantasies by his and his col-
leagues' patients. It is these *récits* that make up the fantasy
materials we will concern ourselves with below.

The Human Subject

But this brings us to another question: is Jung interested
only in those fantasies which he encountered in the course of
his clinical work? And if this is the case, does the method he

devised have any applicability outside the context of the
analytic process that takes place between doctor and patient,
analyst and analysand? These questions require that we specify
the historical/cultural context *from* which Jung's psychology
emerged and *to* which it is intended to speak.

We will begin with the obvious--that Jung's is a psychology
that was fashioned throughout the course of his many years of
clinical work. This means that it emerged from his first-hand
dealings with a limited range of people--those whom he encountered either at Burghölzli Mental Hospital in Zurich, during
the years of his residence there (1900-1909), or in the greater
number of cases, as a result of his private psychiatric practice.[8]

But if Jung's analytical and clinical work constitutes the
primary experiential matrix from which his psychological
thought originated, we cannot disregard a second source that
complements and in many ways interfuses with this major one--
viz. his own personal fantasy-life. The best evidence for this
is naturally his autobiography, *Memories, Dreams, Reflections*,
which attests to the intimate interconnections between his life-
experience and life-work.[9]

It would seem then that Jung's life-experience and life-
work interacted in such a way as to lead him to devise a
consistently employed method with which to interpret fantasy
processes. That this method, however, emerged from his
encounters with a relatively limited range of persons does not
exclude its relevance for a wider range of people. Indeed we
would maintain that Jung intended it to be of use to any person
who, in his search for self-understanding and self-integration,
felt a need to reflect upon and attune himself more deeply to
his imaginative life. And so to our mind the human subject in
question when his psychology offers an account of personal
fantasy processes is the analysand only in the most privileged
instances. For he presumed that the need for a greater degree
of attentiveness to and involvement in one's imaginative life
was deeply felt by an ever growing number of persons in his
time and culture.

Jung constructs for us an exemplary portrait of such
persons in his essay "The Spiritual Problem of Modern Man":

>...the man we call modern, the man who is aware
of the immediate present, is by no means the average
man. He is rather the man who stands upon a peak, or
at the very edge of the world, the abyss of the future
before him,...The modern man--or let us say again, the
man of the immediate present--is rarely met with, for
he must be conscious to a superlative degree. Since
to be wholly of the present means to be fully conscious
of one's existence as a man, it requires the most
intensive and extensive consciousness, with a minimum
of unconsciousness....He alone is modern who is fully
conscious of the present.[10]

This intensification of consciousness brings with it an alienation from the primitive dimensions of one's humanity:

>The man who has attained consciousness of the
present is solitary. The "modern" man has at all times
been so, for every step towards fuller consciousness
removes him further from his original, purely animal
participation mystique with the herd, from submersion
in a common unconsciousness. Every step forward means
tearing oneself loose from the maternal womb of
unconsciousness in which the mass of men dwells.[11]

Inseparable from this alienation is a concomitant estrangement
of the present from the past:

>Only the man who is modern in our meaning of the
term really lives in the present;...The values and
strivings of...past worlds no longer interest him
save from the historical standpoint. Thus he has
become "unhistorical" in the deepest sense and has
estranged himself from the mass of men who live
entirely within the bounds of tradition.[12]

We find here a stark portrait of a man who, while very much
present to himself, is for that very reason distant from all
else. And so modern man pays a heavy price for the acute reaches
of self-awareness he attains--he is estranged from his "primi-
tivity," from his fellow man, and from tradition and his past.
He is as a result cut off from the wellsprings of his imaginative
life. And this is perhaps the most striking and disturbing
trait of "modernity's distress"[13]--what Jung presumed to be
modern man's loss of contact with and devaluation of those
dimensions of human experience that sustain and nourish one's
imaginative life.

This, then, in brief is the modern man about whom and to
whom Jung's psychology speaks. It is significant to note that
such a man was, for Jung, a phenomenon of the *Western* world in

a pre-eminent sense. Jung's proclivity to freely interchange
the expressions "modern man" and "Western man" clearly attests
that this is the case;[14] so also does the fact that he regards
the ethos of modernity as a direct descendant of a historical
process of "despiritualization" set in motion by religion and
culture in their distinctively Western forms.[15] These factors,
then, have led us to identify the historical and cultural context with which his psychology is concerned as a modern/Western
one.

     But in delineating the parameters within which this psychol-
ogy emerged and operated, in "contextualizing" it in this way,
we do not intend to arbitrarily foreclose its applicability or
its relevance to other contexts and cultures; we only mean to
call attention to that context and frame of reference wherein its
relevance is most directly and immediately felt and manifestly
demonstrable. It is well known that Jung, however deeply imbued
with a "Western" spirit and temperament and however committed
to working out its problems, did not remain insularly self-
enclosed within this context. As his autobiography attests, he
felt impelled to turn to non-Western traditions, cultures and
texts--of both the "primitive" and "Eastern" worlds--and to
travel at great lengths in Africa, India, among North American
native peoples, etc.[16] These studies and travels cannot be
dismissed as diversions; by his own account they were instrumental in enabling him to consolidate his central insights and
psychological theories.[17] More importantly, they demonstrate
that Jung envisioned the universal applicability of his find-
ings--of his understanding of the structure and dynamics of the
psychic life of man. Indeed, as we shall see, he proposed
hypothetical constructs and sought for evidence (and fashioned
a method with which to interpret it) in a life-long effort to
vindicate this vision.

     And yet cross-cultural studies constituted but one phase
(albeit a very significant one) of this life-work. Jung was, in
fact, full well aware of the limits and even dangers of invading
"Oriental palaces that our fathers never knew," of "feigning a
legacy to which we are not the legitimate heirs," of cultural
vagabondage and religious eclecticism.[18] Such an awareness
reveals in yet another way that the audience he had in mind

remained a predominantly Western one; and it testifies to his
conviction that Western man could ill afford to disregard or
deny his cultural legacy, no matter how acutely problematic it
proved to be for him.

That he was primarily and existentially concerned, then,
with one culture, with his *own* culture, with its ethos and
problems, cannot and should not lead us to conclude that Jung
was so single-mindedly absorbed by it that he remained indiffer-
ent to and unaffected by the values, ideals and achievements of
other neighboring and distant cultural worlds.

But at this point a critical question might well be raised:
is the universal thrust of Jung's psychology not compromised by
his existential involvement in and indebtedness to a particular
cultural matrix? We are not yet prepared to address ourselves
to this issue, however, not at least pending having familiarized
ourselves more extensively than heretofore with Jung's psychological work and method.[19] For the moment we wish simply to call
attention to his special concern for those persons who suffered
most from "modernity's distress." We will argue that Jung's
interpretation of fantasy is designed as a cultural corrective
for this distress, and that he deemed it potentially relevant to
all those persons in modern Western culture who have come to be
estranged from their imaginative lives.[20] This would include
those who have lost touch with their imagination altogether,
those who stand in danger of this loss, and even those who,
although living in relative harmony with their imagination, seek
to deepen their attunement to it and/or overcome the difficulties
they may experience in interpreting its contents and integrating
their meaning into their own patterns of living.

The Need for Interpretation

These reflections should give us a general idea of the
nature of the human subject about whom and to whom Jung's
psychology speaks. We need now to turn to a further question:
what value does Jung place on an interpretive approach to
fantasy? Some might argue that his intent is simply to enable
persons to experience, to feel, to become aware on a mute, pre-
reflective, unthematized level of the depth of meaning of their
fantasy life. If this is the case, one might wonder whether to

his mind engaging in an extended interpretive process of one's
fantasies is but a luxury which some may wish to indulge in,
but which is not really instrumental in furthering personal
development.

Evidence for this reading of Jung is not difficult to find
for those who would wish to appeal to it:

> ...in the case of a real settlement [with the uncon-
> scious] it is not a question of interpretation: it
> is a question of releasing unconscious processes
> and letting them come into the conscious mind in the
> form of fantasies. We can try our hand at interpreting
> these fantasies, if we like. In many cases it may be
> quite important for the patient to have some idea of
> the meaning of the fantasies produced. But it is of
> vital importance that he should experience them to the
> full and, insofar as intellectual understanding belongs
> to the totality of experience, also understand them.
> Yet I would not give priority to understanding....
> For the important thing is not to interpret and
> understand the fantasies, but primarily to experience
> them.[21]

Yet others will note his statement that:

> ...there are times when, as I have often seen, a
> dream that is not understood can still have a com-
> pensatory effect, even though as a rule conscious
> understanding is required on the alchemical principle
> "*Quod natura relinquit imperfectum, ars perficit*"
> (what nature leaves imperfect, the art perfects).[22]

There are numerous texts that can be brought forth to
support either of these two emphases in his thought. His tendency to alternate between them reflects his clear recognition
of the importance of *both* an experiential and an interpretive
mode of approach to fantasy. There can be no doubt that he
values highly the former; in fact, as the first passage cited
above indicates, he assigns a clear priority to experience over
understanding. That he does so corroborates with his view of
symbolic expressions, the emotional effect of which, we have
noted, "does not depend on conscious understanding."[23]

But we will argue that this priority cannot be taken as a
measure of the value Jung accords to interpreting fantasy. Let
us first consider his insistence on the need to assume a
conscious standpoint vis-à-vis the unconscious:

> ...a real settlement with the unconscious demands a
> firmly opposed conscious standpoint.[24]

> The products of the unconscious are pure nature....
> nature is not, in herself, a guide,...So it is with
> the guiding function of the unconscious. It can be
> used as a source of symbols, but with the necessary
> conscious correction that has to be applied to every
> natural phenomenon in order to make it serve our
> purpose.[25]

> In the final analysis the decisive factor is always
> consciousness, which can understand the manifestations
> of the unconscious and take up a position toward
> them.[26]

These passages suggest that the value Jung assigns to understanding fantasy is co-extensive with the need and value of a
heightened consciousness vis-à-vis the unconscious.

The forcefulness and seriousness with which he reiterates
the importance of "conscious understanding" is indicative of
the fact that he views the attempt to attain and consolidate
it as one of the indispensable ethical tasks of human life.
Note, for example, his statement:

> Before the bar of nature and fate, unconsciousness is
> never accepted as an excuse; on the contrary there are
> very severe penalties for it. Hence all unconscious
> nature longs for the light of consciousness, while
> frantically struggling against it at the same time....
> ...Something empirically demonstrable comes to
> our aid from the depths of our unconscious nature.
> It is the task of the conscious mind to understand
> these hints. If this does not happen, the process
> of individuation will nevertheless continue. The
> only difference is that we become its victims and
> are dragged along by fate towards that inescapable
> goal which we might have reached walking upright,
> if only we had taken the trouble and been patient
> enough to understand in time the meaning of the
> numina that cross our path.[27]

Here Jung is asserting that the process of individuation--of
discovering one's path, of becoming oneself[28]--is facilitated
and intensified if one takes it seriously and reflects on it,
i.e., interprets its meaning and course. While referring to it
as a "natural process" consisting of "a sequence of fantasy-
occurrences which appear spontaneously in dreams and visions,"[29]
at the same time he conceives of it as something to be self-
consciously and deliberately pursued and cultivated:

> The process of coming to terms with the unconscious
> is a true labour, a work which involves both action and
> suffering....The natural process by which the opposites

> are united came to serve me as a model and basis for
> a method consisting essentially in this: everything
> that happens at the behest of nature, unconsciously
> and spontaneously, is deliberately summoned forth
> and integrated into the conscious mind and its
> outlook.[30]

We see, then, that Jung thematizes this whole process of
personal development as an *opus*, a struggle, in which one's
consciousness strives to *differentiate* itself from the unconscious, in order to come into a more effective and balanced
relationship with it.[31] Ideally, the process consists of
dialectical alternations between unconscious and conscious
forces, first the one and then the other taking the lead and
acting their parts, dialogically.[32]

Jung's autobiography offers vivid testimony of how such
a dialogue emerged in his own life. In the pivotal chapter,
"Confrontation with the Unconscious," he describes the impasse
he came to at the mid-point of his life and how he overcame it.
At first there seemed

> ...no technique whereby I might get to the bottom of
> my inner processes, and so there remained nothing for
> me to do but wait, go on with my life, and pay close
> attention to my fantasies....Thus I consciously
> submitted myself to the impulses of the unconscious.[33]

He goes on to relate his experience of utterly letting go, and
then of falling, as in a madness, into a bottomless, dark world
of fantasies. And yet he eventually found himself on solid
ground, a stability that was reached only by means

> ...of a rigorous process of *understanding*. I saw
> that so much fantasy needed firm ground underfoot,
> and that I must first return wholly to reality. For
> me, reality meant scientific comprehension. I had to
> draw concrete conclusions from the insights the
> unconscious had given me—and that task was to become
> a life work.[34]

These passages testify to the fact that in his own life
Jung felt compelled to alternate between giving in to the sway
of his fantasies, and taking up a firm stance vis-à-vis them.
It is as if he could not simultaneously effect both modes of
approaching fantasy, as if the one had to precede or follow the
other. In fact he suggests as much elsewhere:

> After...[the fantasy] has been faithfully observed,
> free rein can be given to the impatience of the
> conscious mind; in fact it must be given or obstruc-
> tive resistances will develop. But each time the
> fantasy-material is to be produced, the activity of
> consciousness must be switched off again.[35]

And so it would seem that each mode is necessary for personal
growth in Jung's view, that each must counter-balance and
complement, without interfering with, the other. On the one
hand the desire to understand must be suspended for there to be
a true "letting go";[36] and yet, on the other, a passive
absorption in one's fantasies has at some point to be broken
if their meaning is ever to be integrated into one's conscious
functioning.[37]

     Thus, the alternating emphasis on one and then the other
of these approaches to fantasy in his writings cannot be
dismissed simply as an ambiguity; rather we find it truer to
his thought to interpret it as expressive of an intent to respect
the integrity, need for, and distinct value of each of them.
We may conclude then that Jung understands the experience of and
interpretation of fantasy as complementary agents, as necessary
partners in a unified psychological process of growth and self-
realization; that he views the emergence of fantasy contents
into consciousness and the interpretation of their meanings as
two distinct, and yet inter-related components of a process of
"continual conscious realization,"[38] of unending assimilation
and integration of one's unconscious world into consciousness.
It is as if each agent must respect the integrity of the other,
and at the appropriate time give in to its sway. Presumably
the sense of timing that enables one to shift from "letting go"
to "taking up a conscious stance" vis-à-vis one's fantasy life
varies with each individual, and is determined by the contingencies of his or her personal circumstances.

     To recapitulate, we have found that the value Jung assigns
to an interpretive approach to fantasy is most clearly manifest
in his emphasis on the moral exigence to understand "the meaning of the numina that cross our path" lest we be "victimized"
by a process whose "goal we might have reached walking upright."
We have sought to demonstrate, then, that he does in fact value
highly the role of interpretation in the process of coming to

selfhood, and that the need to assume an interpretive stance
towards fantasy is closely allied in his mind with the need to
understand, with the need to adopt "a firmly opposed conscious
standpoint" vis-à-vis the unconscious.

Our purpose in these preliminary remarks has been to
indicate some of the factors that led Jung to devise a consistently employed method with which to interpret fantasy materials.
Chief among these are: 1) the central place fantasy processes
and contents assumed in his own personal experience as well as
in the experience of his patients; 2) his understanding of the
cultural problematic of his time, which he conceived to be
rooted in modern man's estrangement from the life of the
imagination; 3) his life-long desire to develop psychological
resources which would help overcome this estrangement; and
4) his belief that personal development could be more meaningfully sustained if in-formed and guided by a deliberate and
methodical interpretive process.[39] In short, we have found that
Jung's method emerged from personal and professional needs,
from personal and clinical experience, that it took shape as a
result of his determined efforts to reflect on the lived process
of interpretation this range of experience involved him in. We
have argued that it was the very nature of this experience and
of the tasks and aims of Jung's clinical work that impelled him
from a series of ad hoc interpretations of fantasy to a systematic interpretive method.

The Method in Search of a Name

With these preliminary reflections in mind, we are now
prepared to turn to an explication of the components of this
method. In what follows *method* will be conceived of as a set
of inter-related intellectual operations employed in a consistent manner throughout the analysis or study of a designated
realm of phenomena.[40] With this notion of method as our guide,
we will attempt, in turning to Jung's extensive and wide-ranging
interpretive work on fantasy, to bring to light the most characteristic and recurrent features of this work. Once having
discovered what these features are, we will then evaluate the

extent to which they constitute the nucleus of an interpretive
method, i.e., a consistently employed inter-related set of
interpretive steps or operations.

We begin our account by returning to what we have said
above of Jung's reliance on the *symbolic attitude*. To our mind
this interpretive device is fundamental to the very nature of
his method; it is the *conditio sine qua non* of the interpretive
process. For unless one engages in this process with a predisposition to discover in one's fantasy life a symbolic dimension
of meaning, it cannot succeed in furthering the larger process
it is designed to subserve--viz. personal development.

We will argue, in fact, that the whole of Jung's method of
interpreting fantasy is best understood as an extended attempt
to draw out the consequences that follow from a symbolic reading
of it. If this is the case, then all that we have said in
Chapter II of his understanding of symbol will have a direct
bearing on his interpretation of fantasy. We may anticipate,
then, that Jung, in attributing symbolic significance to fantasy-
images, will assign to them the very same powers that he assigns
to symbols: the power to convey, while yet concealing, a depth
of meaning by virtue of having originated from an unconscious
ground; the ability to transform psychic energy by means of their
mediation between opposing psychic forces; and concomitant with
this, the ability to actualize the nascent future of the developing self. All of these powers center on an ability to disclose
a depth of meaning in the life-situation of the personal self.
And so we would expect that his symbolic reading of fantasy will
be strongly predisposed "to assume that it purports, or signifies, something different and still greater";[41] and more importantly, that it will construe this "something still greater" as
"a subliminal picture of the actual psychological situation of
the individual,"[42] as "a concentrated *expression of the total
psychic situation*."[43]

But in order to better understand the extent to which this
method centers on a symbolic reading of fantasy--on what we may
henceforth call a *symbolics* of fantasy--we need to examine those
points in Jung's writings where he is most forthright and
declarative in his attempts to conceive of it as a whole. For

the most part these passages occur in works written during the years 1915-1923, a period that manifests a strong drive on his part to bring his psychology to intellectual and methodological self-definition. This drive can best be understood as an out-growth of his long and bitter debate with his friend and colleague Freud, a debate that first broke into the open in 1912 with the publication of Jung's *Wandlungen und Symbole der Libido*,[44] and that persisted unabated throughout the lives of the two men.

We do not intend to enter into a discussion of the histor-ical details of this extremely important chapter in the develop-ment of depth psychology;[45] we refer to it here only in order to point out that the debate occasioned the first sustained attempts on Jung's part to articulate and thematize the theo-retical bases of his own psychological style and method. For there emerged in the works composed and published during this period a series of inter-related distinctions--viz. analytic/synthetic, reductive/constructive, causalistic/finalistic, etc.[46]--that Jung had not previously employed. It seems certain that these terms were designed to differentiate his method from the method he attributed to Freud. We would expect, then, that an examination of the meaning he assigned to them will reveal what he understood to be distinctive about his own method.

Underlying all of these distinctions is the oft-reiterated distinction between sign and symbol. We have noted that for Jung a sign is simply "an analogous or abbreviated expression of a known thing."[47] Carried to an extreme limit, a *semiotic* style of interpretation would become a routinized process of "decoding" the meaning of psychic contents in terms of one's prior assumptions about what they re-present. In Jung's view, such an approach loses sight of the "not yet known" quality, the peculiar obscurity of meaning, that characterizes psychic phenomena.[48] Given his concern to accord to this obscurity or opacity a central significance in its own right, it is not surprising that he came to reject a strictly semiotic interpre-tive method and to advance an explicitly symbolic one.

But what of the other terms Jung appealed to at this time? It seems that they are all designed to add forcefulness to his adherence to a symbolic standpoint. This is most manifest in

the definitions affixed to the conclusion of *Psychological
Types*. As regards *reductive*, he states:

> I employ this expression to denote that method of
> psychological interpretation which regards the
> unconscious product not from the symbolic point of
> view, but merely as a *semiotic* expression, a sort
> of sign or symptom of an underlying process.
> Accordingly, the reductive method treats the
> unconscious product in the sense of a leading-
> back to the elements and basic processes,...
> Hence, the reductive method is orientated back-
> wards..., whether in the historical sense or in
> the merely figurative sense of a tracing back of
> complex and differentiated factors to the general
> and elementary. The methods of both Freud and
> Adler are reductive, since in both cases there is a
> reduction to elementary processes either of wishing
> or striving, which in the last resort are infantile
> or primitive. Hence the unconscious product neces-
> sarily acquires the value of a merely figurative
> or unreal expression, for which the term "symbol"
> is really not applicable.[49]

In contrast to this, Jung sets forth an alternative method:

> *Constructive* means "building up." I employ
> "constructive" and "synthetic" in describing a
> method that is opposed to the reductive. The
> constructive method is concerned with the elabor-
> ation of unconscious products (dreams, fantasies,
> etc.). It takes the unconscious product as a basis
> or starting point, as a *symbolical* expression, which,
> stretching on ahead as it were, represents a coming
> phase of psychological development....
>   ...The aim of the constructive method, there-
> fore, is the production of a meaning from the
> unconscious product which is definitely related
> to the subject's future attitude.[50]

We would add that Jung makes use of the distinction
between *causal* and *purposive* or *finalistic* with the same
purposes in mind:

> ...fantasy needs to be understood both causally as
> well as purposively. With the causal explanation
> it appears as a *symptom* of a physiological or
> personal condition, the resultant of previous
> occurrences; whereas, in the purposive interpre-
> tation, fantasy appears as a *symbol*, which seeks
> with the help of existing material a clear and
> definite goal; it strives, as it were, to distinguish
> or lay hold of a certain line for the future psycho-
> logical development.[51]

That Jung employed all these distinctions interchangeably
testifies to the similar meaning he assigned to them. Note,
for example, the following:

> The Viennese school interprets the psychological
> symbol semiotically, as a sign or token of certain
> primitive psychosexual processes. Its method is
> analytical or causal. The Zurich school recognizes
> the scientific possibility of such a conception but
> denies its exclusive validity, for it does not inter-
> pret the psychological symbol semiotically only but
> also symbolistically, that is, it attributes a
> positive value to the symbol....
>   The method of the Zurich school, therefore, is
> not only analytical and causal but synthetic and
> prospective, in recognition of the fact that the
> human mind is characterized by *fines* (aims) as well
> as by *causae*.[52]

This espousal of a "symbolic," "constructive," "synthetic"
or "purposive" method in contradistinction to a "semiotic,"
"reductive," "analytic," or "causal" one constitutes a consistent
theme in his writings from 1912 on.[53] And there can be no doubt
that the method from which he sought so earnestly to distinguish
his own is none other than that he attributed to Freud himself:
"The essential thing in Freud's reductive method is to collect
all the clues pointing to the unconscious background, and then,
through the analysis and interpretation of this material, to
reconstruct the elementary instinctual processes."[54] "Elementary instinctual processes" is the key expression here, in terms
of which all psychic processes and contents are explained. In
short, it is the "something known" that these contents, as signs,
are deemed to represent.

But it is probable that Jung's debate with Freud stemmed
less from his distrust of the category "instinctual processes,"
from the particulars of Freud's sexual theory of libido and
instinct, and more from his reluctance to accord to any one
explanatory principle a pre-eminent position in his psychology.[55]
For to do so, in his view, would invite one to disregard the
plurality of meanings underlying the life of the psyche. And
this would lead one to fall prey to the temptation and presump-
tion of attempting to give an exhaustive account of what is best
regarded as inexhaustible and ultimately unfathomable.[56]

It is beyond the purposes of this study, however, to pursue
all the ramifications of Jung's break with Freud; we wish simply

to emphasize that their conflict resulted, happily, in a much
more sustained attempt on Jung's part to thematize the nature
of the interpretive method that had emerged from the discoveries
and insights of his psychological work. It would appear, then,
that his psychological thought and method assumed the particular
form they did largely as a result of the existence of an antag-
onistic principle--viz. the "Viennese school."

But this is not to imply that Jung's rejection of the
analytic or causalistic method was total and unequivocal. At
several points in fact he affirms its utility, even if, in so
doing, he insists on denying its "exclusive validity."[57] Note,
for example, his assertion that:

> Through reductive analysis of this expression nothing
> is gained but a clearer view of the elements originally
> composing it, and though I would not deny that increased
> insight into these elements may have its advantages,
> it nevertheless bypasses the question of purpose.
> Dissolution of the symbol at this stage of analysis
> is therefore a mistake. To begin with, however, the
> method for working out the complex meanings suggested
> by the symbol is the same as in reductive analysis.[58]

Jung implies here that the distinction he draws between analytic
and constructive modes of interpretation is more complicated
than a matter of simple opposition. We would suggest, then,
that his professedly constructive method not be viewed as
excluding altogether the interpretation of fantasy in terms of
its immediate personal antecedents. In fact, as we soon shall
see, we will argue that his running debate with Freud, and his
propensity to set his own method over against Freud's, should
not obscure the subtlety with which he incorporates into his
method elements of the analytic-causal approach he ostensibly
spurned.

The Method at Work

Jung's unspoken indebtedness to his intellectual progenitor
should alert us to the fact that the names he employs to differentiate his method from Freud's, and the way he defines them, in
and of themselves, provide an insufficient means with which to
assess his method. Accordingly, we shall attempt in what follows
to take account of the way he actually goes about interpreting
fantasy materials. We shall seek to discover Jung's method "in

act." This requires that we enter into concrete instances of
his interpretive work, that we attend less to what he says of
his method, and more to what he does with it.

Jung's writings abound with dream and waking-fantasy texts,
and with their interpretation. It is difficult to select
examples from the wealth of material available for a number of
reasons. Perhaps the major problem in so doing is the danger of
excising the fantasy from the personal context in which it is
so inextricably embedded. This is why we have selected two
examples which include the person's associations to the fantasy
images, for this will insure that the fantasy, and the life-
situation from which it springs and to which it speaks, are
viewed in terms of each other. Ideally each fantasy image
shquld be interpreted in terms of the continuous stream of
fantasy material that has previously surfaced in the course of
the interpretive process;[59] but it is not possible to give an
exhaustive account of material so extensive in nature.[60] Rather
our purposes here are more modest--to present two isolated
examples, wherein we may detect the more salient features of
Jung's interpretive method at work.

Although Jung's psychology is very much concerned with
waking fantasies, the majority of examples he cites in his
writings are dreams. We have thus selected two dreams for study
here. This should not, however, lead us to overlook the fact
that Jung conceives of dreams as fantasies; *fantasy* is the more
inclusive and all-encompassing category, within which dreams
are subsumed.[61]

We have chosen as our first example a woman's dream, in
which "someone gave her a wonderful, richly ornamented, antique
sword dug up out of a tumulus."[62] It is with the woman's
reaction to the dream, more than with the dream itself, that the
interpretation begins; in and of itself the dream has little
meaning apart from her associations to it.

The image of the sword brings to the dreamer's mind two
principal associations: "her father's dagger, which he once
flashed in the sun in front of her" and "a Celtic bronze
sword," which she associates with her own ancestry. Jung adds
that "her father was in every respect an energetic, strong-willed

man, with an impetuous temperament, and adventurous in love
affairs." And in view of the fact that he died at an early
age, the strong affect with which she responds to the memory of
the flashing dagger becomes the most salient datum to be interpreted, in that it is indicative of an extremely high (unconscious) valuation of her father.

It would appear then that the discovery of the sword
beneath the mound reveals a desire on the woman's part to re-
experience the energy and force of her (lost) father's
personality. Jung offers this as an *analytical* interpretation.
By means of it, a crucial aspect of the present dilemma of the
dreamer is illumined--we are told that "she has never been able
to accept a man like her father and has therefore chosen
weakly, neurotic men against her will." The analytical interpretation suggests this is so, because of a certain (unconscious)
fixation on her father, a fixation that she was unable to out-
grow as a result of his early death. The fact that she associates her *father's* dagger with the sword, and that the image
carries with it a strong affective tone that she traces to her
experience of having seen him once flash it in the sun, presents
the dreamer with an occasion by which to re-discover the meaning
of the buried past that was her father, and in so doing, to
achieve an insight into the make-up of her present situation.

But Jung, pursuing the ramifications of the woman's
reference to her Celtic ancestry, extends the interpretation
much further than this. We are told that she is proud of this
ancestry, a feeling, moreover, that seems to have found expression in the sword image's rich ornamentation. This aspect of
the dream imagery suggests that the woman's longing for her
lost past involves much more than a need to re-experience her
personal father.

And here we reach the most distinctive and radical feature
of Jung's interpretive method: the extension of the meaning
of the image beyond the immediate context provided by the
individual's personal history into the wider context of cultural
meanings imbedded in the collective past of mankind. For the
sword belongs not only to the father, but to the ancient
heritage of the Celts. Thus the fact that it is a "wonderful,
richly ornamented, antique sword" evokes and mysteriously invests

it with a rich fund of meaning. Moreover, the sword is dug up
out of a "tumulus," i.e., an earthen mound serving as a primitive burial site, and not simply a grave as we know it today.
This suggests then that the affective power of the imagery
extends beyond the immediate pull of her own (infantile) past,
carrying with it reverberations that echo back to the "ancient
heritage of the human race."

The *constructive* interpretation of the dream Jung advances
attempts to make use of these reverberations in elucidating the
meaning the sword holds for the woman. When viewed solely as
belonging to the father, it can be taken to represent his power,
his sexuality, or more significantly, his *will*-power; "Her
father's weapon was a passionate, unbending will, with which he
made his way through life." It is evident that she needed to
re-establish some contact with this power, but that her "strong
resistances towards her father" in her conscious life made an
appropriation of it difficult. But Jung maintains that the
sword is no ordinary sword, that it is not simply a weapon of
the will, a means of forceful action, but also, by virtue of
the ancient heritage it embodies, a weapon of insight and
wisdom. This is the dénoument in the interpretation, the point
at which the woman comes to see that will alone may lead to the
adventurism and impetuousness she rightly feared in her father,
while will acting in concert with her intelligence could, as
opposites conjoined, lead her out of her present impasse.

On one level, then, the sword can be interpreted as an object
of the dreamer's regressive longing for her lost father, a
longing, to be sure, that is expressive of a true need to rediscover and appropriate his energy and will. Such an interpretation, as far as it goes, is constructive, inasmuch as the
dream is viewed purposively; that is, insofar as it brings the
dreamer to an awareness of this need, and in so doing sanctions
and legitimates it. But it fails to take account of the further
reaches of meaning in the imagery that the dream makes accessible
to her. These reaches are intimated in the perhaps less notice-
able aspects of the dream imagery: viz. that it is an ornamented,
antique sword, not merely an unadorned one, and that the grave
is a particular kind of grave, i.e., a tumulus.

In summary, Jung interprets the dream as expressive of the woman's need to rediscover a kinship not simply with her father, but with a whole realm of experience and meaning to which she is linked by virtue of her ancestry. Her longing for the personal past that is epitomized in the figure of her father is thus made to serve as a means of access to the more substantial fatherhood provided by the ancient heritage of man.[63]

As a further example, we will take the following dream of another woman patient:

> She is about to cross a wide river. There is no bridge, but she finds a ford where she can cross. She is on the point of doing so, when a large crab that lay hidden in the water seizes her by the foot and will not let her go. She wakes up in terror.[64]

The woman's associations to the imagery of the dream reveal an awareness that she is progressing too slowly in life, as well as a frustration in the face of difficulties she wishes, but is unable, to surmount. She associates the river with the obstacle that is blocking her progress, while the ford represents to her a possible means by which to overcome it, "to cross in safety." She also suggests that this means is the analytic treatment she has undertaken.

The main affect stemming from the dream (terror) is triggered by the emergence of the crab from the water and its seizure of her foot. Because the crab provides the major dramatic element in the dream, we would expect that the interpretation of the dream will depend primarily on the meaning attributed to it. But the dreamer's associative processes are somewhat tentative and broken as regards the crab, which makes its interpretation more difficult. She does, however, mention two things about it: first she links it to its Latin name, *cancer*, which evokes in her memories of the disease by which a close friend of hers had died. In addition, she tries to account for her fear of the crab by portraying it as "an animal that walks backwards--and obviously wants to drag me into the river."

We are also told that at the time of the dream, the dreamer had had a bad argument with a friend, a woman to whom she had a

very close attachment. Their relationship in fact had a
homosexual tone to it, and was characterized by sentimentality
as well as violent quarreling. Jung adds that the course of
the analysis had revealed "an exaggerated, fantastic relation
to her mother," which, after her mother's death, had been
transferred to her friend.

Beginning with an analytical mode of interpretation, Jung
points to the obvious analogy between the situation the dream
depicts and the dreamer's current situation with her friend.
It is apparent from her analysis that she needs to extricate
herself from the exhausting cycle of sentimentality and irrita-
bility she forever lived through with this friend. The dream
imagery reconfirms what she is already well enough aware of--
that she is facing a specific difficulty, that she is firmly
resolved to overcome it (to undertake the crossing of the river),
that she has at her disposal a means of overcoming it (the ford,
which she suggests represents her analytic treatment), and yet
that a seemingly inexplicable obstacle thwarts her purposes,
prevents her crossing. The moment she ventures forward, a crab,
intruding into an otherwise hopeful scene, rises up from the
river and "seizes" hold of her. Terror, not progress, is the
result. The imagery of the dream, then, aptly captures and
distills the essence of the dreamer's situation--she has clearly
reached an impasse. Either she stays on the river-bank, in
which case she is stalemated, or she may attempt a crossing, in
which case she will only be intercepted and presumably dragged
into the river water.

Thus far, the interpretation simply re-presents the
conscious situation of the dreamer. But it does her little good
to be told what she already knows--that she remains in the grip
of an unworkable and unsatisfying relationship. It is at this
point that Jung expands the interpretation in what he calls a
constructive or synthetic direction, by looking for further
levels of meaning which may underlie the dream images and their
personal antecedents.

He does so by probing more deeply into the enigmatic image
of the crab. On one level it is obvious that it represents
the specific obstacle that renders difficult and frightening
the crossing. This obstacle can be viewed simply as the friend

who holds the dreamer in her clutches. On a deeper level,
however, it represents a less easily identifiable *regressive*
force, a pull of the past, the dreamer's reluctance to let go
of her friend (a reluctance that hearkens back to the fear of
losing her mother's embrace). On still another level it
expresses the erotic-sexual desire that draws her to her friend
as well as to her mother. Jung, however, while alluding to all
these meanings, and without denying the distinctly sexual
coloration of the image, is more concerned to construe the force
it represents as "an undisciplined, undifferentiated, and not
yet humanized part of the libido, which still possesses the
compulsive character of an instinct, a part still untamed by
domestication. For such a part some kind of *animal* is an
entirely appropriate symbol." He sees this "untamed," "compulsive" libido at work in her attachment to her friend, as well
as to her mother: "The common factor is a violent, sentimental
demand for love...an overpowering infantile craving."

Moreover, the fact that the crab "lay hidden in the water"
points to the repressed nature of this untamed libido. Interpreting the woman's association of the crab with cancer, Jung
points out that her other friend who had died of the disease
lived an active, "merry" life full of adventures with men.
Apparently the dreamer had always viewed this death as punish-
ment for the woman's frivolous life, in such a way as to reinforce her distrust and denial of her own "frivolous streak."
He infers then that the dreamer's repression of her libido only
serves to keep it in its untamed state, and the more untamed it
remains, the more it will act to draw her downward and backward
from her life's true needs and demands.

Normally, Jung would sanction a giving in to the pull of a
regressive force,[65] a heeding of the movement of the image's
energy back into the hinterlands of the psyche. But in this
particular case the overpowering affect of dread and terror
counselled against such a letting go; it was the woman's fear of
the crab and not the crab itself that had to be heeded. Jung
interprets this fear purposively, then, as an entirely apt and
appropriate feeling-response in view of the power that the
unconscious and its dynamic contents held for her at the time.

But to better understand how he comes to link the image of the crab to a primitive, "untamed" libidinal force, we need to take note of the fact that he amplifies the dream imagery and the dramatic situation it portrays in terms of the myth of the hero and his battle with the monster of the deep, who emerges from the waters and is engaged in mortal combat at water's edge.[66] Jung's recourse to this mythic pattern and particularly to the motif of danger that pervades it serves the dreamer well, for it provides her with a useful backdrop against which she may more easily come to the realization that she is not yet ready for an assumption of the hero's role. The dangers of the crossing are yet too great: "The unconscious powers are still inauspicious and obviously expect more work and a deeper insight from the dreamer before she can really venture across."[67]

In summary, the meaning the dream holds for the woman's immediate situation centers on the warning it sounds against a premature attempt on her part to undertake the crossing, to forge the solution for her dilemma. At the same time, the dream speaks to her prospective situation, in intimating that when the time is more auspicious, overcoming her difficulty may require a real struggle with the "monster of the deep," with the libido-source that is the crab.

In retrospect one can now understand why expanding the meaning of the image of the crab is crucial to the dreamer's ability to perceive how to deal with her present dilemma. For if she had viewed it merely as an analogue of her friend, she may well have reduced its significance in her eyes to that of an irksome obstacle, to be overcome at all costs, and the sooner the better. If it were simply a friend that was holding her back, why should she not reject her and her desire for companionship with her once and for all, and proceed ahead with the tasks that awaited her? A constructive interpretation of the dream, however, enables her to see that such a tact would be highly self-destructive; for it would tempt her into a precipitous crossing, in utter disregard of both her unconscious fears and her desire for her friend/mother.

In Jung's view the only way "across" would be to enter into the pull of this seemingly infantile desire, until the point is reached when its hidden purposes could be deciphered. As

long as the object of her longing is interpreted simply as "my
friend" or "mother," she will resist it, viewing it as operating at cross-purposes with her development. But by amplifying
the meaning of the crab and thereby viewing it as an "untamed
bit of libido" in herself, the interpretive process presents
her with an occasion to achieve a deeper rapport with a more
"tamed" instinctuality.

The Three Components of the Method

Having looked closely at two concrete instances of Jung's
interpretive method "in act," we are better prepared to delineate what we have found to be its three most distinctive
components: 1) the interpretation of fantasy in terms of its
personal antecedents, which extend from the present situation
of the individual back into his or her infantile past; 2) the
expansion of its meaning by virtue of the move from a personal
to a collective past; and 3) the interpretation of this expanded
meaning as revelatory of the specific needs and requirements of
the person's on-going development. Although we have seen the
central role each of these steps played in both of the examples
of Jung's interpretive work examined above, we will now articulate more systematically what each entails, in such a way as to
point to the underlying logic that impels Jung from a personal
to a collective and then back again to a personal context.

The Personal Past

The first step in the interpretive process aims to bring
to light what we have called the personal antecedents of the
fantasy imagery. These may include recent events in the person's
life, aspects of his or her over-all life-situation, or obscure
or traumatic events of the person's more distant past. These
antecedents emerge in the course of the person's associations
to the fantasy material.

It is at this point in the interpretive process that
experiencing and interpreting the fantasy are most contiguous
with each other. For the activity of free association exhibits
the same inner dynamic that the fantasy itself does--a regressiv
movement of psychic energy. Operative in each is a "letting go"

or a giving in to the affect bound up with the fantasy. We
have seen, for example, how the image of the sword evoked the
dreamer's long submerged feeling for her father, and how the
image of the crab evoked terror. In each case the interpretive
process required a surrender to the affect underlying the image,
a surrender which carried the dreamer backward into her past.
By virtue of freely associating memories, images, and other
experiences with those depicted in the fantasy itself, the
dreamer regresses to a more infantile level, thereby enabling
her to rediscover aspects of her experience long ago lost.
The crab's grip first brings to mind the woman's friend, and
then, almost imperceptibly, her mother's embrace. There is a
movement, then, from the more immediate personal antecedents to
the more distant ones, from the present-just-become past to the
infantile past.

The first step of the interpretive process retraces this
movement from immediately prior events and situations in the
person's life back to his or her more remote experiences. In
the course of this retracing the fantasy-image is broken down
into its underlying components, i.e., various "feeling-toned
contents" (or complexes[68]), which in turn point to the primary
"instinctual processes" that lie at the root of the psychic
conflict or problem in question. In each example discussed
above we have seen how disturbances of these primary processes
carried the dreamer to an impasse in her conscious life--in
the first instance, an unconscious erotic tie to the woman's
father brought about the difficulty; in the second, it was "a
violent, sentimental demand for love."

In short, this, the first component of Jung's method, construes the fantasy imagery as a re-presentation of particular
facets of one's personal experience. At this point the interpretive process proceeds by unearthing the personal antecedents
and the primary instinctual processes that underlie the person's
affect-laden associations to the fantasy material. It is here
that Jung's reliance on and assimilation of the analytical
method he attributed to Freud and ostensibly rejected is most
apparent.

From the Personal to the Collective

We now come to the pivotal step of the method--the expansion of the interpretive context from a personal to a collective one. This expansion is brought about by means of what Jung calls *amplification*, an operation whereby the fantasy imagery and the person's associations to it are extended into a wide range of seemingly unrelated mythic, religious and other cultural materials.[69]

We can better understand what such an operation involves by taking account of the sense in which it is a natural outgrowth of the first, and more analytical, step of the method. The continuity between the two is most apparent in the dynamic at work in the person's associations to the fantasy imagery. We have found that Jung views this dynamic as a regressive one, in which the energy and affect[70] bound up with the fantasy draw the person back into ever more infantile states of his or her past life. Perhaps the most remarkable feature of Jung's psychology, however, is his claim that this regressive movement does not find its term in infancy at all, but carries one beyond it into archaic levels of meaning that touch upon those of the ancient heritage of man.[71] The interpretive process, then, does not culminate in the discovery of the instinctual forces and/or disturbances that underlie the imagery. For there is a mysterious sense in which the attempt to interpret it as a historical (biographical) re-presentation of one's infantile being is self-negating, inasmuch as a whole plethora of meanings is opened up in the course of the process that cannot be accounted for by the analytical mode of interpretation that led to their discovery.

Accordingly, this second step of the method involves an entirely different interpretive strategy, one that is designed to amplify and elucidate the further reaches of meaning that one's associations to the imagery evoke. At this point in the interpretive process it is the analyst who indulges in free association, who enters into the spirit and drift of the patient's own associations, pursuing their ramifications beyond the dimensions of his or her personal life-experience.

Here we reach that point in our account of Jung's method where a brief word is necessary with regard to his use of the

notion *archetype* as an interpretive device. It is beyond the
purposes of this study to enter into a detailed discussion of the
terminological and epistemological problems and controversies
that have surrounded his adoption of this term.[72] Rather we
wish here to emphasize the unmistakeable intent that is mani-
fested in the way he makes use of it--to draw attention to the
recurring patterns of meaning and form that underlie man's
imaginative life. In fact it is clear that for Jung the existence of these patterns is so widespread as to be well nigh
universal.

As an interpretive device the archetype serves the important function of undergirding and reinforcing the person's
perceptions of the correspondences and parallels in meaning and
form between the fantasy imagery on the one hand and a collective world of imagery on the other.

The second step of the interpretive process, then, involves
a weaving together of personal and collective worlds of imagery,
or more specifically, an amplification of the former in terms
of the latter. This inter-weaving is made possible by an
elucidation of the correspondences in meaning and form that are
found to underlie both worlds. The archetype is simply posited
as the necessary ground and nucleus of the meaning these two
worlds hold in common.

The discovery and elucidation of these universal patterns
of meaning set in motion profound consequences: the person in
question is emboldened to regard his or her individuality not as
eccentricity or atomicity, but affirmatively as a form and
means of participation in the collective life of man. A kind
of self-fulfillment is made possible by virtue of which:

> This widened consciousness is no longer that touchy,
> egotistical bundle of personal wishes, fears, hopes,
> and ambitions which always has to be compensated or
> corrected by unconscious counter-tendencies; instead
> it is a function of relationship to the world of
> objects, bringing the individual into absolute, binding,
> and indissoluble communion with the world at large.[73]

From the Collective Back to the Personal

But Jung presumed the therapeutic value of the move to the
collective to be ultimately contingent upon the person's ability

to actualize and integrate the expanded meanings opened up by
it into his conscious life. And this brings us to the third
component of his method: the interpretation of these meanings
in terms of the needs and requirements of the person's psychic
development.

    This, the culminating step of the interpretive process,
consists essentially of hitting upon the particular meanings in
the course of the fantasy's amplification that best suggest
new possibilities for one's own development. We have seen, for
example, how the expansion of the meaning of the sword beyond
the strictly personal (or biographical) realm served to bring
the woman to an awareness of her need to forge an alliance
between her intelligence and the will-power that was her
father's. In other words, this aspect of the method enables
the individual to identify and integrate the meaning the fantasy
holds for his or her present and future life; it is the point
at which the psychological purposes of the interpretive process
are brought to fruition.

    For Jung, then, the interpretation of fantasy culminates
when the individual discovers a way to live out, i.e., integrate
into his or her conscious life, this meaning:

>   The wordless occurrences which are called forth
>   by regression to the pre-infantile period need no
>   substitutes; they demand to be individually shaped in
>   and by each man's life and work. They are images
>   sprung from the life, the joys and sorrows, of our
>   ancestors; and to life they seek to return, not in
>   experience only, but in deed.[74]

And so the ethical imperative to understand the meaning of one's
fantasy life must eventually give way to an even more pressing
task, which we may call *appropriation*:

>   As soon as ever we begin to map out the lines of
>   advance that are symbolically indicated, the patient
>   must begin to proceed along them. If he remains
>   hypocritically inert, his own inaction precludes
>   any cure. He is in truth obliged to take the way
>   of individual life which is revealed to him, and to
>   persist in it until and unless an unmistakeable
>   reaction from his unconscious warns him that he is
>   on the wrong track.
>   Whoever is incapable of this moral resolution,
>   of this loyalty to himself, will never be relieved
>   of his neurosis....
>   ...Infallibly, in the last resort, it is the
>   *moral factor* which is decisive for health or for
>   disease.[75]

Assessment

To recapitulate our findings, we have discerned three distinct intellectual operations to be at work in Jung's interpretation of fantasy materials--their interpretation in terms of 1) the personal past, 2) the collective past, and 3) personal becoming. But to gain perspective on how these operations, taken together, constitute the nucleus of his interpretive method, we need to discover the logic that makes of these three steps an *inter-related* set of operations. In short, having differentiated these operations one from another, we need now to seek out the unity of conception and purpose that underlies them and that justifies our having ascribed to them the term *method*.

We will begin our assessment by reflecting once again on what perhaps is the most distinctive feature of the method: the way the interpretive process moves in deliberate and consistent fashion from a personal to a collective context and back again. What is it that impels Jung to broaden so radically the interpretive context? If his psychological purposes are to free the individual to a greater propensity to appropriate "the lines of advance that are symbolically indicated" in his fantasy life, then why need such a long detour through the archaic past of the psyche be taken at all? What would happen if the method were to stop short of this shift in standpoint, confining itself instead to a strictly personal context of meanings and associa- tions? In order to answer these questions, we need to return to the two dreams discussed above. We have seen how in each case the introduction of a wider interpretive context is absolutely critical to the outcome of the interpretive process, and by extension, to the success of the analytic treatment itself. In the sword dream, for example, were it not for the greater sense of perspective this expanded context made possible, the woman would have construed her present needs merely as an index of a child-like longing for a long deceased father. As a result her regressive longing for the past would be viewed as the problem to be overcome, or worse, to be avoided at all costs. And her fears of giving in to a devalued "infantilism" would then stand her in danger of attempting pre-maturely and arbitrarily to sever all her links with the past. The delicate

point of reconciliation that the dream imagery forges between
her conscious desire to "progress" and her unconscious impulses
to regress would be rent asunder.

We are suggesting, then, that the move from the personal to
the collective past is an attempt on Jung's part to give sanction
and freer scope to one's regressive longings, and to "capitalize"
on their purposive nature. For these longings, if heeded and
followed to their term--to the archaic-collective heritage of
mankind--ultimately enable the person to gain greater perspective on the limitations and values of her personal past, and
thereby, ironically, serve to free her from its sway.

In short, the interpretive process, in moving from personal
to collective and back again, is at one and the same time following and retracing the shifting currents of psychic energy backwards into the hinterlands of the psychic past and forwards in
the direction of the individual's prospective development. And
so we are now able to see retrospectively that the inner logic
of Jung's method centers on one of the basic tenets of his
thought--viz. that psychic processes manifest simultaneously a
double movement to the past and to the future: "The psychological moment is Janus-faced--it looks both backwards and
forwards."[76]

It is evident, then, that the method, in moving from a
personal to a collective sphere of imagery and back again, is
faithful to what Jung held to be the alternately regressive and
progressive shifts and turns in the flow of psychic energy. In
inter-weaving and mediating between personal and collective, as
well as past and future poles, it reflects the dialectical nature
of the human psyche's regressive/progressive dynamisms.

But it is not only these alternating movements between past/
future and personal/collective that give to the method a distinctly dialectical character; it is also the fact that throughout the whole of the interpretive process the two poles *self* and
fantasy are alternately viewed in terms of each other. Initially
the fantasy is interpreted in terms of the historical background
of the personal self; ultimately, however, the personal self is
interpreted in terms of the fantasy. It would seem, then, that
in the course of the interpretive process, the method is turned
on its head, that it undergoes its own reversal. The reversal

comes with the third step, when the meaning of the personal
self's prospective development is sought in the fantasy imagery.
At this point the fantasy is no longer interpreted; rather it is
made use of to interpret that from which it emerges and to which
it refers--the personal self. The object of interpretation consequently shifts from *fantasy* to *self*. This is not surprising,
in view of the fact that the purpose of the method is fundamentally a psychological one--to elucidate the fantasy's meaning
in such a way as to enable the individual to come to a better
understanding of his life-situation, and concomitantly to a more
effective way of actualizing his *self*.[77] No doubt such a purpose
led Jung to conceive of the interpretation of fantasy from the
very beginning as a task necessarily subservient to a more
extensive project of *self*-interpretation.

Ultimately, then, fantasy is made to serve the needs of
the developing self. It follows that Jung accords to fantasy a
capacity to speak to the whole of a person's life-situation, and
more specifically, to shape the path of his or her prospective
development. This *shaping* power of fantasy would remain
inaccessible, however, apart from the interpretive process
itself, that is, apart from the depth of meaning unearthed by
the second step of this process. It is this depth of meaning,
and not the fantasy as such (i.e., the fantasy prior to its
amplification) that enables one to decipher "the lines of
advance that are indicated."

Put somewhat differently, the second and third steps or
stages of the interpretive process work hand in hand with each
other. For it is only by virtue of the person's discovery of
resonances in his fantasy-life that reverberate back to the
collective heritage of man that his own sense of self is enriched; and it is only by virtue of this enriched self-awareness
that he is able to redirect his energies to an actualization of
a future commensurate with that sense of self.

Accordingly, we may conclude that Jung's method is pre-
eminently designed to bring persons to an awareness of two
inter-related capacities inherent in their fantasy-life: an
enriching and a *directing* or *shaping* power. The expansion or
amplification of the fantasy imagery's meaning that the method
effects not only serves to enrich one's life, but concomitantly
to direct it forward.

With these reflections in mind, we are better able to
understand how the three steps of the method, when taken together, constitute what we have called a *symbolics* of fantasy.
Let us take each of them in turn, and attempt to specify how it
serves the purposes of a symbolic reading of fantasy.

Although the first step--interpreting fantasy in terms of
its personal antecedents--in and of itself stops short of an
explicitly symbolic mode of interpretation, it nonetheless
paves the way for it. For it reveals the futility of all
attempts to elucidate exhaustively the whole range of meanings
underlying the affects and images set in motion by the person's
associations to the fantasy material; it reveals the impossibility, in fact, of construing these meanings exclusively in terms
of the experiences and memories of one's personal past. We have
found that for Jung interpretation on the analytic level is a
self-transcending, self-abrogating process that carries one
beyond itself, beyond a strictly personal context and world of
imagery, into a collective one. The first component of the
method, then, functions in such a way as to demonstrate the
need that an analytic or *semiotic* reading of fantasy give way
to an explicitly *symbolic* one.

The second step of the process--the amplification of the
fantasy's meaning in terms of patterns of imagery and meaning
of a collective kind--takes up where the first step leaves
off. Pursuing an ever-widening realm of associations and
reverberations back into the archaic-collective past, it seeks
to bring the person to a greater awareness of the abundance of
meaning that inheres in his imaginative life. It is at this
point in the process that the fantasy's capacity to enrich
personal being comes most directly into play; this capacity
accrues to fantasy by virtue of the depth of meaning it embodies.
Now to unearth and elucidate this meaning is to draw upon
fantasy's symbolic significance. For, as has already been made
sufficiently clear in Chapter II, a chief, if not the chief,
characteristic of symbolic expressions, in Jung's view, is the
fact that they embody and convey a *depth* dimension of meaning.

But this meaning does not become meaning *for* the person
until it is perceived to be revelatory of the "lines of advance"
of one's developing selfhood. And it is at this, the third

step of the process, that the other principal characteristics
Jung assigns to symbolic expressions--viz. their transforming
power and their prospective meaning--can be seen to apply to
fantasy as well. And so we cannot but conclude that fantasy
images, when subjected to the rigors of an interpretive process
conceived of and carried out in the light of the method we have
outlined here, show themselves to be inherently symbolic
expressions.

In the foregoing we have delineated the distinctive
features of the interpretive method Jung devised and relied
upon throughout the course of his clinical work, and argued
that its underlying logic centers on the way each of its three
steps shows itself to be designed above all else to bring
persons to a greater awareness of and readiness to appropriate
and live out the symbolic dimension of meaning underlying their
imaginative lives. We are now prepared to move our argument
one step further by designating this method hereinafter as a
hermeneutical one. Such a designation is appropriate for a
number of reasons: for one, any method that is primarily
interpretive in character is *a fortiori* hermeneutical, inasmuch
as the term hermeneutics is generally taken to refer to the
art and method of interpreting. On this most general level,
however, little explanatory value is provided by the term; the
burden of explanation is merely transferred from one term to
another, from *hermeneutics* to *interpretation*.
The meaning accorded the latter then becomes determinative.
We would propose that it be conceived of as the task of deciphering the multivalent meanings inherent in all human phenomena,
whether behavior, language, culture, traditions, etc. Given
this perspective, any humanistic or social-scientific discipline
involved in such a task can be properly termed *hermeneutical*.
We are by no means presuming, however, that this skeletal
notion in and of itself could ground an exhaustive account of
the nature of hermeneutical inquiry and reflection. Rather
we are simply articulating the manner in which the term will be
made use of in all that follows below. The notion we are
advancing here carries with it a particularity of viewpoint:
viz. one that is predicated on the assumption that a wide range

of human phenomena manifest a distinctly multivalent or symbolic
character.   And thus it is limited by this viewpoint; i.e., it
is not designed to embrace or accommodate all hermeneutical
theories.

Central to this notion of hermeneutics, then, is the view
that its nature is necessitated by the peculiar nature of that
which is interpreted.   If the object of interpretation is
characterized by a multivalence of meaning, it will resist the
ready grasp of man's understanding.   And if this is the case,
it is not to be expected that interpretation would yield
insight with perspicuous or intuitive immediacy.   Rather it
will proceed by means of the painstaking task of deciphering,
i.e., of disengaging particular valences or dimensions of
meaning from the phenomena in question.

In short, we are here conceiving of hermeneutics in a way
that is consonant with the nature of that which is interpreted,
i.e., of *method* in a way that is consonant with *content*.   This
consonance between method and content, between the hermeneutical
and the symbolic, serves to alert us to the specificity of
meaning we are assigning to the term *hermeneutics*:   those modes
of human reflection are best termed hermeneutical which are
explicitly designed to interpret the symbolic dimensions of
meaning underlying human life and culture.

With this notion in mind, the propriety of viewing Jung's
method as a hermeneutical one becomes all the more apparent.
For we have already discovered his abiding concern with the
symbolic ranges of meaning he presumed to be inherent in man's
psychic life, and in particular, in his fantasy life.   Hence,
inasmuch as his method aims above all else to elucidate this
meaning, it seems pre-eminently suited to bear this designation.

And yet it would be more precise to term it a *psychological*
hermeneutic, inasmuch as its larger purpose is to further self-
understanding and, concomitantly, personal development.   Such a
designation accords with the fact that Jung's symbolics of
fantasy attempts to bring to light the shape of the individual
life-story that lies hidden in the "depths" of fantasy.

The term "psychological hermeneutic," however, in and of
itself does little to point out what is most distinctive about
the method; and so we would appeal to yet another designation

here: *restorative*.[78] To conceive of the method as a
restorative hermeneutic serves to add emphasis to our finding
that it provides one with a means by which to rediscover,
retrieve, and re-appropriate the fullness of meaning that lies
buried in Western man's collective past. Perhaps the most
remarkable of all the method's many features we have reviewed
above is its ambitious attempt to enable modern man to partake
anew of the fullness and richness of this collective world of
imagery and meaning that is forever receding into the past.

We deem it fitting, then, to make use of this term here,
for in a singular way it serves to draw our attention to the
fact that Jung's method seeks to restore to modern man that
which he is most prone to lose precisely by virtue of his being
modern--a sense of the value that this collective world of
imagery and meaning holds for him. And in so doing, it seeks
to re-vitalize the whole of his imaginative life. And in
re-vitalizing and re-plenishing this life, it envisions ultimately a "restoration of...the whole human being."[79] By
restoring to modern man the fullness of *meaning* that underlies
his imaginative life, the method brings about, if only
incipiently, the fullness of *being* embryonic in the human
personality.

We have now reached a decisive point in our inquiry,
where many of our observations can be brought together. We
have seen how this method moves dialectically between the poles
personal and collective, past and future, self and fantasy.
And we have now noted how, in amplifying the meaning of one's
imaginative life, it serves to enrich one's being and to pave
the way for a "restoration of the total personality."[80] We
would suggest, then, as a means of gaining perspective on the
import of all of our findings, that it is this interaction
between *meaning* and *personal being* that Jung's psychological
hermeneutic seems peculiarly designed to effect. Moreover,
this would accord with our conclusion in Chapter II that
symbolic knowing and personal becoming proceed in conjunction
with each other. Only now we are better able to understand why
such a conclusion remained provisional pending a study of Jung's
interpretive method: because symbolic knowing for Jung is

initimately bound up with an interpretive process, a process
that involves the whole of the human psyche's imaginative life
and contents.

In summary, we have suggested that Jung's psychological
hermeneutic, in viewing the depth of meaning underlying one's
imaginative life as revelatory of the shape of one's emerging
selfhood, functions as a bridge between imagination and personal
being. Accordingly, we have envisaged its ultimate significance
to center on the restoration of man's imaginative life to the
very heart of his being. We would expect that these findings
would carry with them significant implications for religious
studies in general and Christian theology in particular,
implications that would perhaps have their most direct bearing
on religious anthropology. But we are not yet prepared to
spell out these implications, and until we are able to do so,
we would do well to regard this last point as not yet a
conclusive one.

CHAPTER IV

JUNG'S PSYCHOLOGY OF DOCTRINE

In this chapter we come to the heart of our concern in
studying Jung--his interpretation of Christian doctrine. We
will proceed first by surveying those factors in Jung's
experience and work that awakened in him a compelling interest
in Christian doctrine; secondly, by analyzing in some detail
one paradigmatic instance of his interpretive work in the field
of Christian doctrine--his study of the Trinity; and finally by
evaluating our findings in this chapter in the light of conclusions previously reached.

In the preceding chapter we have sought to demonstrate
that Jung's lifelong concern and work with the fantasy processes
of his patients led him to fashion a psychological hermeneutic
with which to interpret and give direction to the whole of a
person's imaginative life and being. By moving here from fantasy
to doctrine, we shall be able to determine the extent to which
Jung relied upon the self-same hermeneutical method in interpreting materials lying outside the immediate context of his
clinical work. For we shall have at our disposal a wealth of
evidence stemming from two of the most important domains of
Jung's psychological studies; and if this evidence reveals the
very same set of intellectual operations at work in both of them,
we shall have done much to strengthen our case that these operations, taken together, give to the whole of his interpretive
work a unity and consistency of intention and performance.

From Fantasy to Doctrine

We will begin our study by seeking to determine why it was
that Jung, a psychologist and primarily a clinical psychologist,
would undertake a study of doctrinal materials. Is it possible
to isolate those factors in his personal experience and work
that impelled him to address himself to religious as well as
clinical materials, to doctrine as well as fantasy? We need
not look long and hard to come to an initial answer to this

question. For we have already seen that Jung deems it essential
to amplify fantasy in terms of imagery of a mythological and
religious nature. It is evident, then, that his interest in
religious materials and their meaning is inseparable from his
concern with fantasy; it is grounded in the very workings and
dynamic of his method of interpreting fantasy materials, in
the shift from a personal to a collective context that this
method undertakes.

It is not simply the requirements of his method, however,
that lead Jung to embark upon his extensive studies of religious materials. There is also a psychohistorical reason that
works hand in hand with this methodological exigence: his
own personal life-experience awakened in Jung a compelling and
abiding need to take account of a wider realm of imaginative
expressions. He tells us in his autobiography that after the
most intensive years of confrontation with his own fantasies
(1913-1917), he was left with

> ...an extreme loneliness....I felt the gulf
> between the external world and the interior world
> of images in its most painful form....
> However, it was clear to me from the start that
> I could find contact with the outer world and with
> people only if I succeeded in showing--and this would
> demand the most intensive effort--that the contents
> of psychic experience are real, and real not only as
> my own personal experiences, but as collective
> experiences which others also have. Later I tried
> to demonstrate this in my scientific work, and I
> did all in my power to convey to my intimates a new
> way of seeing things. I knew that if I did not
> succeed, I would be condemned to absolute isolation.[1]

It is clear, in view of this testimony, that Jung's
propensity to inter-relate personal and collective experiences
and imagery was expressive of a desire to find some confirmation
for his innermost experiences in the life-experiences and cultures of others. An entire chapter in his autobiography
elaborates how he dealt with this need,[2] tracing his fascination
throughout a period of thirty to forty years in his life first
with Gnosticism, then with alchemical literature, and finally
with Christian doctrine. Note, for example, his avowal of the
discovery

> ...that analytical psychology coincided in a
> most curious way with alchemy. The experiences of

> the alchemists were, in a sense, my experiences,
> and their world was my world. This was, of course,
> a momentous discovery: I had stumbled upon the
> historical counterpart of my psychology of the
> unconscious....When I pored over these old texts
> everything fell into place: the fantasy-images,
> the empirical material I had gathered in my prac-
> tice, and the conclusions I had drawn from it. I
> now began to understand what these psychic contents
> meant when seen in historical perspective. My
> understanding of their typical character, which
> had already begun with my investigation of myths,
> was deepened.[3]

This discovery paves the way, in fact, for an insight of
critical importance to Jung's later work: "...it became clear
to me that without history there can be no psychology."[4]

This insight served to vindicate and intensify Jung's
personal interests in a broad range of cultural and religious
materials. His preoccupation with personality theory and
clinical materials, so dominant throughout the middle years of
his life (1910 to 1936), increasingly gives way, and a torrent
of publications on specifically religious texts and themes
follows. The first of these is his commentary on *The Secret of
the Golden Flower* (originally published in 1929),[5] a work which
reflects Jung's new-found fascination with the world of alchemy.
A series of more ambitious works on the subject appear throughout the years 1936-1955, as well as a scattering of works on
folklore, Near Eastern mythology, Buddhism, etc.[6] More important for our purposes, however, are those works given to a
treatment of explicitly Christian themes; spanning the same
period of time, they accompany and in many instances are inter-
woven with his alchemical writings. Chief among them are
"Psychology and Religion," "A Psychological Approach to the
Dogma of the Trinity," "Transformation Symbolism in the Mass,"
Aion, and "Answer to Job."[7] It is apparent, then, that Jung's
own life-experience, his immersion in and preoccupation with
his personal world of fantasy at the mid-point of his life,
shaped profoundly the manner in which his thought developed,
and led him ineluctably to take account systematically and
methodically of a vast array of religious literature and
phenomena.

The Religious Situation

     Jung's efforts in this regard spanned well-nigh fifty years.
We will not presume in this chapter to survey the whole sweep
of his explorations, for our special concern is doctrine and
Jung's interpretation of same. We need, however, to place in
context his work in this domain, in such a way as to clarify the
nature of the relationship between his interest in Christian
doctrinal expressions on the one hand and religious materials of
whatever tradition on the other. We shall approach this task
by highlighting what Jung understood to be the central characteristics of the religious situation of his time and culture. In
so doing we will return to and extend our remarks on his views
of modern man and Western culture in general.

     For Jung this religious situation is an acutely problematic
one. It is rooted in modern man's inability to befriend his
imaginative processes and to incorporate them into his consciousness of self. Alienation ensues, and so does a "bankruptcy"
and "poverty" of the soul[8]--a benumbing sense of spiritual
loneliness and destitution. This pervasive sense of spiritual
malaise constituted what was to Jung's mind the most significant
symptom of the cultural and religious problematic of his time.
His writings tend to view this malaise as the outcome of
centuries of decline in the Christian churches' power to mediate
religious meaning and experience:

          We all know how...piece after piece collapsed, and
     how the alarming poverty of symbols that is now the
     condition of our life came about....
          I am convinced that the growing impoverishment
     of symbols has a meaning. It is a development that
     has an inner consistency. Everything that we have
     not thought about, and that has therefore been
     deprived of a meaningful connection with our develop-
     ing consciousness, has got lost....We have let the
     house our fathers built fall into decay, and now we
     try to break into Oriental palaces that our fathers
     never knew. Anyone who has lost the historical symbols
     and cannot be satisfied with substitutes is certainly
     in a very difficult position today: before him there
     yawns the void, and he turns away from it in horror.[9]

     Jung links this "historical process of...despiritualiza-
tion"[10] to the iconoclastic temper set in motion by the
Protestant Reformation:

> Protestantism, having pulled down so many walls
> carefully erected by the Church, immediately began
> to experience the disintegrating and schismatic
> effect of individual revelation. As soon as the
> dogmatic fence was broken down and the ritual lost
> its authority, man had to face his inner experience
> without the protection and guidance of dogma and
> ritual, which are the very quintessence of Christian
> as well as of pagan religious experience.[11]

> The iconoclasm of the Reformation...quite
> literally made a breach in the protective wall of
> sacred images, and since then one image after another
> has crumbled away. They became dubious for they
> conflicted with awakening reason....
> The history of Protestantism has been one of
> chronic iconoclasm. One wall after another fell.[12]

It is evident from the passages quoted above that the frame of
reference Jung relies upon in depicting this process is the
whole development of the Judaeo-Christian religious tradition
in the Western world. More importantly, he accounts for it by
appealing to what he holds to be the evolution of consciousness
nurtured by the iconoclastic impulses of this tradition:
"Every extension and intensification of rational consciousness...
leads us further away from the sources of the symbols and, by
its ascendancy, prevents us from understanding them. That is
the situation today."[13]

It is this "intensification of rational consciousness"
that gives rise to the religious as well as the cultural situation of modernity, that engenders and perpetuates modern man's
sense of estrangement from the principal forms and structures
of his religious traditions. This estrangement, this spiritual
destitution, is the presupposed "given" in all of Jung's religious writings. It is their starting-point, the problem they
attempt to overcome, a problem, we are told, that cannot be
evaded without evading the burdens of consciousness:

> It seems to me that it would be far better stoutly
> to avow our spiritual poverty, our symbol-lessness,
> instead of feigning a legacy to which we are not the
> legitimate heirs at all. We are, surely, the rightful
> heirs of Christian symbolism, but somehow we have
> squandered this heritage....
> ...spiritual poverty seeks to renounce the false
> riches of the spirit in order to withdraw not only
> from the sorry remnants--which today call themselves
> the Protestant Church--of a great past, but also from
> all the allurements of the odorous East; in order,

> finally, to dwell with itself alone, where, in the
> cold light of consciousness, the blank barrenness
> of the world reaches to the very stars.[14]

In short, we are proposing that we regard Jung's psychological studies of religious materials first and foremost as a
response to the problematic nature of the religious situation
of his time,[15] a response that was designed ultimately to
contribute to an overcoming of modern man's spiritual "bankruptcy." We have already had occasion to emphasize in Chapter
III that Jung's interpretation of fantasy purports to speak
only to those people in the Western world who are modern in the
fullest sense of the word--to those whose consciousness has
outstripped itself, who have fallen prey to the greatest degree
of alienation from the cultural traditions, institutions and
symbolic forms that for so long had a hold on the collective
mind of the West. We may now extend the point and add that the
same holds true for his psychology of religion; it is intended
to be of value primarily to those people who have experienced
a spiritual loss, a barrenness of soul, and to a debilitating
extent:

> I am not...addressing myself to the happy possessors
> of faith, but to those many people for whom the
> light has gone out, the mystery has faded, and is
> dead. For most of them there is no going back, and
> one does not know either whether going back is
> always the better way.[16]

It is developed from its very outset with a particular problem
and a particular audience in mind. And it is designed as a
means of helping those most directly implicated in this problem
to overcome it.

We must take care, then, to approach Jung's psychology of
religion with this "therapeutic" aim clearly in mind. And so,
an appeal to his deep personal and theoretical interests in
religious questions is not enough, in and of itself, to
adequately account for the earnestness with which he applied
his psychological tools to the study of religious materials.
We must include among these factors his therapeutic intent--
his desire to alleviate the spiritual malaise that so beset
the culture of his time.

Jung's Special Interest in Christian Doctrine

If in the foregoing we have set forth some of the factors
that led Jung to interpret a rich variety of religious materials,
we have yet to attempt to put into perspective the particular
place doctrinal interpretation assumed in the whole of this
work. It is to this task that we now turn.

We will begin by delineating what he means by the term
doctrine. It is characteristic of his style of reasoning that
he provides the reader with no straight-forward definition of
the term. His frequent use of it, however, permits us to
identify the nucleus of meaning he assigns to it.[17] For Jung,
doctrine signifies any historically fixed and formalized
expression of the Christian faith or tradition. It is precisely
the fixed and formal nature of doctrinal expressions that
distinguishes them from other kinds of religious expression.
Jung the psychologist is fascinated with this their most
distinctive feature. Why is it and how is it that doctrine has
attained to its fixity of form? As we shall come to see, it is
ultimately to universal forces in the human psyche that Jung
will appeal in answering this question. In his view the enduring stability and indeed the authority of Christianity's central
doctrinal expressions depend primarily on these psychic forces.[18]
And so it is not surprising that questions relating to the
ecclesiastical warrants for the authoritative nature of Christian
doctrine are not at issue for Jung.

That this is the case serves to clarify why it is that he
sees fit to interchange freely the terms dogma and doctrine.[19]
According to traditional usage, doctrine attains the status of
dogma when its form and content are specified and ratified by
ecclesiastical bodies.[20] Jung, however, is not interested in the
role of church authority in the formation of dogma/doctrine, and
so he is disinclined to differentiate the meaning of the two
terms. In fact his fluid use of them indicates that the more
specific of the two--*dogma*--holds for him a meaning which is
co-extensive with the meaning of the more general term--*doctrine*, a meaning, in other words, which is much broader than
that ascribed to it by theological and ecclesiastical tradition.
And so, in what follows we will transliterate all of Jung's

references to dogma and to doctrine as simply "doctrine," in
order to avoid the appearance that we are differentiating what
he himself does not deem it necessary to differentiate.

We need now to turn from these terminological questions to
a more pressing one: how was it that Jung came to accord to
doctrine a privileged place in the whole of his interpretive
work in the field of religion? What was it about doctrine, as
one genre of religious expression among many others (e.g.,
ritual, myth, prayer, mysticism, art, ethics, etc.), that so
deeply absorbed his attention, that so compellingly elicited his
psychological scrutiny?

We will argue that Jung's special interest in doctrine is
a natural outgrowth of his general concern with the religious
problematic of his time. In order to understand how this is the
case, we need to return to and extend what we have said of this
problematic above. We have already noted what for Jung is chief
among the causes, as well as symptoms, of modernity's spiritual
malaise: the pervasive erosion and decline in the power of
religious forms and institutions to mediate meaning. Such an
erosion is disturbing to Jung, for he shows himself to have a
keen appreciation for the positive role played by such forms and
institutions in the psychological development of Western man:

> There are any amount of magical rites that exist
> for the sole purpose of erecting a defence against the
> unexpected, dangerous tendencies of the unconscious....
> Since the dawn of humanity there has been a marked
> tendency to limit this unruly and arbitrary "super-
> natural" influence by means of definite forms and laws.
> And this process has continued throughout history in
> the form of a multiplication of rites, institutions,
> and beliefs. During the last two thousand years we
> find the institution of the Christian Church taking
> over a mediating and protective function between these
> influences and man.[21]

In his psychology of religion he returns again and again to the
"mediating and protective" powers of religious "rites, institutions and beliefs" vis-à-vis the uncontrollable, the unconscious
and the supernatural dimensions of human experience: "All man's
strivings have...been directed towards the consolidation of
consciousness. This was the purpose of rite and dogma; they
were dams and walls to keep back the dangers of the unconscious,
the 'perils of the soul.'"[22]

We see in these statements an attempt to relate the
origins, development and decline of religious forms to a presupposed evolution of consciousness. Jung argues that these
forms have played a vital role in mediating between the classical and medieval mind on the one hand and the primordial ground
of religious experience on the other. They were able to do so
because they succeeded in interposing a permeable screen between
the conscious and unconscious poles of Western man's psychic
and religious life, thereby permitting him to sustain his participation in the "depth" dimension of this life, while at the
same time protecting him from its more awesome and potentially
demonic reaches. Such mediation, to Jung's mind, served the
indispensable need of safeguarding and nourishing a consciousness which was still young, fragile and which remained in
constant danger of dis-integration. And yet he clearly recognizes that a distinctly different exigence manifests itself in
the modern period: an iconoclastic drive to break down the
mediating forms and structures of religion, to overcome the
distance between consciousness and the unconscious wellsprings
of religious experience.[23] How, then, can this need for mediation and this need to overcome it be reconciled?

As we shall see, there is a strong tension between these
two seemingly antithetical emphases in Jung's psychology of
religion. This tension is especially manifest in what Jung says
of doctrinal expressions, which find themselves in a peculiar
position when faced with the iconoclastic impulses of the modern
ethos and spirit. On the one hand, their fixity and stability
of form would appear to render them less vulnerable than other
kinds of religious expression to a general erosion and breakdown
of religious forms. On the other hand, they stand to lose the
most in such a situation, for their identity depends upon a
maintenance of their form intact.

Experience and Doctrine

Perhaps the peculiarities of this situation can best be
clarified by elaborating here on what Jung perceives to be the
dialectic at work between experience and doctrine. Time and
time again he juxtaposes these two terms.[24] A study of the
passages in which he does so reveals an ambiguity in the way he

construes the relationship between them. On the one hand he
emphasizes the consonance between experience and doctrine:
"...the dogmatically formulated truths of the Christian Church
express, almost perfectly, the nature of psychic experience.
They are the repositories of the secrets of the soul."[25] On
the other hand he contrasts and even opposes the two: "A dogma
is always the result and fruit of many minds and many centuries,
purified of all the oddities, shortcomings, and flaws of individual experience. But for all that, the individual experience, by
its very poverty, is immediate life, the warm red blood pulsating
today."[26] While affirming that Christian doctrinal expressions
represent and express "almost perfectly" Western man's religious
experience, he at the same time implies that they stand in danger
of becoming distanced from this experience, if and when its
dimensions and patterns evolve. We shall attempt, when we take
up Jung's study of the Trinity, to draw out the implications
of this dual emphasis in his interpretation of doctrine.

     For the moment we wish simply to point out that his percep-
tion of the inherent harmony that existed in former times between
experience and doctrine does not lead him to disregard the dissonance that threatens to intervene and that in fact has already
intervened to a considerable extent between the two. The anomaly
of this modern-day dissonance in face of what had previously
been a striking degree of congruence perplexes and fascinates
Jung. In what ways and guises does this dissonance emerge?
When do doctrinal expressions thematize experience? When do they
clash with it? How might new lines of inter-relationship between
doctrine and experience be forged? These are the problems that
led Jung into the years of effort that his interpretive work in
the field of Christian doctrine comprised. These are the problems his psychology of doctrine wrestled with and hoped to
resolve.

     The nature of the task they were to involve him in is
forcefully articulated in his short work, "Psychology and Religion," where he states:

          To gain an understanding of religious matters, probably
          all that is left us today is the psychological approach.
          That is why I take these thought-forms that have become
          historically fixed, try to melt them down again and
          pour them into moulds of immediate experience. It is

certainly a difficult undertaking to discover connecting links between dogma and immediate experience of
psychological archetypes, but a study of the natural
symbols of the unconscious gives us the necessary
raw material.[27]

Here Jung's open avowal of the kind of venture he envisioned
reveals its audacity and radicality: his is an interpretation
of doctrine which we may now anticipate to be a *re*-interpreta-
tion, and one, moreover, which begins with a process of
de-construction--with a "melting down" of age-old doctrinal
forms--and culminates in a re-casting of new ones.

On one level, then, Jung's purposes in undertaking a study
of Christian doctrine can only be described as iconoclastic;
for he shows himself to be relentless in his determination to
break down the traditional forms and to wrest from them the
experiences that lie buried within them. It is almost as if he
is more bent on accelerating the historical process of the
declining power of religious forms than he is interested in
arresting or overcoming it. And yet, on another level, he shows
himself to be intent on re-forging the very same "connecting
links" between experience and doctrine that the iconoclastic
thrust of his method breaks down! In the study of this method
"in act" that we are now readying ourselves to embark upon, we
shall come to see that both of these purposes and ways of functioning are in fact true to it and central to it. In short, we
may anticipate that Jung's interpretation of doctrine will move
in both *iconoclastic* and *re-constructive* directions, and that
the one aspect cannot be properly assessed without taking
account of the other. Nor, we need add, can either of these
purposes be reconciled with the romanticist's attempt to rescue
from the corrosive acids of modernity the pristine form of
doctrine in all its splendor in order to secure and preserve an
unchanging form and meaning for all time.

But our aim here is not to assess the import of what we
have yet to examine at close hand; it is, rather, to orient
ourselves to this examination by attempting to explain what it
was that led Jung to accord to his interpretation of doctrine a
privileged place in the whole of his psychology of religion.
We have suggested that one of the chief reasons for his so
doing was his desire to understand the dialectical interplay

between religious forms and experiences, and in particular
between the most historically fixed of these forms, i.e.,
doctrines, on the one hand, and the changing patterns of these
experiences on the other.

Personal Factors

But this is not the only reason; indeed, the whole range
of mutually inter-acting and reinforcing factors--psycho-
historical, therapeutic and theoretical--that awakened in him
a general interest in religion also contributed to his special
interest in doctrine. Of these three sets of factors, the
psychohistorical is particularly worthy of note here. In order
to take sufficient account of it, we need to return to and
extend our earlier remarks on Jung's life-experience as recorded
in *Memories, Dreams, Reflections*.

Here Jung recounts the despair he came to during his
adolescence as a result of his efforts to find in Christianity
confirmation for his visionary experiences of childhood.[28]
Specifically, it was the event of first communion that stretched
the disproportionality between his inner religious experiences
and his confessional, church experience to the point where faith
in the latter was shattered:

> This was called the "Christian religion," but none of
> it had anything to do with God as I had experienced
> Him....
>   What about the failure of Communion to affect me?
> Was that my own failure? I had prepared for it in all
> earnestness, had hoped for an experience of grace and
> illumination, and nothing had happened. God had been
> absent. For God's sake I now found myself cut off
> from the Church and from my father's and everybody
> else's faith. Insofar as they all represented the
> Christian religion, I was an outsider. This knowledge
> filled me with a sadness which was to overshadow all
> the years until the time I entered the university.[29]

Moreover, Jung's difficulties in assimilating or accepting
the teachings of the Christian faith were intensified by the
fact that his father, a Reformed pastor, suffered from a crisis
of purpose which centered in a persisting, gnawing religious
doubt.[30] Jung writes bitterly of the disappointments occasioned
by his attempts to enter into theological dialogue with him:

> Theology had alienated my father and me from one
> another. I felt that I had once again suffered a
> fatal defeat,...He struggled desperately to keep
> his faith. I was shaken and outraged at once,
> because I saw how hopelessly he was entrapped by
> the Church and its theological thinking. They had
> blocked all avenues by which he might have reached
> God directly, and then faithlessly abandoned him.[31]

Especially painful for him was his father's intellectual abdica-
tion before the mystery of the Trinity; while Jung was intrigued
by the problem of "a oneness which was simultaneously a threeness," his father refused to reflect on it.[32] Perhaps we can
trace the root of Jung's continuing interest in the Trinity and
his eventual study of it to this refusal and this pain.

The whole of his autobiography reveals that his intellectual
drive to penetrate the mysteries of the Christian faith, heightened by his strong sense of the discordance between the richness
of his visionary experiences and the meaninglessness of the
public worship of his church, impelled Jung in his later years
to take up a systematic study of Christian doctrine.[33] And so
it was his personal fate to return at the end of his long life
to the religious problems and wounds that had afflicted him in
its beginnings. Jung's extensive forays into Gnostic and
alchemical texts, comparative mythology and folklore, and even
Far Eastern religions notwithstanding, it is ultimately to his
own tradition that he returns. His personal need to come to
terms with Christian doctrine, then, was co-extensive with a
need to come to terms with his own historicity, with the cultural and religious ethos of late nineteenth-century Europe,
with a Christianity that had been refracted through the prism
of the Swiss Reformed Protestantism of his family, time and
place.

The Trinity as Paradigm

Our above remarks have attempted to demonstrate how our
study's move from fantasy to doctrine is true to the exigencies
of Jung's personal and intellectual development. We have main-
tained that these exigencies led Jung inexorably into an
extensive re-interpretation of Christian doctrine. We would
hope that the foregoing will serve as a suitable backdrop

against which we may present an account of the content and
method of this interpretive work.

Our account will center on an exposition and evaluation
of Jung's study of the Trinity, "A Psychological Approach to
the Dogma of the Trinity."[34] We are limiting the scope of our
inquiry to this particular instance of Jung's doctrinal work
for the following reasons. First, rather than attempting to
survey cursorily all of his writings in this domain, it has
seemed preferable that we select one given instance from among
them, in order to better be able to encounter at close hand
the specifics of his method in act.

Secondly, we have already alluded to the fact that his
curiosity vis-à-vis the mystery of the Trinity and his father's
inability to shed light on it deeply impressed Jung in his
youth and awakened in him a determination to understand it.
This determination testifies to the importance he attached to
the doctrine; clearly, he perceived in his early years that it
occupied a pivotal place in the Christian faith and world-view.
We would expect, then, that his principal work on the Trinity
would provide us with an invaluable distillation of his mature
thinking on the whole of the Christian doctrinal tradition. We
will not be disappointed in this expectation, for we will find
that this work does in fact incorporate within it much of what
Jung says elsewhere of the whole gamut of issues this doctrinal
tradition raises for him--Christology, evil, redemption, the
relationship between nature and spirit, etc.[35] Indeed, it provides us with a far more integrated and finished statement of
his psychology of doctrine than can be found in any of his other
writings. For these reasons, then, we have singled out Jung's
study of the Trinity, and will make of it a paradigm for the
whole of his interpretive studies of Christian doctrine.

Before proceeding, one further preliminary remark is in
order: in moving from *fantasy* to *doctrine*, from one genre of
human expression to another, we are entering into an interpretive context distinctly different from that which we have dealt
with heretofore. We have seen that fantasy processes, in Jung's
view, emerge from, reflect and thematize the life of a person;
they speak about and to the personal self. The personal self,
then, is the locus and context of the interpretive process.

Doctrinal expressions, however, emerge from the collective life
of a whole culture; they reflect and thematize this life.
Concomitant with a shift from fantasy to doctrine, then, is a
shift from a *personal* to a *collective* context of meanings and
experiences. We need to keep this point clearly in mind
throughout all that follows, because it carries with it significant repercussions for each step of the interpretive process.

Jung's Interpretation of the Trinity

In turning now to our analysis proper of "A Psychological
Approach to the Dogma of the Trinity," we will employ an order
of exposition which corresponds to the structure of the work
itself: we shall first consider the historical antecedents to
the Trinity; secondly, Jung's argument for the archetypal basis
of the "three-in-one" motif; then his discussion of the specifically Christian form of this motif; and finally, his interpretation of the Trinity's meaning for Western man and culture
today.

Historical Antecedents

The beginning section of the work, "Pre-Christian Parallels,"[36] seeks to bring to light the many precursors to the
specifically Christian form of the doctrine. Jung finds these
precursors in Near Eastern and classical mythology, philosophy
and religion. He appeals to sources as diverse as the triadic
deities of ancient Egyptian and Babylonian religions, the Pythagorean philosophy of numbers and Plato's *Timeaus*. Because his
elucidation of the parallel meanings and forms underlying these
materials provides Jung with a foundation for everything that
is to follow, we need to take careful note here of what he finds
to be significant in them.

As regards the triadic gods of the ancient Near East, it is
the nature of the relationship between the three figures that
most keenly interests him. He notes the monotheistic orientation evident in the Egyptian and Babylonian affirmation of the
essential unity between the first and second figures, who were
imaged in both cultures as "Father" and "Son."[37] The third
figure is viewed primarily as a relational force, as that which

binds together the father and son.[38] These materials will serve
Jung as a backdrop against which to present his views of classical Christianity's affirmation of the *homoousios* formula.

What, then, of Pythagorean philosophy? What relevance does
it hold to Jung's inquiry? He finds in it a resource with which
to think out in more speculative and less figurative terms the
now abstracted problem of unity in diversity. How does division
emerge from unity? And how can the two be reconciled with each
other? Jung sees in Pythagoras' speculations on the mystical
meaning of the numbers one, two and three a means of conceptua-
lizing the "splitting up" of being into the "one" and the
"other."[39] And although these speculations do not resolve the
philosophical and existential dilemma posed by this loss of
unity, they nonetheless articulate it with a clarity that had
not been previously attained. In short, Jung discerns in this
thought-world a profound reflective awareness of the emergence
of cosmic conflict, of moral division, of the warring tension
of opposites.

He is also indebted to Pythagorean thought for its notion
of "threeness" as a representation of the hoped for resolution
between all conflictual pairs:

> In the third, the tension is resolved and the lost unity
> is restored....Three is an unfolding of the One to a
> condition where it can be known--unity become recogniz-
> able; had it not been resolved into the polarity of
> the One and the Other, it would have remained fixed in
> a condition devoid of every quality.[40]

He emphasizes, however, that "the third" is but a depiction of
a resolution that is yet to be achieved; in and of itself, it
is but a logical, a notional solution to the problem.

Jung's dissatisfaction with such solutions leads him, to
the reader's astonishment, to press beyond them altogether and
to introduce what on first reading might appear to be a fanciful
and even contrived idea--the idea of "the fourth." The philosophical resource that he employs in introducing it is Plato's
Timaeus, whose opening words reverberate throughout Jung's
writings: "One, two, three--but where, my dear Timaeus, is
the fourth...?"[41] Tantalized by this question, Jung returns
forever and again to it.

But it is his Trinity article which goes the furthest lengths towards answering it. For it is in wrestling with the trinitarian doctrine that he comes to sense the full weight of Plato's cryptic assertion that something is "missing" in human existence as it is lived and understood. What is this missing "fourth"? Jung suggests that Plato's own life and thought provide us with the best clues for an answer:

> Plato certainly did not lack spirit; the missing
> element he so much desired was the concrete realiza-
> tion of ideas. He had to content himself with the
> harmony of airy thought-structures that lacked
> weight, and with a paper surface that lacked depth. [42]

In so stating, Jung shows himself to be wary of the Platonic tradition of Western philosophy; it is a tradition, he implies, that invites and reinforces Western man's depreciation of the concrete world, of the experiential and material bases of mental and ideational reality.

The Archetypal Basis of the Trinity

We shall see when we arrive at the nucleus of the article that both Pythagoras' idea of the third and Plato's intimation of a (missing) fourth will be instrumental in Jung's amplifica-tion of classical Christianity's representation of the triune God. But the immediate question we must raise here is: why does his study begin with these materials and his analysis of them? By way of response we will first note that in introducing historical antecedents to the Trinity at the very outset of his study, Jung does not mean to construe a cause and effect relation-ship between the two. He does not seek to explain the origins of one by recourse to the other, or to the whole interplay of cultural and historical forces in ancient and patristic times. Rather his aim, in bringing to light the oftentimes startling parallels between the Trinity and its prefigurations in the religions of the Near East, is to provoke in the mind of the reader the question: might not all these expressions share a common psychic origin? Might they not all emerge from similar or even the same psychic needs and roots? This is the question that comes to the fore in the course of reading the first three chapters. [43] Jung seeks his answer to it in the "indestructible

foundations of the human mind,"[44] the "structural dominants" of
which he calls *archetypes*, a designation that depends upon a
prior postulation of a certain invariability, a trans-historical
structure in the human psyche.[45] And so, having first appealed
to the existence of a demonstrably triadic motif or pattern
underlying a wide range of religious and cultural materials,
Jung then proposes construing it as a "structural dominant" of
the psyche, as "...an active archetype operating beneath the
surface and throwing up triadic formulations."[46] That he does
so testifies to his desire to call attention to what are presumed to be the universal dimensions of meaning underlying the
doctrinal form.

It is at this point that we reach the first critical
juncture in Jung's study--the attempt to bring to light and to
explicate the Trinity's universal ground of meaning. Because
this step in the interpretive process will carry with it important consequences for everything that follows, we would do well
to present here a brief assessment of what it entails. How is
it that Jung can attribute such universality of meaning to a
historically conditioned expression? How does he move from the
cultural context of the Western mind to the "indestructible
foundations of...mind" as such, from the contingencies and
idiosyncracies of the former to the essential structures of the
latter?

The fact that Jung is not careful to differentiate the
former from the latter and tends, indeed, to amalgamate the two
only compounds the problems raised by these questions. While
locating Christian doctrine in its context and while arguing
that it is a portrayal of psychic forces and factors that have
emerged in the Western world and that are characteristic of
that world, he at one and the same time can and in fact does
regard this doctrinal tradition as an expression of "the nature
of psychic experience," of "the psyche as a whole," and, indeed,
as we shall see, "as a symbol that comprehends the essence of...
the human."[47] The reader is left to sift out for himself the
extent to which the collective psyche of Western man is identifiable with or discordant with an essential psyche that Jung
appeals to and envisions, but that he is disinclined to thematize in clear, conceptual terms.

But this is not to suggest that Jung is unaware of the need to justify such an appeal. For his recourse to an archetypal ground of meaning is clearly an attempt to bring to light his belief, his "wager,"[48] that the range of meanings embodied in Christian doctrine transcends the cultural and even religious milieu out of which it emerged. He states, in concluding his study of the Trinity, that: "A knowledge of the universal archetypal background was, in itself, sufficient to give me the courage to treat 'that which is believed always, everywhere, by everybody' as a *psychological fact* which extends far beyond the confines of Christianity."[49] But at the same time we will see that the Trinity thematizes the self-understanding of this milieu, even while transcending it. Jung will find, then, in Christian doctrine a paradigmatic expression both of the *Western* psyche and of the psyche *as such*.

Inasmuch as his psychology of doctrine proceeds on these two tracks concurrently, we will inevitably face difficulties in interpreting him. For he will invite the belief that he is according to Western culture and consciousness and to the Christian tradition a privileged status from which to move to a vision of the "essential" psyche and nature of man. It is our considered view, however, that this would be to misconstrue Jung's purposes.[50] For Western culture is but one matrix out of which a more "global" or universal consciousness can emerge and find expression. And to Jung's mind no culture in principle remains closed to a trans-cultural or universal dimension of consciousness, simply because it is axiomatic for him that the psyche of any person or culture is open to worlds of meaning which transcend the confines of a person's or a culture's life-experience.[51] It is this openness which makes possible the realization of a more universal and less idiosyncratic form of consciousness within particular cultural milieus.

In the Western world the co-existence of universal and idiosyncratic elements within Western consciousness generates, by Jung's account, tensions which complicate and yet prove creative for the evolution of Western man's self-understanding. Jung's keen interest in these tensions constitutes, we feel, a significant range of evidence with which to dispel the impression that because he discerns the elements of a universal consciousness

to be at work and to come to expression in Western consciousness, he thereby identifies the two. It is no doubt true and
regrettable that Jung's failure to differentiate clearly and
forthrightly the one from the other invites this reading of
him. To our mind, however, it is a *mis*-reading, not only
because Jung recognizes that the elements of a universal consciousness manifest themselves in any and all cultural contexts
and not exclusively in the West (inasmuch as it is axiomatic
for him that a trans-cultural, self-transcending dynamic is at
work in the human psyche wherever it is found), but also
because he is intent on showing that these elements do not find
their full expression in the West. They come to the fore in the
Western mind in but fragmentary ways and are filtered through
and even distorted by the ethos in which they appear, even while
they succeed, at least in part, in transforming it. Consequently, that he discerns a universal dimension to be at work in the
hinterland of the Western psyche, that he perceives therein the
dim outlines of an "essential" psyche in its still nascent form,
cannot lead us to infer that Jung uncritically bestows on the
Western experience and mind an authoritative status; neither can
it permit us to infer that he would presume to equate the
Western psyche with the psyche as such.

     We need now to take up again our examination of the particu-
lars of Jung's doctrinal work. Thus far we have followed Jung
in his move from the Trinity's historical antecedents to its
archetypal ground, a move which succeeds in transforming the
interpretive process into an explicitly psychological one. For
now the Trinity is regarded as expressive of certain psychic
factors that are presumed to attain to a universal scope, and no
longer mrely as the outcome of a particular nexus of cultural
and historical forces.
     In short, we may view the first stage of this interpretive
process--the elucidation of historical materials which display
forms parallel to that of the Trinity--as propaedeutic to Jung's
explicitly psychological interpretation. It serves the largely
negative function of demonstrating the futility of specifying
the origins and meaning of the doctrine in terms of its antecedents, while yet fulfilling the positive purpose of rendering

more plausible the hypothesis that there is a universal ground
of meaning underlying the particularity of the doctrinal form.
And it is this hypothesis that enables Jung to bring doctrine
out of the realms of history and theology proper into the domain
of his own psychology. It paves the way for what will be the
principal task of his interpretive work--his efforts to disclose
and to elucidate the psychic dimensions of meaning inherent in
the doctrinal form.

   We would reiterate here that we are using the term *psychic*
in accord with the way we understand Jung to use it. We have
argued in Chapter II that psychic reality in Jung's view encompasses the full range of man's mental, spiritual and affective
processes, in both their conscious and unconscious dimensions.
In what follows, then, we will employ the expression *psychic
meaning* as a means of designating that which signifies and
thematizes, even if only latently and mutely, psychic reality,
whether it be embodied in personal or collective forms. It is
that which holds meaning for an embodied human psyche because
it represents it to itself. It "speaks" to, about and therefore
for a particular human subject in a particular time and place,
in a given historical and cultural matrix. The human subject in
question may be an individual, a *personal* self (as has been the
case in preceding chapters), or (as is the case here) a people
or culture, what can best be termed a *collective* self, a
construct we will employ below to refer to the whole of Western
man's cultural and collective life and development.

Father-Son-Spirit

   We need now to examine how Jung elucidates the psychic
meaning of the Trinity. He boldly proposes viewing the doctrine
as a representation of an evolution of consciousness, an evolution which spans three distinct moments. Each of the three
persons, Father, Son and Spirit, is regarded as representative
of a specific stage in "a process of conscious realization continuing over the centuries."[52] We shall summarize what he says
of each of these stages in turn.

   The first, "the world of the Father," is depicted as the
world of man as child. It is a world "characterized by a
pristine oneness with the whole of Nature," a oneness which

precludes doubt, criticism, reflection, i.e., the functions of differentiated consciousness.[53]

But Jung asserts (and here he shows his indebtedness to Pythagorean thought) that the first strivings of consciousness already signal that this "world" has given way to another. For the very phenomenon of consciousness, of the desire to conceive, to grasp this pristine oneness is an index of its loss. And so primal unity and harmony are surpassed or rather subverted by a new age: "...that state of perfection in which man was still one with the Father,...was lost forever, because an irreversible increase in man's consciousness had taken place."[54] Division and conflict are born, and with them the world of the Other or the Son, who is perceived to stand in opposition to the One:

> ...once the question is asked: "Whence comes evil,... why must man suffer?" then reflection has already begun to judge the Father by his manifest works, and straightway one is conscious of a doubt, which is itself the symptom of a split in the original unity. One comes to the conclusion that...the Father cannot be the sole principle of the cosmos. Hence the One has to be supplemented by the Other.[55]

While the Son symbolizes division, doubt, and consciousness itself, the third person represents a reconciling, healing, unifying force: "As he is the third term common to the Father and the Son, he puts an end to the duality, to the 'doubt' in the Son. He is, in fact, the third element that...restores the One."[56]

This "process of conscious realization" is presumably set in motion wherever human consciousness is born; it has, in other words, as Jung's language above suggests, a universal scope. We shall find, however, that his ultimate purpose in delineating this evolution of consciousness is to reveal the extent to which Western man today is implicated in it.

This, then, in skeletal form, is the means Jung adopts to open up the Trinity to its underlying psychic meaning, to begin the process of retrieving this meaning from its age-old doctrinal form. The result is a *displacement* of the doctrine from its familiar context of meaning--an explicitly religious and theological one--into a context and frame of reference seemingly foreign to it. Since the whole of the interpretive process centers on this act of displacement, we will pause once

again in our exposition and offer here a preliminary assessment
of its implications.

The question inevitably raised by this reading of the
Trinity is whether or not Jung simply chooses arbitrarily and
willfully to ignore the obvious--the fact that the doctrine
speaks of and refers to the nature of the divine, as experienced
and understood in the Christian tradition. We will maintain
that he in no way denies this more manifest level of meaning and
reference. On the contrary, he explicitly affirms, in concluding his study, that "...the Trinity lays claim not only to
represent a personification of psychic processes in three roles,
but to *be* the one God in three Persons, who all share the same
divine nature."[57] Clearly, then, he is not offering an interpretation of the Trinity that would make of it nothing more than a
representation of these "psychic processes." And so, to our
mind, this interpretation cannot rightfully be construed as an
attempt to pre-empt its full range of meaning(s) to his own
concerns. We have found, rather, that Jung, in focusing on the
Trinity's psychic dimensions of meaning, far from overlooking or
even denying other of its dimensions, in fact shows a deep
respect and deference for them:

> These considerations have made me extremely
> cautious in my approach to the further metaphysical
> significance that may possibly underlie archetypal
> statements. There is nothing to stop their ultimate
> ramifications from penetrating to the very ground of
> the universe. We alone are the dumb ones if we fail
> to notice it. Such being the case, I cannot pretend
> to myself that the object of archetypal statements
> has been explained and disposed of merely by our
> investigation of its psychological aspects.[58]

But a critical question remains: what is the relationship
between these two "levels" of meaning? This is a question that
is by no means incidental to our inquiry, for Jung is unable to
move directly into a psychology of doctrine without passing
through its manifestly theological content. This means that his
inquiry must of necessity deal explicitly with the Trinity *qua*
representation of the divine, even if only in its initial stages.
For it is none other than the manifest, ostensive meaning of the
doctrine (as set forth in the "Athanasian" creed, which for
"purposes of...discussion" Jung adopts as his model[59]) that

must be shown to disclose, while yet concealing, a psychic
dimension of meaning. Consequently, he does not by-pass its
manifest meaning, but rather begins with it. And so initially
he interprets the three persons as moments of a "life-process
within the Deity,"[60] but subsequently extends the theme of
process beyond the divine in order to apply it to man himself.[61]
In short, the insight that the Trinity portrays a life-process
within man--an evolution of consciousness--is mediated by means
of an analysis of its more explicit portrayal of the "life-
process within the Deity."

The upshot is that categories of the divine are made to
collapse into psychological and anthropological categories, a
task that is not accomplished without considerable ambiguity.
For Jung proceeds from the former to the latter circuitously
and dialectically. In the sections "Christ as Archetype" and
"The Holy Ghost,"[62] for example, he interprets the Christ-image
as an expression of the archetype of the hero or self: "The
content of all such symbolic products is the idea of an overpowering, all-embracing, complete or perfect being," a being
who so far transcends the individual mind and his ego that "the
conscious mind can form absolutely no conception of this totality."[63] Immediately thereafter, he declares that man's archetypal images of the self are indistinguishable from his images
of God: "...as one can never distinguish empirically between
a symbol of the self and a God-image, the two ideas, however
much we try to differentiate them, always appear blended together."[64] In the same vein, he writes: "...self-realization--
to put it in religious or metaphysical terms--amounts to God's
incarnation."[65] At times he affirms an incarnational language
of God-become-man, while at other times he stands this language
on its head and speaks of a spiritual process of divinization
that is taking place in man.

Although the freedom with which Jung interweaves theological
and anthropological images and constructs may appear to court
serious misunderstanding, we will argue that his ultimate purpose
in so doing is to effect a transposition of the former into the
latter. This way of reading him is borne out by the order of
exposition followed in Chapter IV of his study ("The Three Persons
In the Light of Psychology"), which begins with the incarnation

proper, with the second person of the Trinity, wherein God
becomes man, and then moves to the third person, wherein man
becomes God, only finally to recast this divinization process
into a process of self-realization.[66] In the course of his
exposition Jung draws upon the biblical and patristic theme
that the Holy Spirit's in-dwelling in man makes possible a true
partaking of the divine nature: "...the Holy Ghost breathes in
man, too, and thus is the breath common to man, the Son, and
the Father. Man is therefore included in God's sonship, and
the words of Christ--'Ye are gods' (John 10:34)--appear in a
significant light."[67] Man's spiritual life and destiny are
here envisaged as constituent elements of the trinitarian drama,
intrinsically and intimately related to the life of the divine.
And so Jung concludes that "...the Trinity...discloses itself
as a symbol that comprehends the essence of the divine *and* the
human. It is, as Koepgen says, 'a revelation not only of God
but at the same time of man.'"[68]

Jung's psychological interpretation, then, cannot and does
not disregard the doctrine's theological content and frame of
reference. That he places his major emphasis on the less than
obvious--on the latent as distinct from the manifest meaning of
the doctrine, on its disclosure of "the essence of...the human"--
does not lead him to deny or to lose sight of the obvious--that
it speaks of God. Accordingly, we would maintain that Jung's
transposition of theological into anthropological and psychological constructs, far from divesting them of one dimension of
meaning in deference to another, actually serves to bring one
to an intimation of the abundance of meaning that inheres in
them.[69]

Its Meaning for the West Today

After developing at some length the idea of the Trinity as
a "...collective process, representing a differentiation of
consciousness that has been going on for several thousand
years,"[70] Jung turns to an explication of the meaning it might
hold for Western man today. The task is complicated by what we
have already noted to be his keen awareness of the waning
communicative and mediating power of historically fixed and
formalized religious expressions in the modern period. In

Jung's view there is no way to circumvent or blind oneself to
modernity's prevailing religious spirit and temperament. Nor,
on the other hand, may one consign to the past those religious
forms that continue to outlive the ages in which they were born.
The tension between age-old forms and ever-changing patterns of
experience must be faced and reckoned with. Jung's efforts to
do so embolden him to take what surely is the most radical and
startling of the several strategic steps taken in the course of
this study--the attempt to recast the very form and structure
of the trinitarian doctrine.[71]

In order to understand how and why Jung embarks on this
course, we need first to return to and elaborate on what we have
found to be the crux of his "psychologization" of the Trinity--
his account of its portrayal and dramatization of "a process of
conscious realization continuing over the centuries." Jung
argues that modern man in the West is deeply implicated in this
process. This is true largely because the doctrine of the
Trinity has so gripped the Western mind in preceding centuries
that it has succeeded in conforming this mind in important
respects to the model of an evolving consciousness symbolically
portrayed by it. The doctrine, then, has left its mark on
Western man's self-understanding, and to the extent that he has
appropriated and lived in accord with the dictates of this
self-understanding, he has shaped and styled his own evolving
consciousness to fit the trinitarian model. He has striven to
embody, to become, to take on the model. As a result modern
man can find in the doctrine an expression of what pre-modern
Western man strove to become and to some extent succeeded in
becoming. The Trinity provides him not only with a thematization
of what his ancestors strove to become, but also with a reflection of what they collectively--and he as a consequence--have
actually become.

On one level, then, Jung's elucidation of the Trinity's
psychic dimensions of meaning is designed to enable modern man
to retrieve its thematic and expressive power. His is a psychology of doctrine that challenges the modern age to take new
stock of the Christian tradition and its doctrinal legacy, to
rediscover the ways it gives voice to its own cultural and
religious past, to a living past that continues even today to
shape Western man's collective selfhood.

In short, it is the collective selfhood of Western man that
is at stake in Jung's psychological reading of Christian doctrine. But before examining which specific aspects of this
developing selfhood are at issue here, we will take up anew a
question we have raised earlier. How is Jung's concern to
demonstrate the universality of meaning inherent in doctrine
reconcilable with his claim that it emerges from, embodies and
speaks to the particularities of Western man's religious and
cultural history?

In returning to this question here, we need first to recall
that for Jung an archetypal or universal ground of meaning can
manifest itself in principle in any person or culture, and that
any cultural form of expression can be shown for that reason to
be not only self-reflective, but also self-transcending. If
Western man, then, images himself in Christian doctrinal
expressions, he is also concurrently imaging more than himself.
He is imaging not only an acculturated self, but an ideal or
archetypal self as well that has yet to be attained.[72] This
archetypal self is in part realized, at least to the degree
that a particular (in this case Western) culture identifies with
it and lives in accord with it. It is never, however, fully
realized.

In the case of the Trinity, for example, the third stage
in the evolution--a stage which depicts an integral and unified
consciousness, an essential man, a man who is reconciled with
himself, his cosmos and his God--functions as an ideal that
confronts Western man and that he strives to attain. And in
presenting him with a symbolic representation of a fuller kind
of selfhood that he may achieve and that, in fact, he needs to
achieve, the Trinity provides him with a model by virtue of
which he can discern his possibilities and attain a keener
awareness of those factors in his cultural and psychic development that militate against the actualization of these possibilities. A more critical as well as comprehensive self-understanding is thereby brought about--critical, because over-developed
and one-sided modes of adaptation are now more likely to be
perceived as problems; and comprehensive, because a more holistic
feeling for and vision of the collective selfhood of Western
man is conveyed.

And so to our mind it would not be accurate to attribute
to Jung the view that the Trinity, and by extension all of
Christianity's principal doctrinal expressions, are "culture-
bound" simply because they have emerged in and spoken powerfully
and pointedly to a particular cultural milieu. For Jung recognizes that they have acted as transforming leavens within their
cultural context as much as and even more than they have served
to give sanction to its ethos. And it is in this transforming
power, in this capacity to speak of "the essence of...the human"
and to guide persons and cultures (and in particular Western
culture) towards it that Christian doctrine's universal thrust
and meaning is most readily discernible. In this view Christian
doctrine is less bound to its cultural context than this context
is to it.

But Jung's purposes are far from exhausted by his retrieval
of the thematic and expressive power of the Christian doctrinal
tradition. For he is intent on subjecting it to critical
scrutiny as well. And this scrutiny leads him to rethink and
indeed to re-forge the very forms in which it has been cast.
It is here that the iconoclastic and ultimately the re-constructive nature of his psychology of doctrine comes most clearly to
the fore.

We will begin our appraisal of Jung's critical reading of
this tradition's relevance to modern man by taking note of a
singularly striking fact: after all his efforts to rediscover
and to unfathom the transforming power of Christian doctrine,
Jung shows himself to be profoundly troubled by the extent to
which Western man has in past ages been beholden to and shaped
by it! This is not to suggest that he does not appreciate the
positive gains Western man's indebtedness to and fascination
with Christian doctrine yielded in the patristic and medieval
periods. Chief among them was the success with which the
Trinity, in particular, fulfilled two of the major exigencies of
Western man's development and self-understanding: the need to
attain a noetic, spiritual and reflective level of consciousness;[73] and the need to achieve a clear-cut differentiation of
the moral opposites, good and evil, and thereby to exclude evil
from "redeemed" reality.[74] In so doing, it was of inestimable

value in enabling Western man in previous ages to consolidate
his appropriation of the Christian vision.

Ironically, however--and it is at this point that Jung is
led to adopt a self-consciously critical stance towards the
Trinity--the very success with which it conveyed these needs
and ideals served to give sanction to and to reinforce particular aspects of the Western ethos which, however indispensable
in their own time, have contributed to a mode of consciousness
that is now one-sided and that stands in need of developing anew
in distinctly different ways. Or so, at least, Jung contends.
In short, what is a positive asset in one period becomes a
liability in another.

The achievement of a more refined and spiritual and reflective consciousness on the one hand and a keener moral awareness
on the other both set in motion cultural and religious problems
which modern man suffers from and must now contend with. We
need to examine closely how Jung traces the root of these problems back to specific features in the form and content of the
doctrine itself. The first is bound up with the third person,
which is regarded as the foremost expression of the reflective,
abstract nature of the Trinity.[75] Given that Father and Son
are differentiated and then related to each other familially,
the natural way to complete the triad, the "family," would have
been to add as the third a maternal element. It is for this
reason that the presence of the Holy Spirit in the Trinity of
persons can be viewed as an anomaly that breaks up an otherwise
homogeneous pattern. Jung understands its inclusion in the Godhead to have been the outcome of a process of reflection which
raised the attributes "life" and "soul" to an abstract level.
He traces the precursor of this development back to Egyptian
mythology, which pictured the third person of the triad as the
procreative force of the God-head, a masculine giver of life.[76]
The third person of the Christian Trinity, which might have
served as a feminine link between Father and Son, evolves into
a spiritual, rather than a natural or familial entity:

> ...the Holy Ghost is...essentially a product of
> reflection, an hypostatized noumenon tacked on to
> the natural family-picture of father and son...in
> some mysterious and unexpected way, an important
> mental process peculiar to man has been imported
> into it.[77]

The result is that the Trinity takes on an exclusively masculine
character, and is spiritualized beyond the realm of the natural,
the earthly, and the feminine.

But what of the second factor--the need to differentiate
good and evil? What role has the Trinity played in fulfilling
this need? Jung describes the age in which the doctrine reaches
its greatest ascendancy (300-1500 A.D.) as one in which the
struggle between the moral opposites reaches an intense level:

> This opposition means conflict to the last, and it
> is the task of humanity to endure this conflict until
> the time or turning-point is reached where good and
> evil begin to relativize themselves, to doubt them-
> selves, and the cry is raised for a morality "beyond
> good and evil." In the age of Christianity and in the
> domain of trinitarian thinking such an idea is simply
> out of the question, because the conflict is too
> violent for evil to be assigned any other logical
> relation to the Trinity than that of an absolute
> opposite.[78]

Because of the acute nature of this conflict, traditional
Christianity has felt compelled to expel the dark side of God
and man from its central doctrinal affirmations. In the Trinity,
it is the person of Christ and in particular the affirmation of
his sinless nature that testifies most dramatically to this
concern: "...the Christ-figure is not a totality, for it lacks
the nocturnal side of the psyche's nature, the darkness of the
spirit and is also without sin. Without the integration of evil
there is no totality."[79] This absence of a principle of evil in
Christ leads Jung into an amplification of the figures of
Lucifer, the Anti-Christ and the biblical motif of the "warring
brothers" in an attempt to introduce an evil principle into the
Trinity as a constituent element of the divine-human drama that
it portrays.[80]

It is here that we encounter the most provocative element
in Jung's argument: the contention that the trinitarian form
of the doctrine must today submit to its own alteration. It
must undergo a change in symbolization that would make of it a
figure with four structural elements. "Three is *not* a natural
coefficient of order, but an artificial one....The ideal of
completeness is the circle or sphere, but its natural minimal
division is a *quaternity*."[81]

This theme of completeness, of psychic wholeness, is a central one in Jung's psychology; we cannot elaborate on its many ramifications here without entering into a survey of the entire terrain of his thought.[82] It is sufficient for our purposes to be aware of the essential inter-connection Jung makes between the processes of self-realization and individuation on the one hand and the ideal of wholeness on the other. Human becoming, in his view, is the coming into being of an integrated self, of a self that is complete and whole in itself. This is the end to which all of man's developmental processes are tending; it is the end, moreover, for which Western man in the modern period in particular is presumed to yearn.

The brunt of Jung's critique of the Trinity is that it is less than adequate as a symbolic representation of this desired wholeness. It is compelling as a representation of a particular phase in the development of Western man's consciousness and psyche, but limited in its portrayal of the goal of this development. It offers a true portrait of his "life-process," but an incomplete and one-sided one.

But what is the one-sidedness that the introduction of a fourth element is intended to rectify? An answer to this query has already been provided; it is the dimension of worldly materiality, a materiality which embraces within it the maternal and feminine as well as the demonic, that is missing: "The dark weight of the earth must enter into the picture of the whole," if it is to be truly expressive of wholeness.[83] This lacuna, in Jung's view, is endemic to the classical traditions of Christianity; he sees it as a limitation that threatens to undermine Christian doctrine's continuing ability to thematize and symbolically portray the unified consciousness and integral selfhood that Western man needs to make his own.

It is here that the tension between the idiosyncratic and universal components of Western consciousness reaches its most acute point. And it is in the hope of mitigating this tension that Jung engages in his re-constructive efforts and makes bold to modify the trinitarian form of the doctrine. He finds warrant for these efforts by appealing not only to the dreams and fantasies of modern man--many of which, he contends, display to a striking degree an abundance of four-sided or quaternary

figures[84]--but also to a rich variety of mythic and philosophical materials, all of which lie outside of or on the periphery
of classical Christianity, and all of which give evidence of a
similar quaternary symbolic form. Following the lead provided
him by these materials, he proceeds to re-interpret--indeed to
re-cast--the form of the Christian Trinity.

The relation between Father and Son is reconsidered in the
light of the Pythagorean motif of the split between the One and
the Other, in such a way as to make of this split a second phase
in the trinitarian drama. As a result the second person of the
Trinity is broken down into two structural elements--the warring
opposites. The full figure resulting from this reconstruction
then becomes: Father, Son-Devil, Spirit.[85] In short, Jung
finds a way of introducing an additional structural element into
the doctrinal form without thereby disrupting its depiction of
an inter-related unity of three distant phases: "The rhythm
is built up in three steps, but the resultant symbol is a
quaternity."[86] The "fourth," then, does not emerge at the end
of the process, but in its intermediate stage.

At this point we might well ask: how does Jung presume
himself free to reconstruct an historically fixed form that is
a crystallization of centuries of experience? If he is right
in having discerned an archetypal basis in the triadic form,
would not one expect it to remain immutably fixed? In taking
up these questions, we need to emphasize the fact that Jung is
not intent on supplanting one form with another, the Trinity
for a quaternity. Rather his real purpose is to bring to light
the existence of the latter within the very structure of the
former. Far from replacing the one with the other, he in fact
knits the two indissolubly together. Threeness is no less
archetypal than fourness for Jung; he argues that *both* patterns
recur throughout the history of religions and culture, and that
both surface as frequent motifs in dream-materials.[87]

Which of these two patterns will speak most forcefully to
a particular person or culture in a particular time or place
will depend on the contingencies of that person's or culture's
life-history. For the "structural dominants of the mind" are
not static, but constantly in flux; one's imaginative universe

is ever in process. A culture will experience and appropriate
a wide range of archetypal patterns and possibilities in the
course of its development, and it will do so in ways idiosyncratic to, indeed unique to itself. Moreover, cultural as well
as personal development is not free of unevenness, of one-sidedness, of hindrance and conflict.[88] A culture may so orient
itself to one archetypal possibility that it loses sight of
others.

This is precisely what Jung maintains has happened in
Western culture. He perceives, however, in the modern period
the quickening pace of a contrary and compensating develop-
ment--the evolution of a cultural consciousness wherein the
quaternity will gain an ascendancy vis-à-vis the Trinity. It
is as if the "process of conscious realization" which the Trinity
portrays is outstripping the form by which it is portrayed. The
earnestness with which Jung himself reflects upon this evolution
would seem to testify to a desire on his part to impel it closer
towards that critical point which fast seems to be approaching,
that moment when Christian doctrine will either show itself
capable of giving expression to those patterns of experience
that are now buffeting it, or be by-passed by them altogether.

Jung contends, in fact, that we are now entering such a
time, and that we should therefore ready ourselves for and
attune ourselves to significant changes in the ways we image our
individual and collective selves. We would stress, then, that
his attempt to "melt down" and "recast" Christian doctrine is
at its heart an effort to alert modern man to a cultural evolution that is already much in evidence today, and thereby to lead
him to be open to new patterns of symbolization that are proceeding hand in hand with this evolution and that bespeak and
illumine what it portends for his future.

And so what begins as a psychology of *doctrine* eventuates
in a psychology of *culture*, in a critique of the one-sidedness
and lacunae of Western man's consciousness, and concomitantly,
an elucidation of the prospective path of its development. In
short, Jung, in proposing that Christian doctrine submit to a
transmutation of form, is at one and the same time calling
Western man to a transvaluation of his images of and understanding of himself.

But if Jung is convinced that this process of cultural
change will continue to make itself felt and to influence and
even transform Western man's thought-forms and central images,
he shows himself to be less than certain that specifically
Christian forms will evolve *with* this process, perhaps because
of a suspicion that the Christian faith and churches are too
irretrievably committed to the historical fixity and immutability of their central doctrines.[89] But we cannot now anticipate
the extent to which the discordance between these doctrines on
the one hand and Western man's cultural evolution and experience
on the other will increase or decrease. The ways in which the
two interact are obviously numerous, each constituting a specific hermeneutical problem and situation, a particular confrontation between Christianity and culture. Leaving prognostica-
tions of the future aside, we wish simply to stress the point
that the hermeneutic Jung fashions with his own psychological
tools and insights attempts, by entering into the interstices
between doctrine and experience, Christianity and modern/
Western culture, to subvert the isolation of one from the other.

His project, then, is an essentially experimental one; it
in no way presumes the certainty of a successful outcome. It
may be that Christian doctrinal forms will prove too brittle
and will shatter in the course of this cultural ferment; or,
alternatively, they may succeed in absorbing and in-forming it
even as they are carried forward by it. It is no doubt here
that the dialectic of experience and doctrine reaches its most
problematic point: will the dynamics of Western man's cultural
life and evolution continue to by-pass and leave aside the
doctrinal forms of the Christian tradition? If so, Jung's
experiment will surely have failed in its task of mediating the
one to the other. With the advantage of hindsight, some may
well conclude that his method led Jung and perhaps many others
as well beyond the scope and horizon of this tradition altogether. And yet others may find that his experiment will prove
with time to have forged a way for a re-discovery of long
overlooked dimensions of meaning within Christianity and its
abiding doctrinal affirmations. Whatever conclusion one comes
to, however,[90] one cannot fail to note the extraordinary fact
that Jung, with no privileged knowledge of the future at his

disposal, and in the face of his own lifetime of doubts, risked
assuming that the Trinity was not a dying form, that latent
within it, in fact, was an elasticity of form that would enable
it to survive its own transformation, as well as a depth of
meaning that had yet to be actualized and that could still be
instrumental in guiding and shaping cultural and personal growth.

The Unity of Method in Jung's Interpretive Work

   Having examined in depth one paradigmatic instance of
Jung's interpretive work in the field of Christian doctrine, we
need now to put into perspective the methodological underpinnings
of this work. We shall begin by recapitulating the series of
intellectual operations and modes of analysis that we have
found to be instrumental in his interpretation of the Trinity.

   The first of these is Jung's appeal to and elucidation of
the Trinity's various historical antecedents. The major aim
of his so doing is to pave the way for the disclosure of the
doctrine's archetypal or universal ground of meaning. The
postulation of this archetypal ground is a pivotal step in the
interpretive process, for it enables Jung to root the doctrine
in the "indestructible foundations of the human mind." And
this frees him to embark upon an explicitly psychological mode
of interpretation, to construe the Trinity as a doctrine representing an evolution of consciousness that points to and provides a model of the human psyche as such, of "the psyche as a
whole."[91] The disclosure of the Trinity's archetypal basis,
then, serves at one and the same time as the culmination of the
first stage of the process and the point of departure for the
second and most fundamental one--the explication of the psychic
dimensions of meaning inherent in the doctrine. This latter
task carries Jung ultimately into an evaluation of the Trinity's
capacity to speak to the collective selfhood of Western man
today. Herein lies the third and decisive stage of the process,
the one in which the doctrine is made to submit to the severest
of tests--it is hammered hard against the anvil of contemporary
experience.

The Two Interpretive Processes

Having recapitulated our findings in this chapter, we are
now prepared to consider them in the light of those of the
preceding one. Does the psychological hermeneutic that we have
found to be operative in Jung's interpretation of fantasy provide him with the nucleus of the method at work in his interpretation of doctrine? Is the evidence that we now have at our
disposal sufficient to permit us to affirm that we have discovered and identified a common method at work in both domains?
Or, rather, does the weight of the evidence suggest that we are
faced here with two distinct methods, two distinct sets of
tasks, two projects, not one? A definitive answer to these
questions is not ready at hand. For we have encountered a
number of differences as well as similarities in our study of the
ways Jung goes about interpreting fantasy and doctrine. It is
not immediately apparent, then, whether there is a common method
at work here or not. And so it would seem that we must pass in
review and evaluate these similarities and differences if we
are to hope to be able to resolve this issue.

We shall first take up the points of similarity. No doubt
the most striking of these is the similarity of structure that
underlies the two interpretive processes. Both of them exhibit
a structure that is three-fold; both employ a three-fold series
of distinct and yet inter-related intellectual operations.
Moreover, this set of operations appears to function in similar
ways and to fulfill similar purposes, whether it is fantasy or
doctrine that is undergoing interpretation. For both processes
begin with a movement from the figure in question to antecedent
expressions or experiences; both hinge on an elucidation of the
figure's archetypal depth of meaning; and both culminate in an
articulation of the points at which this meaning speaks to and
about a personal or collective self.

These similarities of structure, function and purpose
become all the more apparent if we summarize and synthesize what
we have discovered to be the underlying dynamic of both interpretive processes--that is to say, the movement that carries
each of them from the first to the second and then to the third
of its three parts.

As regards the first of the three--the analysis of the
fantasy's or the doctrine's biographical or historical antece-
dents--we have seen how it demonstrates the impossibility of
evincing without remainder the meaning of the figure in
question. In so doing, it serves to generate an awareness of
the figure's depth of meaning, the scope of which transcends
the history of the person or the culture involved. And it
thereby impels the interpretive process into a distinct mode of
interpretation, one that is specifically designed to elucidate
this depth of meaning.

We have seen, however, that this second phase of the
process paves the way in turn for yet another one. For an
elucidation of this meaning cannot be psychologically effica-
cious, it cannot be therapeutic, unless those involved in the
process are willing and able to draw the lessons from it, to
discern in fantasy or doctrine the "lines of advance...that are
symbolically indicated,"[92] and to allow themselves to be guided
forward by them. And so a third mode of interpretation is
required, one whose chief aim is to decipher the ways these
"lines of advance" speak to the prospective path of man's
personal or cultural life.

In view of the foregoing, it is evident that each phase
of the interpretive process--whether it involves fantasy or
doctrine, a personal or a collective self--feeds into and necessitates its subsequent phase. All three phases are integrally
inter-related and inter-connected.

Assuredly, then, the two interpretive processes display a
number of strikingly similar structural and dynamic features.
These features would seem to point amply and convincingly to
the existence of a common method at work in both of them. We
are unable, however, to state conclusively that what appears to
be the case is in fact the case, not at least pending an evaluation of the ways the two processes differ. For these points
of difference would seem to suggest a contrary conclusion.

We have already alluded to what perhaps is the most important of these points: With fantasy the interpretive context is
a therapeutic one; it centers on the analytic work entered into
by analyst and analysand alike, and ultimately comprises the
whole breadth and depth of an individual's life-story and

experience. Whereas with doctrine, this context encompasses the
cultural and religious situation of the West that Jung confronted
in his own day. And so we are faced not simply with two different genres of human expression, but with two distinctly different
interpretive contexts as well. This difference is a fundamental
one, and in effect dictates that the journeys fantasy and doctrine undergo in the course of their interpretation will differ
in important respects.

This is nowhere more evident than in the second phase of
the two journeys in question. To be sure, in both cases a depth
of meaning is disclosed and elucidated, but the means that are
employed to bring about this disclosure are decidedly different.
With fantasy, we recall that this expansion of meaning is made
possible by a shift from a personal to a collective past and
world of imagery. This shift frees the person involved to
construe his life-story in terms of the wider realm of meaning
embodied in the collective heritage of mankind.

In the case of Christian doctrine, however, such a shift
is neither necessary nor even possible; for Jung presumes, from
the very beginning of the interpretive process, that doctrine,
by its very nature, is a distillate of the collective experience
of an entire culture. The means he employs, then, to open up
and lay bare its hidden reaches of meaning are of necessity
different--he psychologizes it; he explicates the psychic
dimension of meaning underlying the historically fixed form,
thereby bringing to light the ways it represents, however
obliquely, the outlines of a story of Western man's developing
psyche. In short, the one process moves from a personal into a
collective sphere of meaning; the other, from a cultural/reli-
gious into a psychic sphere.

It would seem, then, that the two processes, at this, their
pivotal point, move in well-nigh antithetical directions. But
such a difference, as unmistakeable and irreducible as it is,
cannot lead us to overlook the common purpose that is at work
here: both seek to disclose the depth of meaning inherent in
the figure in question. We would argue, in fact, that it is
precisely at this, their point of seemingly greatest divergence,
that the unity of method underlying the two processes is most
dramatically revealed.

But what prompts us to make this claim? And how, indeed, can we justify it? How can it be that the two processes, starting as they do from different points and moving in different directions, exhibit a unity of method?

Displacement

In an effort to answer these questions, we will look more closely at the common strategy Jung relies on in uncovering and elucidating the depths of meaning that lie hidden in fantasy and doctrine. He is able to bring these hidden reaches of meaning to light only by virtue of the fact that he systematically and methodically *displaces* the figure in question from the context and frame of reference in which it originally finds itself into another, distinct in kind from it. This shifting of contexts sets in motion a whole process of transliterating, even of transferring meanings. The upshot is that fantasy, when displaced from its clinical context, distends the personal into a collective imagination; while doctrine, when displaced from an exclusively theological realm of discourse, opens up the religious mind to the psychic roots of its language and life.

In either case it is an act of displacement that is instrumental in triggering an awareness of the symbolic dimensions of meaning inherent in man's personal as well as his collective, cultural and religious life. This act, this strategy, appears specifically designed to occasion surprise, perhaps even shock, and concomitantly, insight. One is led to experience, understand and affirm: there is more meaning here than has been hitherto fully conscious to me. We can intimate how this insight is catalyzed: much as new meaning is sparked by the emergence of a new metaphor in everyday language. To state something in metaphorical terms, in terms not self-evidently its own, is to perceive and experience it in a fresh way; it is to glimpse previously undetected facets of its meaning and reality.

Jung's strategy of displacement gives every appearance of being a systematic and methodical one--it is a procedure that he employs consistently throughout his interpretive work, whether this work involves him in fantasy materials or doctrinal expressions. That he "psychologizes" in one case (doctrine) and

"mythologizes" in another (fantasy) points, then, to a difference not of strategy or purpose, but of tactics. For the
strategy (displacement) and the purpose (the disclosure of
symbolic reaches of meaning) are the same in either event.

The consequences of Jung's reliance on this common strategy
are extraordinary: Personal and cultural or collective selves,
images and life-stories are made to impinge on and speak to each
other. The distinctions between personal and collective, psychic
and cultural worlds of meaning are relativized. One is led to
perceive hitherto unperceived points of commonality between
them. The world of one's fantasies is no longer an exclusively
private world, an insulated and insular world of experience,[93]
but instead opens one to those motifs and meanings lived, shared
and valued in the collective, ancestral past that is Western
man's. Similarly the Christian doctrinal tradition is no longer
cut off from, extrinsic to, modern man's self-understanding and
experience,[94] but rather is made to impinge directly on his
images and perceptions of himself. In short, the lines of
demarcation between "public" and "private" meaning are blurred.
One is no longer certain of the extent to which one's experience
and representations of it are personally or collectively shaped.

It is clear, then, that this interweaving of worlds of
meaning is integral to Jung's interpretation of fantasy as well
as doctrine; it is intimately bound up with the inner workings
of both of them. Each contributes in its own distinctive way
to the ultimate fusion of these worlds of meaning. In the light
of this finding, it becomes apparent that we cannot conceive of
either interpretive process apart from the other. To our mind
it is essential that they be viewed in conjunction with each
other, as two distinct and yet conjoined poles of one interpretive project, of a project that undertakes to amplify personal
and cultural life-stories in terms of each other. Each pole is
grounded in a particular realm of experience, in a particular
genre of expression. And yet the domain of each is ultimately
broadened to such an extent that it opens into the domain of
the other.

We would maintain, then, that the act of displacement and
the fusion of worlds of meaning that it makes possible testify
perhaps more demonstrably than anything else to the unity of

method that underlies Jung's interpretive work. For the central importance that together they assume in the whole of this work has led us to discern its common purposes as well as the common strategy, modes of analysis and interpretation that are devised to fulfill them.

To be sure, displacement is not the only strategic device Jung relies upon. It is among the more important of them, however; and it is particularly important, given our purposes, that we single it out here, for it serves to demonstrate the common method at work in the two interpretive processes precisely at that point where they appear to be most divergent and least reconcilable. But this methodological unity is not only in evidence at this critical and pivotal point, not merely in the second phase of the process; it is apparent in each of them and in the relationships between them--in short, in all of the structural and dynamic features we have already enumerated.

In conclusion, these findings, taken together, now permit us to state more definitively than heretofore that we have discovered at the heart of Jung's interpretive work a consistently employed hermeneutic--i.e., an interpretive *method*-- which provides it with a unity, intelligiblity, and indeed, we venture to add, an underlying logic.

Retrospectus

Happily, then, we have found what we set out to find. But we have scarcely begun to think out the implications of our findings, to essay the significance of Jung's hermeneutic for religious studies in general and Christian theology in particular. To prepare the way for our doing so, we will bring this chapter to a close by calling attention to some of the more important of our study's findings.

In the foregoing assessment, we have emphasized what is perhaps the most novel, ingenious and distinctive feature of Jung's hermeneutic: the way it serves to lead those involved in its interpretive processes to a discovery of the points of contiguity and commonality between personally and collectively shaped images and worlds. The result is an erosion of the distinction between the two. It would be overstatement, however, to suggest that Jung presumed his own work in and of itself to

have abrogated this distinction. Surely it will continue to
exist as long as people think in terms of it, as long as they
organize and perceive their experience in terms of it. But
this does not detract from the fact that the inner workings of
Jung's method, while presupposing the existence of this distinction, nonetheless function in such a way as to undermine
and ultimately subvert it. His is a hermeneutic that invites
those who feel acutely a disrelation to have interposed itself
between personal and collective worlds and meanings to enter
into an interpretive effort specifically designed to forge anew
lines of inter-connection between the two.

     We would, moreover, reiterate here a related, and by now
no doubt obvious point--the method's interweaving and fusion
of different worlds of imagery and meaning work hand in hand
with a disclosure of their inherently symbolic dimension. It
is of the very essence of Jung's interpretive project to set
free, to disclose symbolic reaches of meaning and to aid one to
attune oneself to and appropriate them. These reaches of
meaning, however, are not ready at hand. One cannot expect to
discover them and draw on their power if one is not willing to
offer up the private world of one's fantasies and the public
world of one's religious beliefs and confessional statements to
the rigors and risks of an interpretive process. A receptivity,
a readiness to undergo and be led by this process is essential
to the success of its outcome. Apart from this process and the
method that in-forms and shapes it, one cannot hope to uncover
the abundance of meaning that lies at the heart of one's imaginative and cultural worlds. For the power of the symbolic, to
repeat, is not ready at hand; one cannot seize hold of it; one
cannot unlock its secrets.

     We recall here Jung's assertion that symbolic expressions
"mean more than they say."[95] In probing this deceptively simple
dictum, we have found how elusive and explosive its import is.
Of what does this "meaning *more*" consist? What is the nature
of this "surplus" of meaning? The results of our study suggest
that one can experience and understand it only by recourse to a
high degree of indirection--by heeding particular genres of
human expression and submitting them to an interpretive method
which, among other things, proceeds by displacing them from

a familiar context and frame of reference into a seemingly
alien one.

For Jung the most privileged of these, the genres of
expression that most unrelentingly detain his attention, are
fantasy and doctrine. He suspects--and his interpretive work
vindicates this suspicion--that they both will serve him well
as exemplary instances of inherently symbolic expressions. And
so he sets about the task of devising a set of procedures, a
series of inter-related intellectual operations--in short, a
method--that is strategically and specifically designed to lay
bare and interpret the "surplus" of meaning inherent in these
expressions.

We have studied at close hand the way he puts this method
to work in the interpretation of doctrinal and fantasy materials.
We have reconstructed its constituent parts and its inner workings. We have reflected on the nature of the tasks it is
designed to perform and the purposes it is designed to serve.
Our efforts, however, to bring to light and to put in perspective the most distinctive features of this method must now
give way to an evaluation of it that focuses explicitly on the
theological uses that might be made of it. We will conclude
our study of Jung, then, by returning to those questions that
first gave rise to it: What can Christian theology learn from
this hermeneutic? What in it invites the theologian's attention and why? How might theology appropriate those of its
elements which it finds particularly valuable? It is to these
questions that we now turn.

CHAPTER V

TOWARDS A THEOLOGICAL APPROPRIATION OF JUNG

In the three preceding chapters we have attempted to enter
as fully as possible into the inner workings of Jung's work
and method; we have heeded the performance of his hermeneutic
"in act" and have attuned ourselves to the purposes and spirit
that animate it. We are now prepared in this, the concluding
chapter of our study, to call attention to the more important
of the many ways we believe religious studies in general and
Christian theology in particular stand to benefit from Jung's
hermeneutic. Concluding assessments in each of the preceding
chapters have laid the groundwork for this endeavor; in what
follows we will presuppose and build upon this groundwork.

We will begin by returning to a by now familiar and obvious
point--Jung's is a *psychological* hermeneutic in its conception,
its purposes and its operations; it originates from his concerns
as a clinical psychologist and is designed to serve those
concerns. No matter how evident this point may appear to be,
we emphasize it here, for no theology can even begin to gauge
the import of this hermeneutic if its psychological character
is not accorded full and explicit recognition. It is not surprising, then, given its fundamentally psychological nature,
that the method would aim to disclose the *psychic* dimension of
meaning underlying whatever it interprets--whether it be literature, fantasy, myth, ritual, doctrine, political ideology, etc.

Our study has sought to focus on how Jung brings his method
to bear on doctrine, on how it is peculiarly suited to illumine
the pre-eminent place this dimension of meaning occupies in the
central doctrinal expressions of the Christian faith and tradition. We would expect that the value of such a method would be
its ability to generate a keener awareness of the presence and
nature of the psychic components of meaning underlying these
doctrinal expressions. And this in fact is how we envision in
its most general terms its value for theology. It remains for

141

us to specify in what follows below *how* and *why* theology can
be expected to benefit from this added awareness.

We will proceed first by delineating and evaluating those
points at which Jung's distinctive reading of doctrine has a
direct bearing on theology's own attempts to interpret and re-
interpret it. Then we will broaden the scope of our inquiry
and attempt to articulate a variety of ways his hermeneutic
method contributes to theological tasks not limited to the field
of doctrinal interpretation per se.

Before proceeding, however, in order to better assure that
we shall be understood in our use of the term *psychic*, we need
to remind ourselves that we have not attempted in the course of
this study to delineate a generic sense of the term, i.e., one
which would apply to all manner of psychological interpretations.
Rather we have chosen to limit ourselves to Jung's understanding
of psychic, for his is a psychology distinctive in its own right
that employs its own distinctive understanding of psychic. It
will be helpful to recall here the most significant features of
his view of the human psyche: first, that it embodies the total
breadth of man's mental and spiritual life, the full spectrum
of his conscious and unconscious functioning; and secondly,
that its processes and contents pertain to the developing self,
to its conflicts, needs and future. Throughout our study we
have returned again and again to the ways Jung's psychology
sheds light on these two aspects of the psyche. It is important
that we keep both of them clearly in mind in what follows, for
they provide him with the constituent elements of his view of
psychic meaning.

To attempt to explicate the psychic components of meaning
underlying a particular doctrine is, given this understanding
of psychic, to attempt to show a) that the doctrine in question
emerges from unconscious as well as conscious factors and forces
in the psyche, and b) that it mirrors and portrays the life-
story of a developing self. These two points--already developed
at length in Chapter IV--will serve as our point of departure
for much of what follows. We will reflect on each of them in
turn, with the aim of articulating what consequences might ensue
were theology to make of them integral elements in its own expli-
cations of the meaning of Christian doctrine.

As regards the first point, it is the central importance
Jung accords to the unconscious reaches of psychic meaning that
most interests us. If it is of the very nature of psychic
meaning that it extends into an unconscious realm, then its
scope will necessarily transcend the horizons of man's awareness. And if this is the case, man will only with the greatest
difficulty be capable of articulating and elucidating this
meaning. He will discover inherent within it a peculiar opacity,
an unspecifiable depth that forever eludes him.

It becomes evident, then, that those theologians who would
take the psychic dimension of doctrinal meaning seriously--
again, given Jung's understanding of psychic--would more readily
take into their purview this peculiar opacity, this "depth"
dimension that underlies the Christian doctrinal tradition. An
immediate consequence follows: to accord to doctrine this depth
of meaning is to re-affirm and provide a fresh vantage-point
from which to think out anew the *symbolic* nature of doctrinal
expressions. In our view this is one of the most noteworthy
gains that would flow from an encounter between contemporary
theology and Jung's distinctive brand of psychological hermeneutics.

But how specifically might this attribution of a symbolic
depth of meaning to doctrine contribute to contemporary theology's efforts to re-interpret its role and place in the past,
present and future of Christian history? We will argue, first,
that it provides a convincing account of what we will call here
the communicative power of doctrine; secondly, that it helps
clarify the nature of the problem of the dis-relation and discordance that seems to have interposed itself between the doctrinal expressions themselves and the lived experience of modern
man (whether or not he conceives of himself as "Christian");
and lastly, that it thereby serves to underscore the critical
importance of theological re-thinking today in insuring the
continuance and vitality of doctrinal development in the future.

1. As regards the communicative power of doctrine, Jung
offers an explanation for how doctrinal expressions can continue
to convey meaning long beyond the point when they appear to
have been eclipsed and consigned to irrelevance. For if Jung is

right in his claim that doctrine is moored in the unconscious
reaches of the psyche, it becomes plausible to maintain that
it is not bereft of meaning simply by virtue of the fact that
this meaning eludes one's conscious grasp. Its meaning may
well live on, totally submerged in the depths of the psyche,
in a dormant, latent state; or it may make itself felt, however
dimly, however fleetingly, in the twilight of one's pre-conscious
states of mind. In either of these ways meaning is present
despite one's inability to give voice to it, to articulate it.
Hence, Jung reminds us that we cannot so readily assume that
doctrine is a "dead letter" for those who no longer explicitly
affirm it to be meaningful to them.

It seems to us theology could well make use of this insight
into the way meaning lives on despite every appearance of meaninglessness, in its need to take account of possible discrepancies between secular man's avowed stance vis-à-vis the Christian
tradition, and the more subliminal, less detectable ways he
resonates to it that do not always find their voice amidst the
thematized "secularistic" viewpoints of the day.

2. But if Jung's psychological-symbolic reading of doctrine
gives some reason to hope that its communicative power, while
waxing and waning, will never reach extinction, this does not
thereby excuse theology from the difficult task of attempting to
fathom the causes of this power's wane in the contemporary period
of Christian history. Here we are faced with a much more troubling and complex problem, whose ramifications are vast and
bewildering: Why is it that doctrine is perceived by so many
people today, whether avowedly Christian or not, as something
alien, as a foreign intruder on our cultural soil, as an awkward
anachronism that appears out of place and out of time in our
contemporary era? And why do many Christians instinctively
recoil from doctrine as from something that has frozen and
rigidified the Christian faith and vision in its classical guise?
To what extent is our cultural mood and self-understanding myopic
here, or to what extent is it paving the way for a liberation
from the myopia of the classical Christian past? Is this mood
revelatory of inherent limitations in the very nature of
doctrine? And if limitations there are, what exactly are they?

Is it that the vehicle itself, the form, the genre is no longer
a suitable means of expression, or does the problem pertain more
to *what* is being expressed than it does to *how* it is expressed?

Contemporary theologians, especially those of Roman Catholic background, are wrestling in concerted and oftentimes
creative ways with these and related questions.[1] In order to
gauge properly the relevance of Jung's reading of doctrine to
these efforts, we need to take up again one of the guiding
threads in our study: the central place the dialectic between
dynamics and form occupies in his thought. For Jung, this dialectic manifests itself throughout the history of doctrine in
the interplay between the fixed form of a doctrine on the one
hand and the "warm red blood" of experience "pulsating" within
it on the other.[2]

In his view this interplay is not always free and easy;
it is subject to all the vicissitudes of history. Doctrine
mediates and channels experience; in the case of the Trinity, it
makes available to succeeding ages the experience of the apostolic and Patristic ages now past. But it also encapsulates this
experience, and the moment the encapsulated form and content of
a doctrine is deemed unchanging, the interplay between dynamics
and form, between experience and doctrine, is disrupted. Experience evolves; the form does not. From this point in time on,
the experience of the past, summed up in its formalized expressions, is cut off from, even as it is represented to and in
succeeding ages. The hermeneutical problem is engendered and
grows as time distends. Past and present no longer interfuse;
and modern man maintains more and more insistently that the
present must take possession of itself by turning away from a
past that formerly had nourished and enriched it.[3] Ironically
doctrine comes to work at cross-purposes with itself; instead
of mediating between past and present epochs of Christian
experience, it becomes a barrier that is interposed between
them, disrupting their interplay and interaction.

And so, although Jung perceives Christian doctrine to be
rooted in Western man's cultural experiences of the past, he
also recognizes the emergence of significant disparities between
doctrine and present-day experience. In Chapter IV we have seen
how he accounts for them in terms of his view of the evolution

of Western man's cultural life and consciousness. Tension and
ultimately a disjunction between evolving experience and unchanging forms result. This, for Jung, is the problem, which
leads him to "...take these thought-forms that have become
historically fixed,...[and] to melt them down again and pour
them into the moulds of immediate experience."[4] It is clear
that this is a radical, bold undertaking, for it implies that
contemporary experience should shape as much as be shaped by
doctrine, that traditional doctrinal forms must not only be re-
interpreted, but also broken down, *re*-formed and reshaped in
the very process of re-interpretation.

Theology, it seems to us, is indebted to Jung for his
having corroborated an insight from his own vantage-point that
much of liberal theology, both Protestant and Catholic, has
long ago articulated, but whose consequences have yet to be
fully clarified even today--viz. that Christian doctrine fails
to convey and evoke meaning at precisely those points where the
experience it embodies and re-presents clashes with contemporary
experience, that the disjunction between doctrine and experience
is more fundamentally a disjunction between changing patterns
within experience.

3. Throughout the last one hundred and fifty years much
of the discussion centering on development of doctrine, so
prominent especially in Roman Catholic circles, has been intimately bound up with this insight.[5] In our view Jung contributes
significantly to this continuing and largely unresolved discussion by clarifying the scope of what doctrinal development
encompasses--it is not simply the addition of new teachings or
definitions to the existing "articles" or "deposit" of faith;
nor is it simply a re-interpretation and a re-actualization of
the depth of meaning latent within the old forms, although this
is a large part of it; it is more fundamentally a re-shaping of
the forms. Development occurs *within the form itself*; moreover,
while rooted in and generated by pre-reflective, indeed subliminal dimensions of experience, it can also be heightened and
ratified by one's own interpretive and reflective participation.
In other words, for Jung development of doctrine, while involving the pouring of new wine into old wineskins, is not simply

this. More importantly it is the corrosive action of the wine
on its skins, the "warm red blood" of our immediate experience
that so eats away the time-worn walls channelling it that only
one of two results may ensue: either total disintegration or
a more resilient and elastic version of the original form.

Which of these two alternatives will materialize--dissolu-
tion or renewal--would seem to depend as much on theology's own
will, imagination, insight and creativity as on the unthematized
moods and perceptions of our culture. Neither of these sets of
factors will alone be determinative of the future of doctrine.
But it is the enormous extent of the present-day disjunction
between the changing patterns of experience and the unchanging
forms doctrine has assumed that in our time, far more than in
most, places its fate in theologians' hands.

To our mind, then, Jung calls theology to make of its
current efforts to reinterpret the *meaning* of doctrine self-
conscious attempts to reconstruct its *form* as well, to "melt
down" and transmute the forms in which this meaning has been
cast. Not to approach the interpretive task with this intent
and aim in mind would in and of itself in Jung's view seal the
fate of Christianity's key doctrinal affirmations; it would
solidify and vindicate the secular culture's suspicion and
perception that doctrine is an ossified and petrified vehicle
of religious truth and expression, the very deadness of which
infects those who are inculcated in its traditions and called
to affirm its truth(s) with a corresponding deadness of spirit
and imagination.

On the one hand, then, Jung's hermeneutic of doctrine
reveals how its richness and depths of meaning, grounded as
they are in the unconscious reaches of the human psyche, live
on despite the doctrinal form's seeming irrelevance; on the
other hand it suggests that the whole Christian doctrinal tradition stands ever in danger of dying the death of a premature
burial at the hands of a culture perilously close to losing
contact altogether with these depths. And thus it falls to the
interpretive mind of the theologian not only to re-actualize,
to find new ways of tapping and retrieving this elusive and
fragile fund of meaning, but also to forge anew the forms which
will contain it and allow it to take root, take hold and grow.

To recapitulate, we have found that this hermeneutic, when
applied to Christian doctrine, clarifies the serious, indeed
the critical nature of the problems theology faces in reflecting
on the meaning of doctrine today, on its relationship with
contemporary experience, and on the possibilities of its continuing development in the face of its apparent rigidity of form.
More importantly, it provides means by which these problems
might be resolved. All of these means, it seems to us, center
on Jung's symbolic reading of doctrine. For to construe doctrine symbolically facilitates, in fact is indispensable to, a
recovery of the full resonances of its meaning. And to accord
it this depth, this abundance of meaning, is to pave the way
for the emergence of more plastic and less static doctrinal
forms. In addition, it is to restore to doctrine its power to
mediate between past and present experience, and between
experience itself and its representation. It is to pave the
way for overcoming what recent Roman Catholic theology has
labelled the "extrinsicism" of the Christian doctrinal tradition,[6] its seeming un-relatedness to man's lived experience,
to those dramatic concerns that give texture and felt meaning
to his everyday existence. In short, this--the distinctive way
in which it grounds and effects a symbolic reading of doctrine--
is one of the principal values of Jung's hermeneutic, and these
are the most important of the theological implications that
follow from it.

What, then, of its second major trait--i.e., the way in
which it relates doctrine to the whole "life-story" and development of what we have called Western man's cultural or collective
selfhood? We will preface our consideration of this theme by
returning to several points previously made.

First we need to recall that for Jung the symbolic reaches
of psychic meaning do not "mean" at all if they are not perceived
to be meaning for one's *self*. In his view it is the peculiar
opacity of the life-processes of the human self that constitutes
the locus of these depths of meaning; as they are disclosed in
the course of interpretation, they are shown at one and the same
time to emerge from the self, but more importantly still, to
speak *to* and *about* it. Psychic meaning, then, inevitably

pertains to the human self. It follows that *psyche* and *self*
are coordinate notions and conjoined realities for Jung. The
psyche, in speaking about a human self, is at the same time
speaking about itself. In short, all psychic activity displays
a fundamental reflexivity to itself.

But the psyche, in speaking to and about itself, cannot but
refer to an incarnate self, to a particular self that is grounded
in a given time and a given place, that is shaped by all the
contingencies and vicissitudes of a personal or cultural life-
history. And so it does not surprise us that Jung, in applying
his hermeneutic to the Christian Trinity, in deciphering its
psychic meaning, finds in its portrayal of a prototypical self
and its evolution an expression which has direct bearing on
Western man and his developing selfhood. In confronting Western
man with a model of an essential self, the Trinity is speaking
of the self he would make his own, of *his* essential self. And
in speaking of this archetypal self, it speaks for that reason
to his actual, empirical self and situation, to the embodied
self or psyche of Western man, rooted as it is in a particular
cultural ethos and faced as it is with a contingent set of
problems and possibilities.

Finally, we need here to reiterate that Jung's "psychologiz-
ing" of doctrine is at one and the same time an "anthropologiz-
ing." This is evident given that his understanding of the
personal as well as the collective self and psyche is animated
by a vision of "the complete actualization of the whole human
being,"[7] by a concern with the "essence of...the human."[8] For
this vision and this concern inevitably involve him in a mode
of speech about the generically *human* as such.

What might theology make of Jung's attempts to psycholgize
Christian doctrine in this way? On the face of it it appears
as if we have reached another point where theological and
psychological aims, priorities and methods are incompatible.
For does not theology begin and end its reflections on the
Trinity with its clear and unmistakeable signification of and
reference to God in three persons? Is not the Trinity nothing
else than a primordial expression of the mystery of God, as
apprehended by the Christian faith and church? If such be the
case, then Jung's contention that it "represent[s] a

personification of psychic processes in three roles"[9] might
invite many to suspect that he is doing violence to the Christian
tradition by re-casting the Trinity into psychological terms.[10]

There is no doubt that his transposition of the doctrine's
clear and manifest reference to the divine into the obscure and
latent reference to "the nature of the psyche" and "the essence
of...the human" is provocative, for on the face of it it seems
to point to an emptying of the divine into the human, a Feuer-
bachian transposition of theological into anthropological constructs that aims to exhaust totally the former in deference to
the latter, that envisions no remainder.

Jung's purposes and method, however, are far more dialectical than this implies, in that for him the transposition is
not intended to be irreversible. In fact we have argued that
his heavy reliance on the symbolic as an interpretive principle
reveals that nothing could be further from his intent than to
presume that his own or any other reading of the Trinity could
ever exhaustively elucidate its meaning.

Nevertheless, the misunderstanding he courts here remains--
some theologians will conclude that to view Christian doctrine
as pre-eminently a psychic phenomenon and expression, to construe
its meaning in terms other than its own, is to make of it something less than itself, to reduce its meaning, or indeed perhaps
even to squander and violate its sacrality. In short, they will
be unable to view his interpretation at this, its pivotal point,
as anything other than an extreme form of psychological reduc-
tionism.[11]

And yet, if there is a danger here, there is an overriding
gain: added forcefulness will be provided to theology's
perennial attempt to reflect on one of the most enduring and
telling elements of the Christian vision--that the mystery of
God is never apprehended apart from an experience of an insight
into the mystery that is man. This is a theme that has emerged
and recurred in countless ways throughout the whole religious
history of Christianity--whether it be in the biblical refrain:
"I shall be your God and you shall be my people,"[12] which so
aptly expresses how a sense of peoplehood and its concomitant
sense of historical consciousness, social responsibility and
self-identity crystallize only in the moment of an intimate

encounter with God; or in the opening declaration of John
Calvin's *Institutes* that knowledge of God and self-knowledge
are mutually reinforcing and therefore inseparable;[13] or in
Karl Rahner's theological method, which declares all theological
statements to be inherently anthropological and vice versa;[14]
or most dramatically of all, in the Christian affirmation of
the Incarnation, which bespeaks the fullest possible conjunction
of human and divine.[15]

    We cannot possibly enter into a discussion of all the
ramifications of this theme here; it accords more with our
interests to limit ourselves to those that pertain to Christian
doctrine and theological interpretations of same. In this
regard we would propose that Jung's *psychological* interpretation
serves to bring back to mind, lest one forget, and reinforce a
genuinely *theological* truth: that the central Christian doctrinal affirmations (viz. the Trinity, together with the Incarnation, which is its fulcrum) have never ceased to express an
image of man precisely in their "imaging" of God, that the one
is expressed in the guise of the other, thereby revealing that
the life of man and God impinge upon each other in the most
radical and intimate of ways--that the mystery of man and the
mystery of God are in their very essence but one mystery.

    This is not to say that Jung's transposition of divine into
human represents something novel in the history of Christian
thought. For we cannot fail to note his indebtedness to and
retrieval of the biblical theme of the Spirit's in-dwelling in
man, together with the Greek patristic theme of incarnation--
God's becoming man--grounding and making possible deification--
man's becoming God.[16]

    But what is most noteworthy about this aspect of his
interpretation is not simply that it echoes age-old insights
long ago articulated, nor that it subsumes them into an explicitly psychological context; rather its import is the new emphasis
given to these perennial themes by virtue of having been re-cast
in this context. It is not so much that Jung transposes talk of
God into talk of man, but how he does it that is important--the
fact that the Trinity is viewed as imaging not man per se, or
man in his essence, but more precisely man in process, man on
the way to his essence, man on the way towards the fullest

possible realization of himself, of his selfhood. This makes of
the classical representation of the Christian God not a static
portrait of man, but a highly dynamic portrayal of his becoming,
of what we have called his "life-processes."

It is remarkable that Jung finds in the principal doctrinal
expressions of the Christian tradition the most powerful and
useful key with which to elucidate the depth of meaning that
inheres in these life-processes. More specifically, it is the
classical representation of the Christian triune God that best
serves him in this task; it is here and nowhere else that he
finds the clues which permit him to unearth an archetypal drama
of an evolving consciousness and to apply this drama to the
problems and possibilities Western man is collectively faced
with.[17]

But it is not simply that Christianity's images of the
divine carry within them hidden meanings which, when deciphered,
will reveal the dim outlines of an essential and integral selfhood; more importantly, such decipherings can be expected to
bring one to an intimation of the mystery of the divine precisely by virtue of having generated a greater awareness of self.
For if Jung's psychology of doctrine reconfirms the view that
the mysteries of man and God are but one mystery, we may infer
that any insight into the one can be shown to pertain to the
other.

Hence it would seem that Jung's perspective on human
becoming eventuates in a view that would make of it a true
partaking of divinity. Such at least is the implication of his
claim that self-images--i.e., images of man's greatest possible
realization, of becoming having reached its end--are at one and
the same time images of God.[18] To our mind this theme in Jung's
thought reveals that his psychology of doctrine leaves itself
open to a reversal of its transposition of divine categories
into human, even if it does not systematically carry it out.

What might ensue were theologians to take up the invitation
offered them here and attempt to effect this reversal? No doubt
human becoming and all of man's varied attempts to understand
it, whether in secularistic or in more traditionally religious
terms, would be invested with a greater degree of sacrality; a
sacred or holy dimension would more readily be seen to inhere

in the very phenomenon of human becoming. For if man's journey
through life, together with his efforts to probe more deeply
into its mystery, are at one and the same time an attempt to
grope his way toward a deeper apprehension of the divine, if
the human and the divine mysteries are co-inherent, then one
cannot help but view human life-processes as fraught with the
highest degree of sacred significance.

At the same time Jung's re-affirmation of such a co-
inherence could contribute in yet another way to overcoming the
"extrinsicism" of the Christian doctrinal tradition, a problem
that Karl Rahner, for one, has claimed besets the doctrine of
the triune God in a way far more vexing than most:

> It is as though this mystery has been revealed for
> its own sake, and that even after it has been made
> known to us, it remains, *as a reality*, locked up
> within itself. We make statements about it, but as
> a reality it has nothing to do with us at all....How
> can the contemplation of any reality, even of the
> loftiest reality, beatify us if intrinsically it is
> absolutely *unrelated* to us in any way?...is our
> awareness of this mystery merely the knowledge of
> something purely extrinsic, which, as such, remains...
> isolated from all existential knowledge about our-
> selves...?[19]

For all those theologians who like Rahner have no choice
today but to wrestle with the spectre of this extrinsicism,
Jung's insight that points of reference to the human psyche or
self and to their processes of becoming are *intrinsic* components
of the Christian doctrine of the triune God can ill afford to
be overlooked. For such an insight sheds new light on the way
doctrine is rooted in human experience, in the whole experiential
matrix out of which selfhood emerges. And by implication this
is to suggest that the primordial religious experiences of the
Christian tradition are experiences in which man comes to stand
before himself--to meet his *self*--even while encountering an
Other. If, then, theology could reconstruct, as Jung does with
the Trinity, the ways Christian man has come to fundamental
moments of self-encounter concurrently with and by virtue of
having formulated his most abiding expressions of the loftiest
of realities, how could such a man continue to feel this
reality foreign to, extrinsic to himself?

    Thus far in our remarks we have focused on the two most
distinctive features of Jung's *psychological* interpretation of
Christian doctrine: his symbolic reading of it and his re-
casting of its theological content into anthropological terms.
We have tried to discern in these features ways theology would
stand to benefit by being in-formed by them. We have argued
that the greatest benefit would come precisely in that realm
where the two enterprises of Jungian psychology and Christian
theology are most contiguous--doctrinal interpretation.

    And yet, that we have limited our focus in the foregoing
to this particular aspect of the theological enterprise should
not lead us to overlook the ways his hermeneutic contributes to
still other of its aspects extending far beyond the realm of
doctrinal interpretation. And so we deem it fitting to broaden
the scope of our assessment by enumerating and evaluating the
most important of these contributions.

    1. We will begin by returning to the guiding thread of our
study--Jung's use of the symbolic as interpretive principle.
We have seen how he relies upon it in his interpretation of
doctrine and fantasy; we need now to extrapolate from these
findings, however, and call attention to the fact that he does
not limit his use of this principle to these domains of his
interpretive work alone. Indeed, he shows himself to be strongly disposed to interpret all psychic phenomena from a symbolic
standpoint: "...*every* psychological phenomenon is a symbol when
we are willing to assume that it purports or signifies something
different and still greater, something therefore which is with-
held from present knowledge."[20] And so we are led to re-affirm
one of the axiomatic tenets of Jung's psychology--that central
to the very functioning of the psyche is its capacity to
generate and give form to symbolic images and meaning.

        ...all pictorial representations of processes and
        effects in the psychic background are *symbolic*.[21]

        Everything psychic has a lower and a higher
        meaning,...Here we lay our finger on the secret
        symbolical significance of everything psychic.[22]

Let us place these assertions side by side with his contention that all human experience, language and culture are
grounded in the human psyche:

> ...it is characteristic of the psyche not only
> to be the source of all productivity, but more
> especially to express itself in all the activities
> and achievements of the human mind.[23]

...the psyche...is the *sine qua non* of all experience.[24]

It then becomes apparent that for Jung all human experience,
all of human life, creativity and self-expression is at one and
the same time inherently *symbolic* and inherently *psychic*. It
is important that we underscore this point here, for it enables
us to envisage what is perhaps the most distinctive feature and
significant achievement of his hermeneutic--the way it succeeds
in forging ineradicable points of linkage between the symbolic
and psychic dimensions of human life.

Moreover, it is precisely because Jung reads whatever he
interprets as a psychic expression--whether it be fantasy, art,
folklore, political ideology, occult phenomena, etc.--that he
is able to attribute symbolic meaning to it. And religious
forms of expression are no exception to this rule. We have
seen, for example, that it is only by virtue of the fact that
he construes doctrine as a psychic phenomenon that he is able
to disclose its "depth" dimension of meaning. But doctrine is
not the only religious form of expression that he psychologizes
and accordingly "symbolizes"; as we would now expect, he does
so with all of the religious phenomena he takes into his purview.
To the extent, then, that he succeeds in demonstrating a) the
psychic nature of such phenomena, and b) the essential inter-
connectedness of psychic and symbolic reaches of meaning; Jung
thereby reconfirms from a fresh vantage-point the growing
recognition of the intrinsically symbolic nature of all religious forms of expression. In so doing, he lends his support
to the consensus that has emerged on this point in religious
studies during the past fifty years.[25]

2. And yet, *that* Jung reads all religious phenomena symbolically is less important than *how* he does so, than how he
applies his view of the symbolic to the study of religious texts

and forms of expression. And so we need to take one last
retrospective look here at the most important and distinctive
features of this view--the capacity of symbols to convey hidden
reaches of meaning, and the way they emerge from and speak to
the developing self. At what points might Jung's understanding
of these characteristics of symbol be of greatest use in theology's efforts to think through the nature of the symbolic
dimension of meaning that is increasingly felt to underlie all
religious phenomena?

As regards the first characteristic, many philosophers of
religion and theologians affirm the communicative power of
symbol as one of its central hallmarks. But it is more difficult
to demonstrate how and why symbols "mean more than they say,"
how and why the reaches of meaning signified in religious
language uncannily transcend the most carefully constructed and
contrived vehicles to which they are entrusted. It strikes us,
however, that depth psychology in general, with its reliance on
the postulate of the unconscious and the success with which it
has marshalled evidence for its reality, and Jung's psychology
in particular, are peculiarly suited to account for this remarkable capacity that seems to inhere in all symbols--symbols convey
while yet concealing this depth of meaning precisely by virtue
of being so firmly rooted in the unconscious depths of the human
psyche.

This is one point where we feel religious studies will
always stand indebted to Jung. As Mircea Eliade has testified:
"Depth psychology has taught us that the symbol delivers its
message and fulfills its function even when its meaning escapes
awareness."[26] In other words, depth psychology makes possible
the recognition that meaning transcends awareness as well as
language, or at least the more intensive levels of reflective
awareness; that meaning can be felt and intimated even when it
is conceptually unspecifiable.

Those theologians who have wrestled with this issue in a
concerted way have frequently sought to resolve it by appealing
to experience in one form or another. For example, Langdon
Gilkey has set forth the view that the power of symbols to
convey meaning depends on their intimate links with human
experience, on their ability to express, illumine and "thematize

our felt and shared experiences."[27] They serve as mediators
between the world of experience and the world of language,
undercutting the disjunctions that are ever prone to emerge
between the two. One finds a similar emphasis in Eliade's
contention that religious symbols emerge from and speak to the
particularities of a concrete human situation. This for him
constitutes their

> ...*existential* value..., that is, the fact that a
> symbol always aims at a reality or a situation in
> which human existence is engaged. It is above all
> this existential dimension that marks off and
> distinguishes symbols from concepts. Symbols still
> keep their contact with the profound sources of
> life; they express, one might say, the "spiritual
> as lived."[28]

We would suggest that Jung's account of how symbols emerge
from and speak to the developing self casts significant light
on what constitutes this "existential" value and meaning of
religious symbolism. We recall here how Jung views the emergence of symbols--they are constellated primarily when critical
junctures and turning-points in a human life are reached, when
conflicts hem in and threaten all future development. This
implies that man is always already engaged when he meets his
symbols, and that they will carry with them the emotional
valences with which his life-situation happens to be charged at
the particular time of their emergence.

Moreover, we have seen that symbols for Jung thematize,
speak to and indeed transform the very same experiential matrix
from which they are born. In other words, the symbolic is
grounded in the whole life of persons and cultures; it emerges
from and speaks to the vicissitudes and needs of the developing
self. It is this then that constitutes the experiential matrix
of symbols, their points of "contact with the profound sources
of life"--in short, their "existential" value and meaning.

3. The way Jung's hermeneutic clarifies the nature of the
existential meaning of symbols, of their rootedness in human
experience, enables us to envision how it could at the same
time serve theology in a much more fundamental way, in one of
its most all-embracing and challenging tasks--the elaboration
of what Langdon Gilkey has called "a secular prolegomenon to

theology,...which begins in our ordinary experience of being
in the world and elicits hermeneutically the meanings for
religious language and its symbolic forms latent within that
experience."[29]

It is remarkable that so many contemporary theologies,
from such a wide variety of vantage-points, have come to affirm
the need to make of this "ordinary experience of being in the
world" a genuine and indispensable source for theological
reflection.[30] We would not presume to delineate here even the
most rudimentary outlines of an adequate and comprehensive
account of human experience. We can, however, indicate what
Jung's direct bearing on such a project would be--he could help
theology specify what particular dimensions of experience
symbols emerge from and thematize. In conceiving of it as
fundamentally an experience of psyche and self, and in conceiving
of psyche and self in developmental terms, i.e., in terms of
their life-processes and becoming, and in viewing these processes, this becoming, as an incipient drama or story, he sets
forth a view of human experience in which the *whole* of it
pertains to and indeed centers on this phenomenon of coming to
selfhood.

That Jung focuses on this phenomenon is not to say that he
thereby attempts or aims to give an exhaustive phenomenology of
the full range of human experience. But it is to point out that
he accords it so central a place in this full range that we
feel no such phenomenology of experience could hope to be
adequate without taking careful account of it. It follows that
contemporary phenomenologies of religious experience or of the
religious dimensions of secular experience will need to come to
terms with Jung's view that the experience of "coming to selfhood" constitutes a vital component of all human, and hence
religious experience.

4. We are now prepared to widen still further the scope of
Jung's applicability to theological tasks. For here we intend
to suggest how his hermeneutic could provide theology with a
fresh perspective from which to reflect upon the very nature of
human becoming, of man in process. This requires that we extend still further our consideration of the privileged place
the phenomenon of coming to selfhood assumes in his thought.

That Jung would view all human becoming, both in its
personal and cultural or collective modalities, as a process
that carries man to his selfhood reveals the profoundly *teleological* orientation of his thought.[31] Human becoming is
innately ordered to an end, to an end, moreover, that is
realizable no matter how fragmentarily experienced and dimly
perceived. Human becoming is a "coming to," and all of man's
life-processes work purposively to facilitate this "coming to."
Here we are brought close to the heart of the vision underlying
Jung's psychology--that all human experience, potentially at
least, is meaningful and intelligible by virtue of being imbued
with this sense of the orderedness of everything in a life-time
to the whole of it.

It seems to us that those metaphysicians and theologians
who make of *becoming* or *process* privotal categories not only
in their view of reality as such, but more particularly in their
view of human reality, would find this account of it inviting.
For by marshalling evidence for the existence of natural mech-
anisms within the human psyche which regulate and guide the
life-process forward, Jung renders more convincing those views
of man which would see a teleological dynamism immanent in all
personal and cultural growth and change. He provides empirical
grounding for such views.

Moreover, we would maintain that his account of human
becoming sheds significant light on the phenomenon of "life-
story"--on the way a person deciphers and gives shape to the
whole of his life-process. In so doing he provides theology
with a much needed resource with which to clarify the meaning
of the category *story*, a task that is called for, we feel, in
view of the widespread currency the term has gained in recent
times in religious studies and the proliferation of usages to
which it could well be subjected in future years.

Here everything we have discovered about the way Jung's
hermeneutic moves from the immediacies of a life-situation into
the personal and historical past only to shift back to one's
present and forward into intimations of the future, of one's
prospective path and being, can be said to have direct bearing
on the phenomenon of "telling one's story." For it is precisely these steps or shifts in the method that serve to etch out

the shape of one's life-process and of the finished self that
emerges in the course of it. Accordingly, we can see in the
method's very underpinnings a means by which persons can bring
to more reflective consciousness and integrate the past, present
and even future patterns of their life-experience. And this,
it strikes us, is what story-telling is all about: discerning
and thereby giving voice to, articulating, the inter-relation-
ships of a sequence of events lived through time.[32]

In our view the value of the kind of personal story-telling
Jung's method engages one in lies in the way it serves to height-
en a sense of the meaningfulness of one's life-experience. It
does this by enabling persons to perceive the inherent orderedness that underlies the totality of this experience. When is
my life-experience felt to be meaningful? When is it not? At
what points is personal change threatening? When does it create
a sense of disorder, of chaos? When a sense of the orderedness
of my becoming? These are ultimately religious questions. We
feel religious studies in general and Christian theology in
particular could find in Jung's understanding of story a useful
resource with which to reflect on them--on the nature of the felt
meaning and sense of purpose that may or may not undergird human
life.[33]

We have found then that Jung attributes an inherent orderedness and purposiveness to human becoming, an orderedness and
purposiveness which give to all of one's life-experience an
intelligibility, a unity, indeed a coherence. But this is not
to imply that it is a coherence easily grasped. To articulate
the story one is living out is an arduous task; it requires
painstaking efforts to hit upon the "right" image and then to
decipher its elusive meanings. The temptation to resort to an
easier way, to fall prey to an eagerness to specify the exact
course of one's development, to adopt a semiotic rather than a
symbolic style of interpretation will be ever present. Jung's
method guards against these dangers by calling one to an explicit
recognition of the symbolic depth of meaning inherent in the
life-process. The story-telling this method makes possible is
thereby moored in this depth; it proceeds from it and may never
leave it behind.

And so we are led to reaffirm one of the most important of our study's findings--that personal becoming and symbolic knowing always proceed in conjunction with each other. We now see more clearly than before how Jung's account of human becoming is utterly dependent upon his postulate that a symbolic dimension is its inevitable concomitant. In fact it should by now be abundantly evident that for Jung such a dimension is *ubiquitous* in human life--it is rooted in the very dynamics of the psyche; it manifests itself in all forms of human expression; it accompanies personal and cultural development at every turn in its path. For Jung, man is nothing if he is not an *animal symbolicum*.[34]

But what is the theological import of this central affirmation in his thought? It is our view that theology could utilize this understanding of man's becoming, and by extension of man himself, in its own efforts to account for the religious dimension of human existence, to reflect on the very nature of *homo religiosus*. No doubt Jung's relevance here will be most manifest to those theologians who acknowledge the existence of a necessary link between the religious and symbolic dimensions of human life. For we would expect such thinkers to find in his universalization of the symbolic dimension, in his propensity to see its manifestations throughout the whole tissue of human life, corroborating evidence and thus added support for their own view that man's religiosity is an essential, indelible component of his being.

This is not to say that Jung himself sets forth an explicit argument for a necessary link between the religious and the symbolic, although many aspects of his thought suggest that he in fact presupposed such a link to exist.[35] Rather it is to maintain that his understanding of the symbolic supplies those theologians, philosophers of religion and phenomenologists of religion who wish to argue for such a link with a very helpful resource and range of evidence. Thus we are able to extend one step further a point we have made earlier--Jung's psychology lends greater forcefulness to the views of those who would argue for the intrinsically symbolic nature not only of religious forms of expression, but also of the *whole religious life and constitution of man*.

We have delineated the most distinctive features of Jung's
understanding of human becoming in such a way as to illumine
their points of applicability to specific theological issues
and tasks. To put our findings in proper perspective, we will
conclude this section by proposing that all of these issues and
tasks pertain to what we will generically call *religious
anthropology.*

We conceive religious anthropology's major task to be an
elucidation of the nature of the religious dimension, impulse,
drive or faculty in human life. Just how universal is this
drive? What does it consist of? How does it manifest itself?
How does it motivate, direct and orient man? These are the
questions it will center on. Many contemporary theologians
recognize that such questions must be raised explicitly and
systematically before the theistic question as well as the whole
content and meaning of a historical revelation can even begin
to be considered.[36]

We would hope and expect that a theological inquiry into
the religious nature of man would be informed by the findings
of psychology, phenomenology and philosophy of religion in this
domain. Jung's psychology, we feel, is particularly relevant
in this regard; his insights into the phenomenon of coming to
selfhood--its rootedness in a symbolic depth of meaning; its
teleological dynamism, i.e., its purposive orderedness to a
realizable end; the sense in which the whole of a life-time
constitutes a unity of lived experience which, when brought to
awareness, begins to assume the form of a story; and the deepen-
ing sense of purpose and meaningfulness of one's life-experience
that ensues--all add forcefulness to those views of human
becoming that attribute to it an inherently sacred, holy and
hence religious dimension.

5. We will conclude by suggesting ways Jung's method
contributes to a deeper understanding on theology's part of the
role and importance of hermeneutical modes of reflection in
religious studies.

At a very minimum this method will lead to a greater
recognition of the need that theology adopt and employ hermeneutical methods whenever it concerns itself with an explication

of the symbolic reaches of meaning underlying the religious
life of man. For to our mind such methods are expressly
designed to deal with the problems and peculiarities entailed
by man's attempt to reflect on these elusive reaches of meaning. In fact we take the very emergence of these methods in
recent times and the widespread attention accorded them in
religious studies as a measure of a new-found respect and
fascination for the symbolic as such. As this interest grows,
so too will an interest in hermeneutics grow. For it is evident that there is increasingly manifest in religious studies
today a natural consonance between content and method, between
the symbolic and the hermeneutical. In view of this consonance
we would propose that the very fact that Jung contributes to a
keener awareness on theology's part of the pervasive power and
presence of the symbolic in all aspects of the religious life
of man cannot but lead at one and the same time to a fuller
recognition of the need that theology avail itself of hermeneutical methods in reflecting on this power and presence.

But how might it do so? At what points and in what ways
would its own modes of reflection assume a necessarily hermeneutical character? We would hope that our own study of Jung
has called attention to two broad areas of the theological
enterprise where the use of hermeneutic methods is particularly
relevant--first, doctrinal studies, in their bearing on both
the historical and systematic branches of theology; and secondly, the large-scale efforts within contemporary theology to
forge a secular prolegomenon with which to explicate the religious horizon of contemporary man's secular experience and self-
understanding. For nowhere more forcefully and convincingly
than in his work on Christian doctrine and on the life and
imagination of despiritualized, secularized modern man does
Jung demonstrate the central place and role of the symbolic;
nowhere more successfully than in these two areas does he apply
his own brand of hermeneutical reflection. We would conclude
then that Jung's findings in both of these areas provide a
strong impetus to theology to engage in explicitly hermeneutical
modes of reflection when addressing itself to either of them.

We wish to clarify, however, that in so arguing, we do not
thereby intend to deny the applicability of hermeneutic methods

to other theological domains. Certainly biblical studies,
for example, rely heavily on a wide spectrum of interpretive
tools and sciences, and thus cannot help but deal with the
hermeneutical questions posed by the use of these tools and by
the very nature of biblical language. But because Jung does
not apply his method to biblical texts in any concerted way, we
have not focused on biblical hermeneutics here. We have not
attempted, then, to enumerate the full range of tasks theological hermeneutics encompasses; rather we have chosen to delineate
only those upon which Jung's own hermeneutic method has the most
direct bearing.

    Nor is this to presume that theological reflection in all
its moments can or should conceive of itself hermeneutically.
Without attempting to inventory all of theology's varied functions and sub-disciplines here, we would nonetheless mention
three points where, in our view, theological discourse leaves
hermeneutical reflection behind, even while relying on its
results: 1) when a hermeneutic of secular man's lived experi-
ence--the attempt to bring to light and inter-relate the patterns
of symbolic meaning of that experience--gives way to an attempt
to conceptualize the religious horizon or dimension disclosed
in these patterns and to theistically ground this horizon (i.e.,
gives way to what we would designate "philosophy of religion");
2) when theology embarks upon what we conceive to be its
principal constructive task--the attempt to inter-relate and
integrate the results of its hermeneutic of contemporary experience with the findings of biblical hermeneutics and a hermeneutic
of Christian doctrine, with the aim of determining the ultimate
meaning and truth of the Christian faith and message;[37] and
3) when theology engages in self-reflection--when it seeks to
establish the ground rules for all its modes of discourse and
inquiry, as well as to differentiate and inter-relate its
various functions and branches (this we would deem to be theological method's major task).

    These aspects of the theological enterprise do not directly
involve hermeneutical methods as we have conceived of them here,
for they are not primarily concerned with explicating the
symbolic dimension of human and/or Christian experience. We
are not claiming then that Jung helps clarify the nature of the

methods theology must employ in these larger tasks, but only
that he brings it to a keener awareness of the hermeneutical
nature of the tasks confronting it in delimited areas--in
doctrinal studies and in its account of contemporary man's
secular experience.

But to argue *that* theology needs to engage in hermeneutical
reflection and to clarify *at what* specific *points* it needs to
do so is not yet to indicate *how* such reflection should be
carried out. How might we best delineate Jung's relevance here?
What bearing does his brand of hermeneutics have on the *way*
theology undertakes its own brand of hermeneutical reflection?

Let us begin with a disclaimer. It should be apparent
that Jung does not present theology with a ready-made theological hermeneutic, nor even with anything approaching a carefully
devised blueprint for such a hermeneutic. And so it is by no
means our intention here to propose that all the aims and tasks
of theological hermeneutics would be fulfilled if theology were
to adopt in its entirety Jung's method. For Jung's is a method
that is not designed to elucidate the full range of symbolic
meanings underlying Christian doctrine and contemporary experience. It does, however, elucidate one particular valence in
this full range--namely the psychic--and demonstrates its pivotal
place in the *multi*-valence of symbolic meaning. To our mind
theological hermeneutics must not only be cognizant of these
many valences, but also undertake to differentiate and inter-
relate them. If this is granted, then Jung's contribution to
such a task becomes obvious: he brings to light the vital part
psychic components of meaning play in this multi-valence.

In making this point we are returning to the point of
departure of this chapter; we are re-articulating the essential
nucleus, the underlying form of the argument we have employed
throughout its several parts--viz. that Jung's is a hermeneutic
peculiarly suited to disclose these components of meaning, and
that this, its chief hallmark, is also its chief theological
value. We have attempted to specify what this value is by
enumerating and reflecting on the ways Jung's method contributes
to a re-thinking of a wide spectrum of theological issues,
problems and tasks. We have seen that all of these issues--the
communicative power of symbols, doctrinal meaning and development,

the dialectic of experience and symbolic forms, the symbolic
nature of human becoming and religious forms of expression--
pertain to the role of the symbolic. And so it should now be
clear, given the consonance we presuppose exists between the
symbolic and the hermeneutical, that each and every one of these
issues will be of direct concern to what we are here calling
"theological hermeneutics." If this is the case, we can conclude that all of the ways Jung contributes to these issues will
at one and the same time have a bearing on theological hermeneutics. Therefore, we need not spell out further how Jung's
own brand of hermeneutics could be of use in theological
hermeneutics; for to do so would simply be to reiterate findings
we have already dwelled on at length. It will suffice here to
underscore our basic point--in its attempts to elucidate the
multi-valence of symbolic meaning underlying religious phenomena,
theological hermeneutics will need to account for its psychic
components, especially in view of Jung's demonstration that
symbolic meaning is moored in the life-processes of the human
psyche.

There is a further consequence that can be expected to
follow from a theological encounter with Jung's hermeneutic and
the keener awareness of psychic meaning that such an encounter
makes possible. It is of less direct, yet wider significance
than any of the implications discussed heretofore--to our mind
an in-depth encounter with and assessment of this hermeneutic
will eventuate in a clearer recognition of theology's need to
take careful account of the whole panoply of hermeneutic methods
and strategems employed in the study of religion. For if
theology can benefit from an assessment of *one* such method, the
case is strengthened that it should in fact reflect systematically on *all* of them.
We view the emergence of these methods throughout the last
one hundred and fifty years as a direct outcome of a growing
interest in and awareness of the plurality of (symbolic) meanings underlying religious phenomena. In fact we would maintain
that the very existence of this plurality requires that a
plurality of methods be employed in elucidating it.

If this is the case, the tasks of theological hermeneutics are compounded and immeasurably complicated, for it becomes apparent that a comprehensive articulation of the full range of valences that make up symbolic meaning would require that theology understand in depth an equally wide range of methods, while also undertaking to differentiate, coordinate and integrate the insights and findings of all of them. No doubt the outcome of such a venture must await a collaborative effort on the part of generations of religious scholars. In the meantime individual thinkers can make their own limited contribution by reflecting on particular hermeneutic methods and on the particular valences of symbolic meaning disclosed by them.

In our view the complexity of this hermeneutical situation and of the tasks it dictates is at the same time theology's opportunity. For taking into its purview this whole bewildering array of methods will enable it to solidify and deepen its understanding of the very nature of symbolic meaning--of the whole spectrum of valences, levels or components that consti- tutes its abundance and elusive depths.

In this study we have examined one such method. We would hope that, in addition to being one small step on the way to the fulfillment of this much larger task, it will also contribute to a greater sense of the need that theology undertake it.

INTRODUCTION

NOTES

[1]We will offer an interpretation of the nature and extent
of Jung's reliance on his intellectual progenitor in Chapter
III, pp. 72-75 and 84 below.

[2]"Jung and Theology: A Bibliographical Essay," in *Spring:
An Annual of Archetypal Psychology and Jungian Thought* (1973),
p. 204.

[3]We shall discuss why he did so in Chapter IV, pp. 102-8
below.

[4]For an explanation of how we construe the meaning of this
term, see pp. 59-61 below.

[5]We will provide a more extensive account of the meaning
we ascribe to this term in Chapter III, pp. 92-93.

[6]An important exception is Peter Homans, whose "Psychology
and Hermeneutics: Jung's Contribution," *ZYGON/Journal of
Religion and Science* 4 (December 1969): 333-55, has been
instrumental in suggesting to us the possibilities inherent
in this way of reading Jung.

CHAPTER I

NOTES

[1]Heisig's "Jung and Theology: A Bibliographical Essay,"
pp. 204-55, is a very useful survey of the whole field of such
literature.

[2]Trans. G. R. Lamb (New York: Sheed & Ward, 1957).

[3]Ibid., pp. 111-12.

[4]Ibid., p. 118.

[5]Ibid., p. 119.

[6]Jung's clearest avowal of this standpoint occurs in
Psychology and Religion: West and East, trans. R. F. C. Hull,
Bollingen Series XX: *The Collected Works of C. G. Jung*, ed.
Sir Herbert Read, Michael Fordham, and Gerhard Adler; William
McGuire, executive editor; vol. 11 (New York: Pantheon Books,
1958), pp. 5-7. See also ibid., pp. 299-310.

[7]Hostie, p. 120.

[8]Ibid., pp. 119-20.

[9]Ibid., pp. 203-4.

[10]Note, for example, his assertion that "...Jung is always
letting himself be dragged beyond the confines of his own rights
and competence....he undoubtedly goes beyond the field of
psychology. And therefore I feel obliged to refuse to
his views,...any real value in connection with the study of
actual dogma." Ibid., pp. 209-10. See also our discussion in
Chapter IV of Jung's proclivity to interchange the terms dogma
and doctrine, pp. 102-3 below.

[11]Hostie, p. 206. Italics added.

[12]Ibid., p. 209.

[13]Hostie, p. 133.

[14]Ibid., pp. 214 and 222.

[15]Peter Homans advances a more explicit acknowledgement of
this fact in his *Theology after Freud: An Interpretive Inquiry*
(Indianapolis: Bobbs-Merrill Co., 1970), p. 218. "Jung's
thought is incredibly elusive, provocative, and rich. He is a
'bridge' figure, one who sees and relates many things, leaving
to others the task of finding a clearly recognizable focus or
center, sacrificing organization to richness."

[16](London: Salisbury Square, 1958).

[17]Ibid., p. x.

[18]Ibid., p. xi.

[19]Ibid., pp. 3-4.

[20]Ibid., p. 81.

[21]Trans. Stanley Godman (Notre Dame, Ind.: University of Notre Dame Press, 1964).

[22]Ibid., p. 172.

[23]Martin Buber, *Eclipse of God: Studies in the Relation between Religion and Philosophy* (New York: Harper & Row, 1952).

[24]Ibid., pp. 78-79 and 82.

[25]Ibid., p. 84.

[26]Ibid.

[27]Ibid., p. 78.

[28]Ibid., p. 86.

[29]Our own interpretation of Jung will differ significantly with Buber; see pp. 118-20 and 147-51 below.

[30]Buber, pp. 78 and 133.

[31]See his *Psychology and Religion*, pp. 5-7.

[32]Ibid., pp. 247-48, 476 and 511-12; *Aion: Researches into the Phenomenology of the Self*, trans. R. F. C. Hull, *The Collected Works of C. G. Jung*, vol. 9, Part 2, 2d ed. (Princeton, N.J.: Princeton University Press, 1968), pp. 194-95; and *Mysterium Coniunctionis*, trans. R. F. C. Hull, *The Collected Works of C. G. Jung*, vol. 14, 2d ed. (Princeton, N.J.: Princeton University Press, 1970), pp. 547-49.

[33]*Two Essays on Analytical Psychology*, trans. R. F. C. Hull (Cleveland: Meridian Books, 1956), p. 301.

[34]See our discussion, pp. 71-75 and 92-94 below.

[35]Buber, p. 135.

[36]Ibid., p. 134. Cf. Jung's statements in *Psychology and Religion*, pp. 511-12, and in "Religion and Psychology: A Reply to Martin Buber," *Spring: An Annual of Archetypal Psychology and Jungian Thought* (1973), p. 200.

[37]"Can a Psychologist Be Religious?" *Commonweal* 58 (September 1953): 583-84; "Jung and the Supernatural," *Commonweal* 55 (March 1952): 561-62; "Two Theologians on Jung's

Psychology," *Blackfriars* 36 (1955): 382-88; and "Theological Reflections," *Journal of Analytical Psychology* 5 (1960): 147-54.

[38]With a Foreword by C. G. Jung (Cleveland: Meridian Books, 1952/1961).

[39](London: Collins, 1960).

[40]See Jung's numerous letters addressed to White during the years 1945-1950 in *C. G. Jung: Letters*, ed. Gerhard Adler and Aniela Jaffé, trans. R. F. C. Hull, Bollingen Series XCV:1, 2 vols. (Princeton, N.J.: Princeton University Press, 1973-75), vol. 1: *1906-1950*, pp. 381-568 passim.

[41]*Soul and Psyche*, pp. 11-31.

[42]"But if their respective fields of inquiry and operations sometimes become a battlefield, this can only be because they are operating on the same ground." Ibid., p. 11.

[43]Included as Section 6 in *Psychology and Religion*, pp. 357-470. See White's discussion of the work in *Soul and Psyche*, pp. 235-40.

[44]For his discussion of the former see Chapter IX, "The Integration of Evil" in *Soul and Psyche*, pp. 141-65; cf. Jung's letter of 31 December 1949 in *Letters*, pp. 539-41, and his foreword to White's *God and the Unconscious*, pp. 18-24. For White's discussion of Jung and the *imago dei*, see *Soul and Psyche*, pp. 45-64, as well as *God and the Unconscious*, pp. 81-100.

[45]*Soul and Psyche*, pp. 51-54.

[46]Ibid., p. 51.

[47]Ibid., p. 61.

[48]See, for example, *Psychology and Religion*, pp. 357-63 and 468-70.

[49]*Soul and Psyche*, p. 54.

[50]See "The History and Psychology of a Natural Symbol" in *Psychology and Religion*, pp. 64-105.

[51]For our view of this challenge, see pp. 127-30 and 142-51 below.

[52]Trans. R. F. C. Hull, Bollingen Series XXI (New York: Pantheon Books, 1950). Schaer's study was written at too early a date (the original German edition appeared in 1946) to be able to treat Jung's later works, such as "Answer to Job" (1952) and his posthumous *Memories, Dreams, Reflections*, ed. Aniela Jaffé and trans. Richard and Clara Winston (New York: Vintage Books, 1963), which are so revelatory of his personal religious outlook.

[53]See "The Psychic Bases of Religion" and "Religion as a Psychic Function" in Schaer, pp. 59-136.

[54]Ibid., p. 62.

[55]Ibid., p. 136.

[56]*Individuation* is the term Jung employs to designate "the process by which individual beings are formed and differentiated; ...having for its goal the development of the individual personality." *Psychological Types*, trans. H. G. Baynes and revised by R. F. C. Hull, *The Collected Works of C. G. Jung*, vol. 6 (Princeton, N.J.: Princeton University Press, 1971), p. 448.

[57]Schaer, p. 197.

[58]See ibid., pp. 158-95.

[59]Ibid., p. 193.

[60]See our own statement of Jung's contribution to this task, pp. 159-60 below.

[61]Schaer, pp. 203-5.

[62](Philadelphia: Westminster Press, 1967).

[63]Ibid., pp. 13-17.

[64]Ph.D. dissertation, University of Chicago, 1964. A digest of the major findings of the dissertation has been published as "The Archetypal Self: Theological Values in Jung's Psychology," in Peter Homans, ed., *The Dialogue Between Theology and Psychology*, vol. 3 of *Essays in Divinity*, ed., Jerald C. Brauer (Chicago: University of Chicago Press, 1968), pp. 221-47.

[65](London: Collier-Macmillan, 1969).

[66]Analytical Psychology Club of New York, *Carl Gustav Jung, 1875-1961: A Memorial Meeting* (New York: Analytical Psychology Club of New York, 1962), pp. 28-32.

[67]Bockus, preface.

[68]Ibid.

[69]Ibid. Cf. Friedrich Schleiermacher, *The Christian Faith*, trans. and ed. H. R. Mackintosh and J. S. Stewart (Edinburgh: T. & T. Clark, 1928), #60, #93, #97:4, #100:2, and #108:1.

[70]Bockus, p. 196.

[71]See pp. 159-60 below.

[72]"The Impact of Pastoral Psychology on Theological Thought," *Pastoral Psychology* 11 (February 1960): 17-23; and "The Theological Significance of Existentialism and Psychoanalysis" in his *Theology of Culture*, ed. Robert C. Kimball (London: Oxford University Press, 1959), pp. 112-26.

[73]Analytical Psychology Club of New York, *A Memorial Meeting*, p. 29.

[74]"[Jung] ...distinguishes between symbols and archetypes. Symbols are the infinitely variable expressions of the under- lying, comparatively static archetypes....That [the archetypes] are preformed in the unconscious as potentialities makes understandable both the wide range of their variability and the traits of a definite structure which limit the possibilities of variation." Ibid., p. 30.

[75]Ibid., p. 31.

[76]"Existentialism and Psychoanalysis," pp. 117 and 123. In so arguing, he shows himself to be more indebted to Freud than to Jung (see ibid., pp. 120-22), but the influence of the latter, if not explicitly acknowledged apart from his theory of religious symbolism, is nonetheless discernible in Tillich's recognition of depth psychology's rediscovery "of the demonic structures that determine our consciousness" (ibid., p. 124), his concern for the *telos* of personal development that is revealed in its pathologies (ibid., p. 119), etc.

[77]Ibid., p. 125.

[78]See "The Impact of Pastoral Psychology," pp. 22-23.

[79]Ibid.; italics added.

[80]"Existentialism and Psychoanalysis," p. 114.

[81]See Dunne, pp. vii-xi and 1-8.

[82]Ibid., p. 205.

[83]Ibid., pp. 112-13; see also pp. 75-83 and 120-26.

[84]Ibid., pp. 141-42, 151-53, and 161-63.

[85]Ibid., pp. 151-53 and 175.

[86]Ibid., pp. 175-77.

[87]The following recent works testify to the growing importance of such efforts: John Dominic Crossan, *The Dark Interval: Towards a Theology of Story* (Niles, Ill.: Argus Communications, 1975); Michael Novak, *Ascent of the Mountain, Flight of the Dove: An Invitation to Religious Studies* (New York: Harper & Row, 1971), pp. 44-88; and John S. Dunne, *Time and Myth* (Garden City, N.Y.: Doubleday & Co., 1973).

[88]See pp. 93, 135 and 157-58 below.

[89]This is more manifestly the case with Dunne than it is with Bockus or Tillich; but it is evident nonetheless in Bockus' concluding chapter ("The Self and Christ," pp. 148-97), as well as in much of Tillich's work. See, for example, his reliance on the metaphor of *depth* in "Religion as a Dimension

in Man's Spiritual Life," pp. 3-9 of *Theology of Culture*; and
"The Depth of Existence," pp. 52-63 of *Shaking of the Foundations* (New York: Charles Scribner's Sons, 1948); and his
discussion of the relation of personality "centeredness" to
ultimate concern in *Dynamics of Faith* (New York: Harper & Row,
1958), pp. 4-22 and 105-11.

[90]See p. 160 below.

[91]See, for example, Schubert Ogden, "What Is Theology?"
Journal of Religion 52 (January 1972): 22-40; David
Tracy, "The Task of Fundamental Theology," *Journal of
Religion* 54 (January 1974): 22-28; Robert W. Funk, *Language,
Hermeneutic, and the Word of God; The Problem of Language in
the New Testament and Contemporary Theology* (New York: Harper
& Row, 1966), pp. xi-122; James M. Robinson and John B. Cobb,
Jr., eds., *The New Hermeneutic*, New Frontiers in Theology,
vol. 2 (New York: Harper & Row, 1964).

CHAPTER II

NOTES

[1]Our introductory remarks to Chapters III and IV will clarify what each of these areas of Jung's thought encompasses and why he attached such great importance to them. See pp. 58-70 and 96-108 below.

[2]*The Archetypes and the Collective Unconscious*, trans. R. F. C. Hull, *The Collected Works of C. G. Jung*, 2d ed., vol. 9, Part 1 (Princeton, N.J.: Princeton University Press, 1969), p. 6n.

[3]*Mysterium Coniunctionis*, p. 468n.

[4]*Psychological Types or The Psychology of Individuation*, trans. H. Gordon Baynes (New York: Harcourt, Brace & Co., 1923), pp. 601-2. Except where otherwise specified, all references to this work are from this edition (which is now superseded by vol. 6 of *The Collected Works*).

[5]*The Spirit in Man, Art, and Literature*, trans. R. F. C. Hull, *The Collected Works of C. G. Jung*, vol. 15 (Princeton, N.J.: Princeton University Press, 1966), p. 70.

[6]See variants of this formula in the following: *Aion*, p. 73; *The Structure and Dynamics of the Psyche*, trans. R. F. C. Hull, *The Collected Works of C. G. Jung*, 2d ed., vol. 8 (Princeton, N.J.: Princeton University Press, 1969), p. 336; *The Spirit in Man, Art, and Literature*, p. 76; and *Mysterium Coniunctionis*, p. 540.

[7]We will take up this question when we discuss what Jung calls the "symbolic attitude"; see pp. 58-61, 152-53 and 159 below.

[8]See Gilbert Durant, *L'Imagination symbolique*, 2d ed. (Paris: Presses Universitaires de France, 1968), pp. 3-15 and 61-68, for an interpretation of Jung's theory of symbolism in terms of the distinction employed in linguistic theory between signifier and signified.

[9]*Two Essays*, p. 299.

[10]*Mysterium Coniunctionis*, p. 468n.

[11]*Symbols of Transformation: An Analysis of the Prelude to a Case of Schizophrenia*, trans. R. F. C. Hull, *The Collected Works of C. G. Jung*, vol. 5 (New York: Pantheon Books, 1956), p. 222.

[12]*Psychology and Religion*, p. 207.

[13]*Symbols of Transformation*, p. 124.

[14]*The Spirit in Man, Art, and Literature*, p. 136.

[15]In fact other theories of symbolism, in particular that propounded by Paul Ricoeur, have called attention more explicitly than Jung himself did to this built-in tension between the hidden and manifest elements of the symbol's content and meaning, or in Ricoeur's terms, between its secondary and primary intentionality. See his *Symbolism of Evil*, trans. Emerson Buchanan (Boston: Beacon Press, 1969), pp. 3-24; and also *Freud and Philosophy: An Essay on Interpretation*, trans. Denis Savage (New Haven: Yale University Press, 1970), pp. 6-19.

[16]*Structure and Dynamics*, pp. 45-46 and 75; and *Psychological Types*, pp. 584-85.

[17]*Symbols of Transformation*, p. 124.

[18]See ibid., p. 77; *Psychological Types*, pp. 601-2; *Structure and Dynamics*, pp. 175 and 336; *Aion*, p. 73; *Psychology and Religion*, p. 207; and *The Practice of Psychotherapy: Essays on the Psychology of the Transference and Other Subjects*, trans. R. F. C. Hull, *The Collected Works of C. G. Jung*, 2d ed., vol. 16 (Princeton, N.J.: Princeton University Press, 1966), p. 175.

[19]We reiterate that we are making use here of terms Durand uses to explicate Jung's understanding of symbol; see *L'Imagination symbolique*, pp. 61-68.

[20]*Psychological Types*, p. 602.

[21]Ibid., p. 601.

[22]*The Spirit in Man, Art, and Literature*, p. 77. See also his statement that "...symbols mean very much more than can be known at first glance"; in *Alchemical Studies*, trans. R. F. C. Hull, *The Collected Works of C. G. Jung*, vol. 13 (London: Routledge & Kegan Paul, 1967), p. 302.

[23]*Alchemical Studies*, p. 302n. In so stating, Jung implies that a symbol's meaning, although felt and dimly apprehended, is not amenable to conceptual categorization.

[24]*Freud and Psychoanalysis*, trans. R. F. C. Hull, *The Collected Works of C. G. Jung*, vol. 4 (Princeton, N.J.: Princeton University Press, 1961), p. 215.

[25]*Psychology and Religion*, p. 255. See also ibid., p. 468; and the statement that "...symbols were never devised consciously, but were always produced out of the unconscious by way of revelation or intuition"; in *Structure and Dynamics*, p. 48.

[26]*The Archetypes*, p. 6n.

[27]"The ground principles...of the unconscious are indescribable because of their wealth of reference, although in themselves recognizable. The discriminating intellect naturally keeps on

trying to establish their singleness of meaning and thus misses
the essential point; for what we can above all establish as the
one thing consistent with their nature is their *manifold
meaning*, their almost limitless wealth of reference, which
makes any unilateral formulation impossible." *The Archetypes*,
p. 38. Perhaps the most comprehensive expositions of Jung's
understanding of the unconscious can be found in "On the Nature
of the Psyche," in *Structure and Dynamics*, pp. 159-234; and
Two Essays, especially pp. 75-89 ("The Personal and the
Collective or Transpersonal Unconscious") and pp. 277-304
("The Structure of the Unconscious"). See also "The Concept of
the Collective Unconscious" in *The Archetypes*, pp. 42-53; and
"The Role of the Unconscious" in *Civilization in Transition*,
trans. R. F. C. Hull, *The Collected Works of C. G. Jung*, 2d ed.,
vol. 10 (Princeton, N.J.: Princeton University Press, 1970),
pp. 3-28.

[28] *Structure and Dynamics*, p. 409.

[29] *The Archetypes*, p. 58.

[30] *Freud and Psychoanalysis*, pp. 331-32.

[31] *The Archetypes*, p. 101.

[32] *Civilization in Transition*, p. 269.

[33] This is especially apparent from a study of *Die Dynamik
des Unbewussten*, vol. 8 of *Gesammelte Werke* (Olten und Freiburg
im Breisgau: Walter Verlag, 1971).

[34] See translator's note in *Structure and Dynamics*, p. 300;
and editors' note in *Psychology and Alchemy*, trans. R. F. C.
Hull, *The Collected Works of C. G. Jung*, 2d ed., vol. 12
(Princeton, N.J.: Princeton University Press, 1968), pp. 8-9.

[35] This evolution can be traced by studying his usage of
these terms in "Über die Energetik der Seele," "Die Struktur
der Seele," "Theoretische Überlegungen zum Wesen des Psychi-
schen," "Geist und Leben," "Das Grundproblem der Gegenwärtigen
Psychologie" and "Seele und Tod," in *Die Dynamik des Unbewussten*.

[36] See, for example, "Psychology and Religion" and "Psychological Commentary on *The Tibetan Book of the Great Liberation*"
in *Psychology and Religion*, pp. 3-105 and 475-508; *Analytical
Psychology: Its Theory and Practice*, *The Tavistock Lectures*,
with a Foreword by E. A. Bennet (New York: Vintage Books, 1968);
"The Concept of the Collective Unconscious" and "Conscious,
Unconscious, and Individuation" in *The Archetypes*, pp. 42-53
and 275-89.

[37] P. 129.

[38] *The Archetypes*, p. 58.

[39] *Civilization in Transition*, p. 270.

[40]*Psychology and Alchemy*, p. 9.

[41]*Structure and Dynamics*, p. 200.   Cf. *The Archetypes*,
pp. 287-88; and *Psychology and Alchemy*, pp. 480-81.

[42]*Psychological Types*, p. 588.

[43]The most systematic of Jung's many attempts to view the
psyche in these terms is his "On the Nature of the Psyche," in
Structure and Dynamics, pp. 159-234. See also "The Structure
of the Psyche," ibid., pp. 283-342; "The Relations between the
Ego and the Unconscious" in *Two Essays*, pp. 133-253; and "Conscious, Unconscious, and Individuation" in *The Archetypes*,
pp. 275-89.

[44]Note, for example, the statement: "As an empirical concept, the self designates the whole range of psychic phenomena
in man. It expresses the unity of the personality as a whole";
in *Psychological Types, The Collected Works*, revised version,
p. 460. See also ibid., editors' note.

[45]See *Two Essays*, pp. 250-55; and *Aion*, pp. 3-7 and 23-35.

[46]*Aion*, pp. 3-7.

[47]*Two Essays*, p. 64. See also *Memories*, p. 350.

[48]*Two Essays*, pp. 311-12 (note #6).

[49]See "The Concept of Libido" in *Symbols of Transformation*,
pp. 132-41.

[50]*Memories*, p. 350.

[51]See *Two Essays*, p. 71; and *Structure and Dynamics*, p. 253.

[52]*Symbols of Transformation*, p. 58; see also *Structure and
Dynamics*, pp. 243 and 253.

[53]*Psychological Types*, pp. 531-33; *Two Essays*, pp. 121, 186-
87 and 322-23 (note #16); *Structure and Dynamics*, pp. 255-57
and 287-88; and *Civilization in Transition*, pp. 18-20.

[54]*Two Essays*, p. 121.

[55]*Structure and Dynamics*, pp. 325-26.

[56]*Two Essays*, p. 58. Note also his assertion that "libido
can never be apprehended except in a definite form; that is to
say, it is identical with fantasy-images." Ibid., p. 227.

[57]We shall take up a related point in Chapter IV, when we
consider the dialectic between *experience* and *form*, between the
dynamic and structural factors that Jung presumes underlie
Christian doctrine and its history and development. See
pp. 104-7 below.

[58]In *Structure and Dynamics*, pp. 3-66; see especially pp. 32-40.

[59]Ibid., p. 32.

[60]Ibid.

[61]Ibid., p. 122.

[62]Ibid., pp. 10-11.

[63]Ibid., p. 96.

[64]Ibid., p. 122.

[65]Ibid., pp. 32-33.

[66]Ibid.

[67]Ibid.

[68]Ibid.

[69]Ibid., p. 35. See also *Freud and Psychoanalysis*, pp. 179-80.

[70]*Structure and Dynamics*, p. 36.

[71]Ibid., p. 41.

[72]*Two Essays*, pp. 62-63.

[73]*Structure and Dynamics*, pp. 38-39 and 47-50.

[74]Ibid., p. 41.

[75]Ibid., p. 42.

[76]Ibid., p. 45.

[77]Ibid., p. 48.

[78]Ibid., p. 47; see also ibid., p. 49.

[79]Ibid., p. 47; see also ibid., p. 25; and *Symbols of Transformation*, p. 226.

[80]*Symbols of Transformation*, p. 224.

[81]*Psychology and Religion*, p. 191.

[82]*Psychological Types*, pp. 326-27.

[83]Ibid.

[84]*Aion*, p. 194.

[85]*Psychological Types*, p. 324.

[86]*Psychology and Religion*, p. 468.

[87]We will return to this point in Chapter III; see pp. 62 and 70 below.

[88]*Psychological Types*, pp. 608-9; see also ibid., p. 326.

[89]Jolande Jacobi's *Complex, Archetype, Symbol in the Psychology of C. G. Jung*, trans. Ralph Manheim with a Foreword by C. G. Jung (Princeton, N.J.: Princeton University Press, 1959), pp. 95-99, offers an interpretation of Jung's notion of symbol that diverges from the one we have presented here. For Jacobi, the conjunction between the symbol's unconscious and conscious components is based upon the conjunction between an image (*Bild*) and a "sense" or meaning (*Sinn*). The latter is "the integrating component of the cognitive and formative consciousness," while the former is "the content, the raw material of the creative, primordial womb of the collective unconscious, which takes on meaning and shape through its union with the first component" (p. 95). Her appeal to the etymology of the German *das Sinnbild*, however, is misleading, in that Jung employs consistently a different term for symbol: viz. *das Symbol*. And while it is suggestive to identify the world of images with the unconscious and the world of meaning with consciousness, Jacobi fails, in so doing, to account for the way the sense or meaning of a symbol is inextricably bound to and incommunicable apart from the particular image or expression itself.

[90]Consider Jung's statement that "it is in...[symbols] that the union of conscious and unconscious contents is consummated" (*The Archetypes*, p. 289), in the light of his contention that symbols "never have an exclusively conscious or unconscious source, but proceed from a uniform co-operation of both" (*Psychological Types*, pp. 605-6).

[91]*Psychological Types*, p. 320.

[92]*Structure and Dynamics*, p. 48.

[93]*Two Essays*, p. 299.

[94]*Freud and Psychoanalysis*, p. 291. See "Prefaces to 'Collected Papers on Analytical Psychology'" in its entirety, ibid., pp. 290-93; and *Structure and Dynamics*, pp. 255-56.

[95]*Structure and Dynamics*, p. 255.

[96]Ibid., p. 336.

[97]*Psychological Types*, p. 326.

[98]*Two Essays*, p. 299.

[99]Here and in what follows we are elaborating on Peter Homans' reformulation of Paul Ricoeur's dictum "the symbol gives rise to thought." In the light of Jung's psychology this dictum is re-cast as "the symbol...gives rise to becoming,

to individuation, to the metamorphosis of personality."
"Psychology and Hermeneutics: Jung's Contribution," p. 353.
Cf. Ricoeur's "Conclusion" to *The Symbolism of Evil*, pp. 347-
57.

[100] See our discussion of Jung's use of these qualifications,
pp. 39-40 above.

[101] *Two Essays*, p. 300.

CHAPTER III

NOTES

[1]*Psychological Types*, *The Collected Works* version, p. 427.

[2]Ibid., p. 433; italics added.

[3]*Psychological Types*, H. G. Baynes (1923) edition, p. 604.

[4]Ibid., p. 603.

[5]*Mysterium Coniunctionis*, p. 540.

[6]It is clear that Jung subsumes dreams within the larger category fantasy, albeit they are thought of as *passive*, as opposed to *active* fantasies; see *Psychological Types*, pp. 574-76.

[7]This is most evident in "The Transcendent Function," *Structure and Dynamics*, pp. 67-91, where Jung discusses specifically waking fantasies; and in "The Technique of Differentiation between the Ego and the Figures of the Unconscious," *Two Essays*, pp. 224-38. For Jung's writings that focus specifically on dreams, see "General Aspects of Dream Psychology" and "On the Nature of Dreams," in *Structure and Dynamics*, pp. 237-97; and "The Practical Use of Dream-Analysis," in *The Practice of Psychotherapy*, pp. 139-61.

[8]On occasion Jung also comments on case-material not his own; the whole of *Symbols of Transformation*, for example, is an extended account of one such case-history.

[9]In this regard, see pp. 68, 96-98 and 107-8 below. See also Peter Homans' discussion in "Psychology and Hermeneutics; Jung's Contribution," pp. 340-43.

[10]*Civilization in Transition*, pp. 74-75; the aforementioned essay is included in full in this volume, pp. 74-94.

[11]Ibid., p. 75.

[12]Ibid.

[13]We are making use here of an expression of Paul Ricoeur's; see his "The Hermeneutics of Symbols and Philosophical Reflection," *International Philosophical Quarterly*, 2 (July 1962): 202.

[14]See *Civilization in Transition*, pp. 77-78, 89 and 92.

[15]See *Psychology and Religion*, pp. 21-22, 45-49 and 85; and *The Archetypes*, pp. 12-15. We shall elaborate on this point in Chapter IV, pp. 99-101 below.

[16]See *Memories*, Chapter IX, pp. 238-88.

[17]See pp. 96-98 below.

[18]*The Archetypes*, p. 15. See also "Yoga and the West," in *Psychology and Religion*, pp. 529-37.

[19]See pp. 113-15 and 122-23 below.

[20]See our assessment of the way Jung's method serves to restore to man that which is lost to him by virtue of his modernity, pp. 93-95, 99-107 and 141-51 below.

[21]*Two Essays*, p. 225.

[22]*Civilization in Transition*, p. 238; see also *Psychology and Religion*, p. 199.

[23]See p. 41 above; and *Freud and Psychoanalysis*, p. 215.

[24]*Two Essays*, p. 226.

[25]*Civilization in Transition*, p. 23.

[26]*Memories*, p. 187.

[27]*Psychology and Religion*, pp. 459-60. See *Symbols of Transformation*, pp. 72 and 231; *Memories*, pp. 192-93; *Two Essays*, pp. 300-02; as well as Jung's statement that: "We must interpret, we must find meanings in things, otherwise we would be quite unable to think about them. We have to break down life and events, which are self-contained processes, into meanings, images, concepts, well knowing that in so doing we are getting further away from the living mystery"; in *The Spirit in Man, Art, and Literature*, p. 78; and: "A practising analyst may be supposed to believe implicitly in the significance and value of conscious realization, whereby hitherto unconscious parts of the personality are brought to light and subjected to conscious discrimination and criticism. It is a process that requires the patient to face his problems and that taxes his powers of conscious judgment and decision. It is nothing less than a direct challenge to his ethical sense, a call to arms that must be answered by the whole personality." *The Practice of Psychotherapy*, pp. 146-47.

[28]See *Psychological Types*, pp. 561-63.

[29]*Two Essays*, p. 90.

[30]Ibid.

[31]See *Memories*, p. 187; and *Two Essays*, pp. 161-65 and 224-38.

[32]*Alchemical Studies*, p. 17; see also "The Transcendent Function" in *Structure and Dynamics*, pp. 67-91.

[33]*Memories*, pp. 172-73.

[34]Ibid., p. 188. See also ibid., pp. 176, 180 and 192-93.

[35]*Alchemical Studies*, p. 17; see also *Two Essays*, pp. 212-14.

[36]*Structure and Dynamics*, p. 82.

[37]See *Freud and Psychoanalysis*, p. 186.

[38]*Two Essays*, p. 231.

[39]By "interpretive process" we mean to refer to the joint project of interpretation analyst and analysand embark upon in a clinical setting and for therapeutic reasons.

[40]The key elements of the notion of method we are advancing here are drawn from Bernard Lonergan's understanding of method, as presented and developed at the outset of his *Method in Theology* (New York: Herder & Herder, 1972), pp. 3-25. Note especially his statement that: "A method is a normative pattern of recurrent and related operations yielding cumulative and progressive results. There is a method, then, where there are distinct operations, where each operation is related to the others, where the set of relations forms a pattern, where the pattern is described as the right way of doing the job"; ibid., p. 4.

[41]*Psychological Types*, p. 603.

[42]*Freud and Psychoanalysis*, p. 240.

[43]*Psychological Types*, p. 555. Note also Jung's statement that the dream is a "spontaneous self-portrayal, in symbolic form, of the actual situation in the unconscious"; *Structure and Dynamics*, p. 263.

[44](Leipzig und Vienna: Franz Deuticke Verlag, 1912); trans. Beatrice M. Hinkle as *The Psychology of the Unconscious* (New York: Moffatt Yard & Co., 1916), and now superseded by *Symbols of Transformation*.

[45]For surveys of the history of depth psychology, see Dieter Wyss, *Depth Psychology: A Critical History--Development, Problems, Crises*, trans. Gerald Onn (New York: W. W. Norton, 1966); and Henri F. Ellenberger, *The Discovery of the Unconscious: The History and Evolution of Dynamic Psychiatry* (New York: Basic Books, 1970). See also William McGuire, ed., *The Freud/Jung Letters: The Correspondence between Sigmund Freud and C. G. Jung*, trans. Ralph Manheim and R. F. C. Hull, Bollingen Series XCIV (Princeton, N.J.: Princeton University Press, 1974).

[46]This period of fresh intellectual creativity corresponds fairly closely to the period of Jung's most intense submergence into fantasy--1912-1919 (see *Memories*, pp. 170-99). It would thus seem that this creative watershed period brought a new freshness not only to his imaginative life but to his theoretical work as well. Some of Jung's most important works in personality theory were begun during this time. The original essays, for example, upon which *Two Essays* later was to be

based, "Neue Bahnen der Psychologie" and "La Structure de
L'Inconscient," appeared in 1912 and 1916 respectively (the
translations of same have been published as appendices to
Two Essays, pp. 257-304). And the essay "On Psychic Energy,"
although not published until 1928, was begun in 1912; perhaps
more than any other of his writings, this article succeeds in
clarifying the nature of Jung's divergence from Freud's understanding of libido and psychic dynamics.

[47]See p. 40 above; and *Psychological Types*, p. 601.

[48]Note his assertion that: "Everything psychic has a lower
and a higher meaning,...Here we lay our finger on the secret
symbolical significance of everything psychic." *Symbols of
Transformation*, p. 50.

[49]*Psychological Types*, pp. 584-85.

[50]Ibid., pp. 536-38; italics added.

[51]Ibid., p. 580.

[52]*Freud and Psychoanalysis*, p. 291.

[53]See, for example, Preface to the first edition of
"Collected Papers on Analytical Psychology," in *Freud and
Psychoanalysis*, pp. 290-93; "The Transcendent Function," in
Structure and Dynamics, pp. 67-91 and especially p. 75; and
"On Psychic Energy," ibid., pp. 3-66 and especially p. 24.
All of these essays first appeared during the years 1916-1928.

[54]*The Spirit in Man, Art, and Literature*, p. 70.

[55]Jung implies as much in *Memories*, pp. 146-69; and also
in *Freud and Psychoanalysis*, pp. 325-37.

[56]We have already noted Jung's deep respect for the
mysterious nature of the psyche; see pp. 42-43 above.

[57]*Freud and Psychoanalysis*, p. 291.

[58]*Structure and Dynamics*, p. 75. See also ibid., pp. 49-
50 and especially pp. 257-58; as well as *Psychological Types*,
pp. 312-13.

[59]See *The Practice of Psychotherapy*, p. 150.

[60]For good examples of Jung's presentation of fantasy-
material serially, i.e., as it occurs throughout the course of
an analysis, see "A Study in the Process of Individuation," in
The Archetypes, pp. 290-354; and "Individual Dream Symbolism in
Relation to Alchemy," Part 2 of *Psychology and Alchemy*, pp. 39-
223. For further examples of isolated cases, see *Freud and
Psychoanalysis*, pp. 237-38; *Two Essays*, pp. 112-20 and 226-36;
Structure and Dynamics, pp. 241-50; "The History and Psychology
of a Natural Symbol" in *Psychology and Religion*, pp. 64-105;
and *Analytical Psychology: Its Theory and Practice*, Lectures 3
and 4, pp. 87-138.

[61]See *Psychological Types*, *The Collected Works* version, pp. 427-33; and p. 61 above.

[62]*Structure and Dynamics*, pp. 75-76 and extended note following. All quotations in the following analysis of Jung's interpretation of this dream are taken from this passage.

[63]For Jung's understanding of the way in which what he calls the *parental-imagos* serves to mediate between the personal and collective worlds of the psyche, see *Two Essays*, pp. 69-77, 136-47 and 195-98; as well as *Symbols of Transformation*, pp. 329-30.

[64]*Two Essays*, p. 91. Our discussion to follow will be based upon the interpretation of the dream Jung presents ibid., pp. 91-112. Except where otherwise noted, all quotations are taken from pp. 92-98.

[65]See pp. 48-49 above.

[66]Jung pursues the psychological ramifications of this mythic motif at greater length in *Symbols of Transformation*, pp. 210-12, 367 and 374-75.

[67]*Two Essays*, p. 112.

[68]See pp. 47-48 above.

[69]*Two Essays*, p. 91; *Symbols of Transformation*, p. xxv; *Psychology and Alchemy*, p. 289; and *Alchemical Studies*, p. 348.

[70]There is a close relationship between *energy* and *affect* in Jung's thought; note, for example, his statement that the "intensity of affect" of psychic contents, that is, their "feeling-tone," can be "expressed in terms of energy," i.e., as a "value quantity"; *Structure and Dynamics*, p. 11. Jung defines *affect* as "...a state of feeling characterized by a perceptible bodily innervation on the one hand and a peculiar disturbance of the ideational process on the other. I use emotion as synonymous with affect"; *Psychological Types*, p. 522. And *feeling* is viewed as "...primarily a process that takes place between the ego and a given content, a process, moreover, that imparts to the content a definite *value* in the sense of acceptance or rejection ('like' or 'dislike')"; ibid., p. 543.

[71]See "The Personal and the Collective (or Transpersonal) Unconscious" in *Two Essays*, pp. 74-89; "Symbols of the Mother and of Rebirth," in *Symbols of Transformation*, pp. 207-73; and his statement: "It must be remembered that the 'mother' is really an imago, a psychic image merely, which has in it a number of different but very important unconscious contents.... regression leads back only apparently to the mother; in reality she is the gateway into the unconscious, into the 'realm of the Mothers.' ...For regression, if left undisturbed, does not stop short at the 'mother' but goes back beyond her to the prenatal realm of the 'Eternal Feminine,' to the immemorial world of archetypal possibilities where, 'thronged round with images of all creation,' slumbers the 'divine child,' patiently awaiting his conscious realization." Ibid., pp. 329-30.

[72]The most important of Jung's many explanations of the term's meaning are: *Two Essays*, pp. 74-89; *Structure and Dynamics*, pp. 200-16; and *The Archetypes*, pp. 3-41, 75-80 and 151-60. Jolande Jacobi provides a thorough account of the development of this notion in Jung's thought in *Complex, Archetype, Symbol*, pp. 31-36.

[73]*Two Essays*, p. 187.

[74]Ibid., p. 89.

[75]Ibid., pp. 300-01.

[76]*Psychological Types*, p. 578.

[77]See p. 44 above for the sense in which we are employing this term.

[78]We are making use here of another of Paul Ricoeur's terms, which he employs in order to characterize one side of what he has perceived to be the "conflict of interpretations" underlying the hermeneutical dilemma that confronts modern man: "The situation in which language today finds itself comprises this double possibility, this double solicitation and urgency: on the one hand, purify discourse of its excrescences, liquidate the idols, go from drunkenness to sobriety, realize our state of poverty once and for all; on the other hand, use the most 'nihilistic,' destructive, iconoclastic movement so as to *let speak* what once, what each time, was *said*, when meaning appeared anew, when meaning was at its fullest. Hermeneutics seems to me to be animated by this double motivation: willingness to suspect, willingness to listen; vow of rigor, vow of obedience." *Freud and Philosophy*, p. 27; see also ibid., pp. 20-36, 460 and 530.

[79]*The Practice of Psychotherapy*, p. 160.

[80]Ibid.

CHAPTER IV

NOTES

[1]*Memories*, pp. 194-95.

[2]Ibid., Chapter VII, "The Work," pp. 200-22. See also Jung's important Foreword to his "Commentary on 'The Secret of the Golden Flower,'" in *Alchemical Studies*, pp. 3-5.

[3]*Memories*, p. 205.

[4]Ibid.

[5]Translated and included in *Alchemical Studies*, pp. 1-56.

[6]Jung's principal alchemical works have been collected and published in *Psychology and Alchemy*, *Alchemical Studies* and *Mysterium Coniunctionis*. See also *Aion*; and "The Psychology of the Transference" in *The Practice of Psychotherapy*, pp. 163-323. The essays on Eastern religious traditions which first appeared during this time have been re-published as Parts 7-9 of *Psychology and Religion*, pp. 475-608. For Jung's studies of mythology and folklore, see the articles collected in Parts 2-5 of *The Archetypes*, pp. 75-272 (all of which first appeared during the years 1948-1954).

[7]With the exception of *Aion*, all of these works have been included in *Psychology and Religion*. See Parts 1, 2, 3 and 6 therein.

[8]*Civilization in Transition*, p. 76.

[9]*The Archetypes*, pp. 13-15.

[10]*Psychology and Religion*, p. 85.

[11]Ibid., p. 21.

[12]*The Archetypes*, pp. 12-13.

[13]*Psychology and Religion*, p. 199.

[14]*The Archetypes*, pp. 14-15.

[15]Jung suggests, in fact, that the whole of modern psychology can be viewed as a historical child of this cultural/religious situation: "Since the stars have fallen from heaven and our highest symbols have paled, a secret life holds sway in the unconscious. That is why we have a psychology today and why we speak of the unconscious. All this would be quite superfluous in an age or culture that possessed symbols." Ibid., pp. 23-24.

[16]*Psychology and Religion*, p. 89. See also Jung's letter to H. Irminger, 22 September 1944: "Have you never noticed that I do not write for ecclesiastical circles but for those who are *extra ecclesiam*? I join their company, deliberately and of my own free will outside the Church." *Letters*, p. 350.

[17]See, for example, those passages in his writings where doctrine is discussed explicitly and at length: "Background to the Psychology of Christian Alchemical Symbolism" in *Aion*, pp. 173-83; "Introduction to the Religious and Psychological Problems of Alchemy" in *Psychology and Alchemy*, pp. 3-37 (and especially pp. 15-18); "Archetypes of the Collective Unconscious" in *The Archetypes*, pp. 3-41 (and especially pp. 11-24); and "Dogma and Natural Symbols" in *Psychology and Religion*, pp. 34-63 (and especially pp. 43-50).

[18]It is for this reason that Jung appeals to Vincent of Lérins' fifth century canon of the *consensus omnium*, and insists with him that those doctrines are true which are believed to be true "always, everywhere, by everybody"; quoted in *Psychology and Religion*, pp. 199-200.

[19]Note, for example, *Aion*, pp. 173-75; and *Mysterium Coniunctionis*, pp. 308-9 and 523.

[20]See the article on "Dogma: Theological Meaning of," by Karl Rahner and Candido Pozo in *Encyclopedia of Theology: The Concise Sacramentum Mundi*, ed. Karl Rahner (New York: Seabury Press, 1975), pp. 352-56. Cf. Jaroslav Pelikan's formulation and discussion of the classical meaning of the term *doctrine* as that which "the church of Jesus Christ believes, teaches, and confesses on the basis of the Word of God"; in *The Emergence of the Catholic Tradition (100-600)* (Chicago: University of Chicago Press, 1971), pp. 1-10.

[21]*Psychology and Religion*, pp. 18-19.

[22]*The Archetypes*, p. 22; see also ibid., p. 12.

[23]See *Psychology and Religion*, pp. 21 and 89; and *Structure and Dynamics*, p. 59.

[24]See *Aion*, pp. 173-83; *Psychology and Religion*, pp. 43-50 and 89; *The Practice of Psychotherapy*, p. 193; and *Mysterium Coniunctionis*, p. 454.

[25]*The Practice of Psychotherapy*, p. 193.

[26]*Psychology and Religion*, p. 50. See also ibid., pp. 45-46; and *Aion*, p. 178.

[27]*Psychology and Religion*, p. 89.

[28]See Chapters I and II of *Memories*, pp. 6-83, and especially pp. 52-59.

[29]Ibid., pp. 55-56.

[30]Ibid., pp. 73, 91-94 and 215.

[31]Ibid., p. 93.

[32]Ibid., p. 52; see also *The Archetypes*, pp. 15-16.

[33]See especially Chapter VII, "The Work," in *Memories*, pp. 200-22.

[34]Originally published as "Zur Psychologie der Trinitätsidee," *Eranos-Jahrbuch* 1940-41, ed. Olga Fröbe-Kapteyn (Zurich: Rhein-Verlag, 1942), pp. 31-64. Revised and enlarged as "Versuch zu einer psychologischen Deutung des Trinitätsdogmas" in *Symbolik des Geistes: Studien über Psychische Phänomenologie* (Zurich: Rascher, 1948), pp. 321-446. The latter is translated and included in full in *Psychology and Religion*, pp. 107-200.

[35]For Jung's interpretation of the Christian understanding of evil, see "Answer to Job"; his Foreword to Victor White, *God and the Unconscious*, pp. 13-25; "Good and Evil in Analytical Psychology" in *Civilization in Transition*, pp. 456-68; and in particular his responses to the letters and questions of Howard L. Philp in the latter's *Jung and the Problem of Evil*, pp. 8-21 and 213-54. For his views on the doctrine of Christ, his fullest statements, apart from his work on the Trinity, can be found in *Aion* and "Answer to Job."

[36]*Psychology and Religion*, pp. 112-28.

[37]Ibid., pp. 113-15.

[38]Ibid., pp. 115-16.

[39]Ibid., pp. 117-19.

[40]Ibid., p. 119.

[41]Quoted ibid., p. 122.

[42]Ibid., pp. 122-23.

[43]Ibid., pp. 112-47.

[44]Ibid., p. 130; cf. ibid., pp. 123-29.

[45]Ibid., p. 149n. See also ibid., pp. 148-52; and pp. 85-86 above.

[46]*Psychology and Religion*, p. 139.

[47]*The Practice of Psychotherapy*, p. 193; and *Psychology and Religion*, pp. 161 and 194.

[48]We are borrowing here a term Paul Ricoeur employs in his discussion of the chimera of a presuppositionless philosophy: "A philosophy that starts from the fullness of language is a philosophy with presuppositions. To be honest, it must make its presuppositions explicit, state them as beliefs, wager on

the beliefs, and try to make the wager pay off in understanding." *Symbolism of Evil*, p. 357; see also ibid., pp. 19-24.

[49] *Psychology and Religion*, p. 200.

[50] To our knowledge, nowhere does Jung explicitly assign this status to Western man. And although one might plausibly argue that he does so implicitly, one could just as plausibly maintain that the Gnostic mind or the Upanishadic tradition or even the consciousness of primitive man provided him with a model for the nature of the psyche more comprehensive than that provided him by his own culture.

[51] It is one of the central aims of our study to clarify how this axiomatic presupposition is put to use in Jung's psychology. See our assessment, pp. 134-36 below; and cf. pp. 85-86 and 88-89 above.

[52] *Psychology and Religion*, p. 194; see also ibid., pp. 129-37 and 180-87.

[53] Ibid., p. 134.

[54] Ibid., p. 135.

[55] Ibid., p. 134.

[56] Ibid., p. 135.

[57] Ibid., p. 194.

[58] Ibid., p. 200. See also ibid., pp. 110-11 of the Introduction.

[59] Note the rationale he provides for so doing: "Not having any theological knowledge worth mentioning, I must rely in this respect on the texts available to every layman. But since I have no intention of involving myself in the metaphysics of the Trinity, I am free to accept the Church's own formulation of the dogma, without having to enter into all the complicated metaphysical speculations that have gathered round it in the course of history. For the purposes of psychological discussion the elaborate version contained in the Athanasian Creed would be sufficient, as this shows very clearly what Church doctrine understands by the Trinity." Ibid., pp. 110-11.

[60] Ibid., p. 136.

[61] Insofar as Jung's psychology speaks of the human psyche as such, it can be said to concern itself with the generically *human* as such. We will return to this point in Chapter V; see p. 147 below (and pp. 42-44 above for Jung's notion of psyche).

[62] *Psychology and Religion*, pp. 152-63.

[63] Ibid., pp. 155-56.

[64]Ibid.   Cf. ibid., pp. 468-69; and *Two Essays*, pp. 250-52.

[65]*Psychology and Religion*, p. 157.

[66]Ibid., pp. 148-63.

[67]Ibid., p. 158.

[68]Ibid., p. 161; quoted from Georg Koepgen, *Die Gnosis des Christentums* (Salzburg: O. Müller Verlag, 1939), p. 194.

[69]We shall return to this point in our concluding chapter; see pp. 146-51 below.

[70]*Psychology and Religion*, p. 180.

[71]See ibid., pp. 164-87.

[72]See our distinction between the empirical and the archetypal self, p. 44 above.

[73]*Psychology and Religion*, p. 193.

[74]Ibid., pp. 174-76.

[75]Ibid., pp. 157-59.

[76]Ibid., pp. 115-16 and 158-59.

[77]Ibid., p. 159.

[78]Ibid., p. 174.

[79]Ibid., p. 156.

[80]Ibid., pp. 168-80.

[81]Ibid., p. 167; italics added.

[82]The following works attest to the central place this theme occupies in Jung's thought: "Conscious, Unconscious and Individuation" and "Concerning Mandala Symbolism" in *The Archetypes*, pp. 275-89 and 355-84; "The History and Psychology of a Natural Symbol" in *Psychology and Religion*, pp. 64-105; and "Individual Dream Symbolism in Relation to Alchemy" in *Psychology and Alchemy*, pp. 174-75.

[83]*Psychology and Religion*, p. 178.

[84]Ibid., pp. 189-90.   See also "A Study in the Process of Individuation" and "Concerning Mandala Symbolism" in *The Archetypes*, pp. 290-384; "The History and Psychology of a Natural Symbol" in *Psychology and Religion*, pp. 64-105; and "Individual Dream Symbolism in Relation to Alchemy" in *Psychology and Alchemy*, pp. 41-223.

[85]See illustrations in text; *Psychology and Religion*, pp. 174-75.

[86]Ibid.

[87]Ibid., pp. 189-90.

[88]See our discussion of psychic conflict, pp. 47-48 above.

[89]See, for example, *Psychology and Religion*, pp. 109-10.

[90]For our own conclusions, see pp. 140-51 below.

[91]*Psychology and Religion*, p. 194.

[92]*Two Essays*, p. 300.

[93]See ibid., p. 187 (and quotation from same, p. 86 above); *The Spirit in Man, Art, and Literature*, pp. 81-82; and *Alchemical Studies*, p. 301.

[94]Note Jung's articulation of the disparity between the two in the following: "The bridge from dogma to the inner experience of the individual has broken down. Instead, dogma is 'believed'; it is hypostatized, as the Protestants hypostatize the Bible, ...Dogma no longer formulates anything, no longer expresses anything; it has become a tenet to be accepted in and for itself, with no basis in any experience that would demonstrate its truth." *Aion*, p. 178. See also Karl Rahner's discussion of the "extrinsicism" of much of the traditional Catholic understanding of the doctrine of the Trinity in his *The Trinity*, trans. Joseph Donceel (New York: Herder & Herder, 1970), pp. 10-15; as well as his critique of same in *Nature and Grace: Dilemmas in the Modern Church*, trans. Dinah Wharton (New York: Sheed & Ward, 1964), pp. 115-19.

[95]*The Spirit in Man, Art, and Literature*, p. 77.

CHAPTER V

NOTES

[1]See, for example, Gregory Baum, *Faith and Doctrine: A Contemporary View* (Paramus, N.J.: Paulist Press, 1969); Avery Dulles, *The Survival of Dogma* (Garden City, N.Y.: Doubleday & Co., 1971); Leslie Dewart, *The Future of Belief: Theism in a World Come of Age* (New York: Herder & Herder, 1966); and Karl Rahner, "The Development of Dogma" in *Theological Investigations*, vol. 1: *God, Christ, Mary and Grace*, trans. Cornelius Ernst (Baltimore: Helicon Press, 1961), pp. 39-77; "Considerations on the Development of Dogma" in *Theological Investigations*, vol. 4: *More Recent Writings*, trans. Kevin Smyth (Baltimore: Helicon Press, 1966), pp. 3-35; and "What Is a Dogmatic Statement?" in *Theological Investigations*, vol. 5: *Later Writings*, trans. Karl -H. Kruger (Baltimore: Helicon Press, 1966), pp. 42-66.

[2]*Psychology and Religion*, p. 50.

[3]"Only the man who is modern in our meaning of the term really lives in the present; ...he has become 'unhistorical' in the deepest sense and has estranged himself from the mass of men who live entirely within the bounds of tradition." *Civilization in Transition*, p. 75.

[4]*Psychology and Religion*, p. 89.

[5]For recent surveys of this discussion in Roman Catholic theology see Owen Chadwick, *From Bossuet to Newman: The Idea of Doctrinal Development* (Cambridge: Cambridge University Press, 1957); Part 3 of T. M. Schoof, *A Survey of Catholic Theology: 1800-1970*, trans. N. D. Smith (Paramus, N.J.: Paulist Press, 1970), pp. 157-227; Frederick E. Crowe, "Development of Doctrine and the Ecumenical Problem," *Theological Studies* 23 (March 1962): 27-46; and Anthony A. Stephenson, "The Development and Immutability of Christian Doctrine," *Theological Studies* 19 (December 1958): 481-532.

[6]See Karl Rahner's use of this term in "Concerning the Relationship between Nature and Grace," *Later Writings*, pp. 298-303; and *Nature and Grace*, pp. 115-19.

[7]*The Practice of Psychotherapy*, p. 160.

[8]*Psychology and Religion*, p. 161.

[9]*Psychology and Religion*, p. 194.

[10]See pp. 11-13, 16-17 and 21-23 in Chapter I above.

[11]See our discussion of Hostie and Goldbrunner, pp. 10-13 and 15-16 above.

[12]Jer. 7:23, 11:4, 24:7, 31:1, 31:33, 32:38; Ex. 6:7;
Lev. 26:12; Ezek. 11:20, 14:11, 36:28, 37:23, 37:27; Zech. 8:8.

[13]"Nearly all the wisdom we possess, that is to say, true
and sound wisdom, consists of two parts: the knowledge of God
and of ourselves. But, while joined by many bonds, which one
precedes and brings forth the other is not easy to discern. In
the first place, no one can look upon himself without immediately turning his thoughts to the contemplation of God, in whom
he 'lives and moves.' ...The knowledge of ourselves not only
arouses us to seek God, but also, as it were, leads us by the
hand to find him. Again, it is certain that man never achieves
a clear knowledge of himself unless he has first looked upon
God's face, and then descends from contemplating him to scruti-
nize himself." *Institutes of the Christian Religion*, trans.
Ford Lewis Battles (Philadelphia: Westminster Press, 1950), I,
i, 1-2; see editor's notes to same, and cf. ibid., II, i, 1.

[14]Perhaps the best summary statement of Rahner's position
is found in his "Theology and Anthropology" in T. Patrick Burke,
ed., *The Word in History* (New York: Sheed & Ward, 1966), pp. 1-
23, where he states: "As soon as man is understood as that
being which has absolute transcendence toward God (and it is
surely obvious that he is such), then anthropocentricity and
theocentricity in theology are not contradictories but strictly
one and the same thing seen from two different aspects, and
each aspect is unintelligible without the other....Speech about
God and speech about man are connected, not only from the point
of view of content, but from the point of view of knowledge itself" (pp. 1-2). See also his assertion: "...if God himself is
man and remains so for ever, if all theology is therefore
eternally an anthropology; if man is forbidden to belittle
himself, because to do so would be to belittle God; and if this
God remains the insoluble mystery, man is for ever the articulate
mystery of God." *More Recent Writings*, p. 116.

[15]Such an affirmation has found lasting expression not only
in the Chalcedonian formula, but also in the letter (449) of
Leo, Bishop of Rome, which did much to shape it: "Therefore in
the entire and perfect nature of very man was born very God,
whole in what was his, whole in what was ours....He assumed
'the form of a servant' without defilement of sin, enriching
what was human, not impairing what was divine: because that
'emptying of himself,' ...was a stooping down in compassion,
not a failure of power. Accordingly, the same who, remaining
in the form of God, made man, was made man in the form of a
servant. For each of the natures retains its proper character
without defect; ...the selfsame who is very God, is also
very man; and there is no illusion in this union, while the
lowliness of man and the loftiness of Godhead meet together."
The Seven Ecumenical Councils, vol. 14 of *A Select Library of
Nicene and Post-Nicene Fathers of the Christian Church*, Second
Series, ed. Philip Schaff and Henry Wace (New York: Charles
Scribner's Sons, 1900), pp. 255-56.

[16]Consider *Psychology and Religion*, pp. 152-63, in the
light of II Peter 1:4: "...he has granted to us his precious and
very great promises that...you may...become partakers of the

divine nature"; Irenaeus: "It was for this end that the Word
of God was made man, and He who was the Son of God became the
Son of man, that man, having been taken into the Word, and
receiving the adoption, might become the son of God.... Or how
shall man pass into God, unless God has first passed into man?
...the Word of God, our Lord Jesus Christ...did, through His
transcendent love, become what we are, that He might bring us to
be even what He is Himself" (*Against Heresies*, III.19:1,
IV.33:4, and V. preface; in *The Apostolic Fathers*, vol. 1 of
The Ante-Nicene Fathers, ed. Alexander Roberts and James
Donaldson [Grand Rapids, Mich.: Eerdmans, 1956]; and
Athanasius: "For therefore did He assume the body originate
and human, that having renewed it as its Framer, He might deify
it in Himself, and thus might introduce us all into the kingdom
of heaven after His likeness....The union was of this kind,
that He might unite what is man by nature to Him who is in the
nature of the Godhead, and his salvation and deification might
be sure" ("Second Discourse against the Arians," No. 70, in
St. Athanasius: Select Works and Letters, vol. 4 of *Nicene and
Post-Nicene Fathers*, Second Series).

[17]We wish to stress once again that it is the religious
situation of Western man to which Jung's psychology of doctrine
is first and foremost addressed. In so doing we do not thereby
intend to deny in principle its relevance to other cultures,
but only to single out the audience Jung had uppermost in mind
in devising it.

[18]*Psychology and Religion*, pp. 157, 190, 194-95, 468-69
and 580-82. See also *Two Essays*, pp. 250-52.

[19]*The Trinity*, pp. 14-15. It is worth noting here that
Rahner makes of this problem the point of departure for his
study of the Trinity; it is the major impetus that leads him to
engage in his re-interpretation. Interestingly enough, his
attempt to overcome the doctrine's disrelation to experience
proceeds by way of recovering what he contends is the original
unity between the immanent Trinity as a representation of God
Himself and the economic Trinity as a portrayal of God in
intimate relationship with man. In other words, for Rahner it
is man's inability to apprehend the intimate nature of the
divine-human conjunction that is responsible for the fact that
Christian doctrine is so often found to be extrinsic to his
experience. See ibid., pp. 21-24, 38-41, 45-48 and 99-103.

[20]*Psychological Types*, p. 603, italics added.

[21]*The Spirit in Man, Art, and Literature*, p. 136.

[22]*Symbols of Transformation*, p. 50.

[23]*The Spirit in Man, Art, and Literature*, p. 85.

[24]*Structure and Dynamics*, p. 139.

[25]Note, for example, Mircea Eliade's assertion that
"...all religious facts have a symbolic character" in "Methodological Remarks on the Study of Religious Symbolism," in

History of Religions: Essays in Methodology, ed. Mircea Eliade
and Joseph Kitagawa (Chicago: University of Chicago Press, 1959),
p. 95; and Langdon Gilkey's statement that "religious language
is thus first and foremost multivalent, or symbolic in a
special sense; ...all religious language has this multivalent
character as symbolic of a sacrality within and yet beyond the
observable world of things and people" in *Naming the Whirlwind:
The Renewal of God-Language* (Indianapolis: Bobbs-Merrill, 1969),
pp. 290-91. Cf. Karl Rahner's *ontology* of symbol, which
predicates that "...all beings are by their very nature symbolic,
because they necessarily 'express' themselves in order to attain
their own nature." *More Recent Writings*, p. 224.

[26]"Methodological Remarks on the Study of Religious
Symbolism," p. 107.

[27]*Naming the Whirlwind*, p. 269 et passim.

[28]"Methodological Remarks on the Study of Religious
Symbolism," p. 102. We would add that this in Eliade's view
represents but *one* aspect of religious symbolism, which, if
taken alone, is unable to account for its specifically religious
function--i.e., the way symbols succeed in "bursting the bonds"
of man's particularity, in opening the immediacies of his life
and history to their universal and transcendent dimension. See
ibid., p. 103.

[29]*Naming the Whirlwind*, p. 260.

[30]See, for instance, Karl Rahner, "Reflections on Methodology" and "The Experience of God Today," in *Theological Investigations*, vol. 11: *Confrontations*, trans. David Bourke (New York:
Seabury Press, 1974), pp. 68-84 and 149-65; Anne Carr, "Theology
and Experience in the Thought of Karl Rahner," *Journal of
Religion* 53 (July 1973): 359-78; Edward Schillebeeckx, "New
Trends in Present-Day Dogmatic Theology" in *Revelation and
Theology*, trans. N. D. Smith, 2 vols. (New York: Sheed & Ward,
1967-68), 2:106-54; Gilkey, *Naming the Whirlwind*, pp. 266-304
and 305-413 ("The Dimension of Ultimacy in Secular Experience");
Tracy, "The Task of Fundamental Theology," pp. 13-14 and 19-22.

[31]This is not, however, to deny the strong importance Jung
ascribes to regression, to heeding and giving in to the archaisms
of the personal and collective past. Here as elsewhere he reads
the psychic life of man dialectically; alternating shifts in
the flow of psychic energy between past and future, as well as
introverted and extraverted poles are necessary if development
is to occur. See our discussion of Jung's notion of regression,
pp. 48-49 above; and his statement on the "teleological
significance of regression" in *Freud and Psychoanalysis*, pp. 179-
80.

[32]I have distilled the skeletal notion of story presented
here from Michael Novak's reflections on its meaning: "A story
is a narrative that links sequences. A story is a structure
for time. A story links actions over time....more profoundly,
it links transformations....It unites past and future. It
supplies patterns, themes, motifs by which a person recognizes

the unity of his or her life." *Ascent of the Mountain*, pp. 49, 53 and 60.

[33]As we have already noted, John S. Dunne is one theologian who has self-consciously followed up on Jung's thinking here. For Dunne, it is precisely the phenomenon of life-story which, when brought to fullest possible awareness, serves to reveal an encompassing story of God. See pp. 31-33 above.

[34]We have borrowed this expression from Ernst Cassirer, *An Essay on Man: An Introduction to a Philosophy of Human Culture* (New Haven: Yale University Press, 1967), pp. 23 f. To propose, however, that it is as apt a designation for Jung's view of man as it is for Cassirer's is not to overlook significant disparities between each's understanding of the symbolic. Cf. Cassirer's Introduction to his *The Philosophy of Symbolic Forms*, trans. Ralph Manheim, 3 vols. (New Haven: Yale University Press, 1953-57), 1:73-114; with the notion of symbol set forth in Jung's *Psychological Types*, pp. 601-10.

[35]Note, for example, the statement with which Jung concludes his study of the Trinity: "Religion is a 'revealed' way of salvation. Its ideas are products of a pre-conscious knowledge which, always and everywhere, expresses itself in symbols. Even if our intellect does not grasp them, they still work, because our unconscious acknowledges them as exponents of universal psychic facts." *Psychology and Religion*, p. 199.

[36]See, for example, Schubert Ogden's argument that "...theology must so interpret the witness of faith as to present faith itself as the decisive answer to the religious question of mankind. This implies, in turn, that the theologian must become fully self-conscious of the structure of this religious question, by understanding in an express, thematic, and conceptually precise way both the question itself and its 'tacit presuppositions.'" "The Task of Philosophical Theology," in *The Future of Philosophical Theology*, ed. Robert A. Evans (Philadelphia: Westminster Press, 1971), p. 81. Note also David Tracy's contention that theology must make of its efforts "...to explicate a preconceptual dimension to our common shared experience that can legitimately be described as religious" a task that is differentiated from and yet ultimately correlated with "...historical and hermeneutical investigations of the Christian fact"; in "The Task of Fundamental Theology," pp. 20 and 29. Cf. Paul Tillich, *What is Religion?* ed. and with an Introduction by James Luther Adams (New York: Harper & Row, 1973); and "Religion as a Dimension in Man's Spiritual Life," in his *Theology of Culture*, pp. 3-9; John E. Smith, "The Religious Dimension of Experience and the Idea of God," in his *Experience and God* (London: Oxford University Press, 1968), pp. 46-67; and Louis Dupré, *The Other Dimension: A Search for the Meaning of Religious Attitudes* (Garden City, N.Y.: Doubleday & Co., 1972).

[37]Our own formulation here derives from key elements of the second and fifth of the (five) theses presented by David Tracy in "The Task of Fundamental Theology," pp. 16-19 and 29-34.

SELECTED BIBLIOGRAPHY

Works by Jung

The Collected Works of C. G. Jung. Editors: Sir Herbert Read, Michael Fordham, Gerhard Adler; William McGuire, executive editor. Translated by R. F. C. Hull (except vol. 6). Bollingen Series XX.

Vol. 4: *Freud and Psychoanalysis.* Princeton, N.J.: Princeton University Press, 1961.

Vol. 5: *Symbols of Transformation: An Analysis of the Prelude to a Case of Schizophrenia.* New York: Pantheon Books, 1956.

Vol. 6: *Psychological Types.* A revision by R. F. C. Hull of the translation of H. G. Baynes. Princeton, N.J.: Princeton University Press, 1971.

Vol. 8: *The Structure and Dynamics of the Psyche.* 2d ed. Princeton, N.J.: Princeton University Press, 1969.

Vol. 9, Part 1: *The Archetypes and the Collective Unconscious.* 2d ed. Princeton, N.J.: Princeton University Press, 1969.

Vol. 9, Part 2: *Aion: Researches into the Phenomenology of the Self.* 2d ed. Princeton, N.J.: Princeton University Press, 1968.

Vol. 10: *Civilization in Transition.* 2d ed. Princeton, N.J.: Princeton University Press, 1970.

Vol. 11: *Psychology and Religion: West and East.* New York: Pantheon Books, 1958.

Vol. 12: *Psychology and Alchemy.* 2d ed. Princeton, N.J.: Princeton University Press, 1968.

Vol. 13: *Alchemical Studies.* London: Routledge & Kegan Paul, 1967.

Vol. 14: *Mysterium Coniunctionis.* 2d ed. Princeton, N.J.: Princeton University Press, 1970.

Vol. 15: *The Spirit in Man, Art, and Literature.* Princeton, N.J.: Princeton University Press, 1966.

Vol. 16: *The Practice of Psychotherapy: Essays on the Psychology of the Transference and Other Subjects.* 2d ed. Princeton, N.J.: Princeton University Press, 1966.

Vol. 17: *The Development of Personality*. Princeton, N.J.: Princeton University Press, 1970.

Analytical Psychology: Its Theory and Practice, The Tavistock Lectures. Foreword by E. A. Bennet. New York: Vintage Books, 1968.

C. G. Jung: Letters. Edited by Gerhard Adler and Aniela Jaffé. Translated by R. F. C. Hull. Bollingen Series XCV:1. 2 vols. Princeton, N.J.: Princeton University Press, 1973-75. Vol. 1: *1906-1950*.

Die Dynamik des Unbewussten. Vol. 8 of *Gesammelte Werke*. Olten und Freiburg im Breisgau: Walter Verlag, 1971.

Man and His Symbols. Edited by C. G. Jung. Garden City, N.Y.: Doubleday & Co., 1964.

Memories, Dreams, Reflections. Edited by Aniela Jaffé and translated by Richard and Clara Winston. New York: Vintage Books, 1963.

Psychological Types or The Psychology of Individuation. Translated by H. Gordon Baynes. New York: Harcourt, Brace & Co., 1923.

"Religion and Psychology: A Reply to Martin Buber." In *Spring: An Annual of Archetypal Psychology and Jungian Thought* (1973), pp. 196-203.

Two Essays on Analytical Psychology. Translated by R. F. C. Hull. Cleveland: Meridian Books, 1956.

"Versuch zu einer psychologischen Deutung des Trinitätsdogmas." In *Symbolik des Geistes: Studien über Psychische Phänomenologie*. Zurich: Rascher, 1948. Pp. 321-446.

Works about Jung

Jung and Religion

Altizer, Thomas J. J. "A Critical Analysis of C. G. Jung's Understanding of Religion." Ph.D. dissertation, University of Chicago, 1955.

Beirnaert, Louis. "Jung et Freud au regard de la foi Chrétienne." *Dieu Vivant* 26 (1954): 95-100.

Bockus, Frank. "The Self and Christ: A Study of Carl Jung's Psychology of the Self and Its Bearing on Christology." Ph.D. dissertation, University of Chicago, 1964.

Brooks, Henry Curtis. "Analytical Psychology and the Image of God." *Andover Newton Quarterly* 6 (November 1965): 35-55.

Buber, Martin. *Eclipse of God: Studies in the Relation between Religion and Philosophy*. New York: Harper & Row, 1952.

Cox, David. *Jung and St. Paul: A Study of the Doctrine of Justification by Faith and Its Relation to the Concept of Individuation.* London: Longmans, Green & Co., 1959.

Dawson, Eugene Ellsworth. "The Religious Implications of Jung's Psychology." Ph.D. dissertation, Boston University, 1949.

Dunne, John S. *A Search for God in Time and Memory.* London: Collier-Macmillan, 1969.

Frischknecht, Max. *Die Religion in der Psychologie C. G. Jungs.* Bern: Paul Haupt, 1945.

Hanna, Charles. *The Face of the Deep: The Religious Ideas of C. G. Jung.* Philadelphia: Westminster Press, 1967.

Heisig, James W. "Jung and the *Imago Dei*: The Future of an Idea." *Journal of Religion* 56 (January 1976): 88-104.

_____. "Jung and Theology: A Bibliographical Essay." In *Spring: An Annual of Archetypal Psychology and Jungian Thought* (1973), pp. 204-55.

Homans, Peter. "Psychology and Hermeneutics: Jung's Contribution." *ZYGON/Journal of Religion and Science* 4 (December 1969): 333-55.

Hostie, Raymond. *Religion and the Psychology of C. G. Jung.* Translated by G. R. Lamb. New York: Sheed & Ward, 1957.

Leonard, Augustin. "La Psychologie religieuse de Jung." *Supplément de la Vie Spirituelle* 5 (September 1951): 325-34.

Michaëlis, Edgar. "Le Livre de Job interprété par C. G. Jung." *Revue de Théologie et de Philosophie* 3 (1953): 183-95.

Moreno, Antonio. *Jung, Gods, and Modern Man.* Notre Dame, Ind.: University of Notre Dame Press, 1970.

Noel, Daniel C. "Still Reading His Will? Problems and Resources for the Death-of-God Theology." *Journal of Religion* 46 (October 1966): 463-76.

Philp, Howard L. *Jung and the Problem of Evil.* London: Salisbury Square, 1958.

Schaer, Hans. *Religion and the Cure of Souls in Jung's Psychology.* Translated by R. F. C. Hull. Bollingen Series XXI. New York: Pantheon Books, 1950.

Spicer, Malcolm. "La Trinité: Essai sur Jung." *Studies in Religion/Sciences Religieuses* 3 (1973/4): 299-319.

Ulanov, Ann Belford. *The Feminine in Jungian Psychology and in Christian Theology.* Evanston: Northwestern University Press, 1971.

White, Victor. "Can a Psychologist Be Religious?" *Commonweal*
      58 (September 1953): 583-84.

_____. *God and the Unconscious*. Foreword by C. G. Jung.
      Cleveland: Meridian Books, 1952/61.

_____. *Soul and Psyche: An Enquiry into the Relationship
      of Psychotherapy and Religion*. London: Collins, 1960.

_____. "Jung and the Supernatural." *Commonweal* 55 (March
      1952): 561-62.

Other

Adler, Gerhard. "A Psychological Approach to Religion." In
      his *Studies in Analytical Psychology*. New York: G. P.
      Putnam's Sons, 1966. Pp. 176-216.

Analytical Psychology Club of New York. *Carl Gustav Jung,
      1875-1961: A Memorial Meeting*. New York: Analytical
      Psychology Club of New York, 1962.

Fordham, Frieda. *An Introduction to Jung's Psychology*. 3rd
      ed. Harmondsworth, England: Penguin Books, 1966.

Goldbrunner, Joseph. *Individuation: A Study of the Depth
      Psychology of Carl Gustav Jung*. Translated by Stanley
      Godman. Notre Dame, Ind.: University of Notre Dame
      Press, 1964.

Jacobi, Jolande. *Complex, Archetype, Symbol in the Psychology
      of C. G. Jung*. Translated by Ralph Manheim with a Foreword
      by C. G. Jung. Princeton, N.J.: Princeton University
      Press, 1959.

_____. *The Psychology of C. G. Jung*. Translated by
      Ralph Manheim. New Haven: Yale University Press, 1962.

Jaffé, Aniela. *The Myth of Meaning in the Work of C. G. Jung*.
      Translated by R. F. C. Hull. London: Hodder & Stoughton,
      1970.

Philipson, Morris. *Outline of a Jungian Aesthetics*. Evanston:
      Northwestern University Press, 1963.

Progoff, Ira. *Jung's Psychology and Its Social Meaning*. Garden
      City, N.Y.: Anchor Press/Doubleday, 1973.

Ricketts, Mac Linscott. "The Nature and Extent of Eliade's
      'Jungianism.'" *Union Seminary Quarterly Review* 25 (Winter
      1970): 211-34.

Singer, June. *Boundaries of the Soul: The Practice of Jung's
      Psychology*. Garden City, N.Y.: Doubleday & Co., 1972.

Background Works

Hermeneutics and Symbolism

Cassirer, Ernst. *The Philosophy of Symbolic Forms*. Vol. 1:
    Language. Translated by Ralph Manheim. Preface and
    Introduction by Charles W. Hendel. New Haven: Yale
    University Press, 1953. Vol. 2: *Mythical Thought*. Trans-
    lated by Ralph Manheim. Introductory note by Charles W.
    Hendel. New Haven: Yale University Press, 1955.

Dillistone, F. W., ed. *Myth and Symbol*. Theological Collec-
    tions, vol. 7. London: S.P.C.K., 1966.

Durand, Gilbert. *L'Imagination symbolique*. 2d ed. Paris:
    Presses Universitaires de France, 1968.

Eliade, Mircea. *Images and Symbols: Studies in Religious
    Symbolism*. Translated by Philip Mairet. New York: Sheed
    & Ward, 1969.

_____. "Methodological Remarks on the Study of Religious
    Symbolism." In *History of Religions: Essays in Methodology*.
    Edited by Mircea Eliade and Joseph Kitagawa. Chicago:
    University of Chicago Press, 1959. Pp. 86-107.

Funk, Robert W. *Language, Hermeneutic and the Word of God: The
    Problem of Language in the New Testament and Contemporary
    Theology*. New York: Harper & Row, 1966.

Homans, Peter. "Psychology and Hermeneutics: An Exploration of
    Basic Issues and Resources." *Journal of Religion* 55
    (July 1975): 327-47.

Lonergan, Bernard J. F. "The Truth of Interpretation." In
    Insight: A Study of Human Understanding. Rev. ed. London:
    Longmans, Green & Co., 1958. Pp. 562-94.

Long, Charles. "Archaism and Hermeneutics." In *The History of
    Religions: Essays on the Problem of Understanding*. Edited
    by Joseph M. Kitagawa. Vol. 1 of *Essays in Divinity*.
    Edited by Jerald C. Brauer. Chicago: University of Chicago
    Press, 1967. Pp. 67-87.

Merleau-Ponty, Maurice. "On the Phenomenology of Language."
    In *Signs*. Translated and with an Introduction by Richard
    McCleary. Northwestern University Studies in Phenomenology
    and Existential Philosophy. Evanston: Northwestern Univer-
    sity Press, 1964. Pp. 84-97.

Novak, Michael. "Culture and Imagination." In *Philosophy of
    Religion and Theology: 1972--Working Papers Read to the
    Philosophy of Religion and Theology Section, American Acad-
    emy of Religion Annual Meeting 1972*. David Griffin, Chair-
    man. Chambersburg, Pa.: American Academy of Religion,
    1972. Pp. 54-63.

Palmer, Richard E. *Hermeneutics: Interpretation Theory in Schleiermacher, Dilthey, Heidegger, and Gadamer*. Northwestern University Studies in Phenomenology and Existential Philosophy. Evanston: Northwestern University Press, 1969.

Ricoeur, Paul. *The Conflict of Interpretations: Essays in Hermeneutics*. Edited by Don Ihde. Northwestern University Studies in Phenomenology and Existential Philosophy. Evanston: Northwestern University Press, 1974.

_____. *Freud and Philosophy: An Essay on Interpretation*. Translated by Denis Savage. New Haven: Yale University Press, 1970.

_____. "Philosophy and Religious Language." *Journal of Religion* 54 (January 1974): 71-85.

_____. *Symbolism of Evil*. Translated by Emerson Buchanan. Boston: Beacon Press, 1969.

Robinson, James M., and Cobb, John B., Jr., eds. *The New Hermeneutic*. New Frontiers in Theology, vol. 2. New York: Harper & Row, 1964.

Underwood, Richard A. "Hermes and Hermeneutics: A Viewing from the Perspective of the Death of God and Depth Psychology." *Hartford Quarterly* 6 (Fall 1965): 34-53.

Depth Psychology

Ellenberger, Henri F. *The Discovery of the Unconscious: The History and Evolution of Dynamic Psychiatry*. New York: Basic Books, 1970.

Erikson, Erik H. "The First Psychoanalyst." In *Insight and Responsibility: Lectures on the Ethical Implications of Psychoanalytic Insight*. New York: W. W. Norton & Co., 1964. Pp. 19-46.

Freud, Sigmund. *An Autobiographical Study*. Translated by James Strachey. New York: W.W. Norton & Co., 1952.

_____. *Civilization and Its Discontents*. Translated by Joan Riviere. Garden City, N.Y.: Doubleday & Co., 1958.

_____. *The Future of an Illusion*. Translated by W. D. Robson-Scott and edited by James Strachey. Garden City, N.Y.: Doubleday & Co., 1964.

_____. *The Interpretation of Dreams*. Translated and edited by James Strachey. New York: Avon Books, 1965.

_____. *An Outline of Psychoanalysis*. Translated by James Strachey. New York: W.W. Norton & Co., 1949.

Glover, Edward. *Freud or Jung*. London: George Allen & Unwin, 1950.

Hall, Calvin S., and Lindzey, Gardner. *Theories of Personality*. New York: John Wiley & Sons, 1957.

Ricoeur, Paul. "The Unconscious." In *Freedom and Nature: The Voluntary and the Involuntary*. Translated by Erazim V. Kohák. Northwestern University Studies in Phenomenology and Existential Philosophy. Evanston: Northwestern University Press, 1966. Pp. 373-409.

Rieff, Philip. *The Triumph of the Therapeutic: Uses of Faith after Freud*. New York: Harper & Row, 1966.

Walters, Orville S. "Theology and the Changing Concepts of the Unconscious." *Religion and Life* 37 (Spring 1968): 112-28.

Whyte, Lancelot Law. *The Unconscious before Freud*. With a Foreword by Edith Sitwell. London: Social Science Paperbacks/Tavistock Publications, 1967.

Wyss, Dieter. *Depth Psychology: A Critical History--Development, Problems, Crises*. Translated by Gerald Onn. New York: W.W. Norton & Co., 1966.

Theological Method

Davis, Charles. "The Reconvergence of Theology and Religious Studies." *Studies in Religion / Sciences Religieuses* 4 (1974/5): 205-21.

Gilkey, Langdon. *Naming the Whirlwind: The Renewal of God-Language*. Indianapolis: Bobbs-Merrill, 1969.

Homans, Peter. *Theology after Freud: An Interpretive Inquiry*. Indianapolis: Bobbs-Merrill, 1970.

Lindbeck, George A. "Theological Revolutions and the Present Crisis." *Theology Digest* 23 (Winter 1975): 308-19.

Lonergan, Bernard J. F. *Method in Theology*. New York: Herder & Herder, 1972.

Macquarrie, John. *God-Talk: An Examination of the Language and Logic of Theology*. London: SCM Press, 1967.

McShane, Philip, ed. *Foundations of Theology: Papers from the International Lonergan Congress 1970*. Dublin: Gill & Macmillan, 1971.

Ogden, Schubert. "What Is Theology?" *Journal of Religion* 52 (January 1972): 22-40.

Rahner, Karl. *Hearers of the Word*. Translated by Michael Richards. New York: Herder & Herder, 1969.

_____. *Theological Investigations*. Vol. 9: *Writings of 1965-1967 I*. Translated by Graham Harrison. New York: Herder & Herder, 1972. Vol. 11: *Confrontations*. Translated by David Bourke. New York: Seabury Press, 1974.

Smith, John E. *Experience and God*. London: Oxford University
     Press, 1968.

Tillich, Paul. "Introduction." In *Systematic Theology*, three
     volumes in one. New York: Harper & Row and University of
     Chicago Press, 1967. 1:3-68.

Tracy, David. "The Task of Fundamental Theology." *Journal of
     Religion* 54 (January 1974): 13-34.

Christian Doctrine

Baum, Gregory. *Faith and Doctrine: A Contemporary View*.
     Paramus, N.J.: Paulist Press, 1969.

Crowe, Frederick E. "Development of Doctrine and the Ecumeni-
     cal Problem." *Theological Studies* 23 (March 1962): 27-46.

Dulles, Avery. *The Survival of Dogma*. Garden City, N.Y.:
     Doubleday & Co., 1971.

Rahner, Karl. *Theological Investigations*. Vol. 1: *God, Christ,
     Mary and Grace*. Translated by Cornelius Ernst. Baltimore:
     Helicon Press, 1961. Vol. 4: *More Recent Writings*. Trans-
     lated by Kevin Smyth. Baltimore: Helicon Press, 1966.
     Vol. 5: *Later Writings*. Translated by Karl -H. Kruger.
     Baltimore: Helicon Press, 1966.

_____. *The Trinity*. Translated by Joseph Donceel. New
     York: Herder & Herder, 1970.

Rahner, Karl and Pozo, Candido. "Dogma: The Theological Meaning
     of." In *Encyclopedia of Theology: The Concise Sacramentum
     Mundi*. Edited by Karl Rahner. New York: Seabury Press,
     1975. Pp. 352-70.

Schillebeeckx, Edward. "New Trends in Present-Day Dogmatic
     Theology." In *Revelation and Theology*. Translated by
     N. D. Smith. 2 vols. New York: Sheed & Ward, 1967-68.
     2: 106-54.

Schoof, T. M. *A Survey of Catholic Theology: 1800-1970*.
     Translated by N. D. Smith. Paramus, N.J.: Paulist Press,
     1970.

Stephenson, Anthony A. "The Development and Immutability of
     Christian Doctrine." *Theological Studies* 19 (December
     1958): 481-532.

Psychology and Religion

Campbell, Joseph. *The Masks of God*. Vol. 1: *Primitive Mythol-
     ogy*. New York: Viking Press, 1970.

Fromm, Erich. *Psychoanalysis and Religion*. New Haven: Yale
     University Press, 1950.

Hillman, James. *Insearch: Psychology and Religion*. New York: Charles Scribner's Sons, 1967.

_____. *The Myth of Analysis: Three Essays in Archetypal Psychology*. Studies in Jungian Thought. Evanston: Northwestern University Press, 1972.

Homans, Peter, ed. *The Dialogue between Theology and Psychology*. Vol. 3 of *Essays in Divinity*. Edited by Jerald C. Brauer. Chicago: University of Chicago Press, 1968.

Miller, David L. "Polytheism and Archetypal Theology: A Discussion." *Journal of the American Academy of Religion* 40 (December 1972): 513-20.

Otto, Rudolf. *The Idea of the Holy. An Inquiry into the Non-Rational Factor in the Idea of the Divine and Its Relation to the Rational*. Translated by John W. Harvey. New York: Oxford University Press, 1958.

Tillich, Paul. "The Impact of Pastoral Psychology on Theological Thought." *Pastoral Psychology* 11 (February 1960): 17-23.

Other

Baum, Gregory. *Man Becoming: God in Secular Language*. New York: Herder & Herder, 1970.

Crossan, John Dominic. *The Dark Interval: Towards a Theology of Story*. Niles, Ill.: Argus Communications, 1975.

Dunne, John S. *The Way of All the Earth: Experiments in Truth and Religion*. New York: Macmillan Co., 1972.

Dupré, Louis. *The Other Dimension: A Search for the Meaning of Religious Attitudes*. Garden City, N.Y.: Doubleday & Co., 1972.

Eliade, Mircea. *The Quest: History and Meaning in Religion*. Chicago: University of Chicago Press, 1969.

Novak, Michael. *Ascent of the Mountain, Flight of the Dove: An Invitation to Religious Studies*. New York: Harper & Row, 1971.

Tillich, Paul. *Dynamics of Faith*. New York: Harper & Row, 1958.

_____. *Theology of Culture*. Edited by Robert C. Kimball. London: Oxford University Press, 1959.

AUTHOR INDEX

Athanasius, 199 n.16
Bockus, Frank, 27-28, 31, 33-34, 35
Buber, Martin, 16-17, 18, 19, 20, 22, 23, 35
Calvin, John, 151, 198 n.13
Cassirer, Ernst, 201 n.34
Dunne, John S., 27, 31-34, 35, 201 n.33
Durand, Gilbert, 177 n.8, 178 n.19
Eliade, Mircea, 156, 157, 199 n.25, 200 n.28
Feuerbach, Ludwig, 17, 150
Freud, Sigmund, 1-2, 14, 45, 73, 75-76, 85, 175 n.76
Gilkey, Langdon, 156-58
Goldbrunner, Joseph, 15-16
Hanna, Charles B., 26, 33
Heisig, James, 2, 171 n.1
Homans, Peter, 169 n.6, 171 n.15, 182-83 n.99, 185 n.9
Hostie, Raymond, 10-14, 17, 18, 20, 22, 23, 26, 35, 36
Irenaeus, 199 n.16
Jacobi, Jolande, 182 n.89, 190 n.72
Koepgen, Georg, 121
Leo, Bishop of Rome, 198 n.15
Lonergan, Bernard, 187 n.40
Lüdemann, Hermann, 25
Novak, Michael, 200-1 n.32
Ogden, Schubert, 201 n.36
Pelikan, Jaroslav, 192 n.20
Philp, Howard L., 14-15, 16, 17, 23, 25, 193 n.35
Plato, 111, 112, 113
Pythagorus, 112, 113
Rahner, Karl, 151, 153, 196 n.94, 197 n.6, 200 n.25
Ricoeur, Paul, 178 n.15, 182-83 n.99, 185 n.13, 190 n.78,
   193-94 n.48
Schaer, Hans, 23-25, 26, 33, 34-35
Schleiermacher, Friedrich, 25, 27
Tillich, Paul, 27, 28-31, 33-34, 35
Tracy, David, 201 n.36-37
Vincent of Lérins, 192 n.18
White, Victor, 20-23, 25, 35

depth dimension of human existence, 105, 143, 144, 156,
  175 n.89. *See also* depth of
  meaning; psychology, depth
depth of meaning, 132, 143;
  in doctrine, 133-35, 143-
  44, 146, 147-48, 152, 155
  (*see also* doctrine, symbolic nature of); in fantasy, 61, 66, 91, 92, 96,
  133-35 (*see also* fantasy,
  symbolic nature of); inherent in psychic life, 41,
  59, 62, 72, 105, 147, 152,
  156, 160, 162 (*see also*
  meaning, symbolic dimen-
  sions(s) of, in psychic
  life). *See also* meaning,
  abundance of; meaning,
  multivalent; meaning,
  symbolic
despiritualization, 65, 100,
  107
differentiation: of consciousness, 121; role of, in
  Jung's method, 69
displacement, 118-19, 135-37
dissociation, 48
divinization, 120-21, 151,
  199 n.16
doctrine: communicative power
  of, 3, 121, 143-44; depth
  of meaning of, 130, 133-35,
  143-44, 146, 147-48, 152,
  155; development of, 143,
  146-47; dialectic between
  experience and, 21, 105-8,
  122, 130, 143, 145-48, 196
  n.94; and dogma, 103-4,
  192 n.20; extrinsicism of,
  148, 153, 196 n.94, 199
  n.19; fixity of form of,
  103, 105, 106, 128, 130,
  145-46, 148; historical
  context of, 114-15, 123-24;
  interpretation of (*see* doc-
  trine--Jung's interpretation of; hermeneutic(s)--
  Jung's, of doctrine; theology, and doctrinal interpretation); Jung's notion
  of, 103-4, 192 n.18; Jung's
  psychology of, 3-4, 5, 110,
  122, 129, 151, 199 n.17
  (*see also* Trinity, Jung's
  psychologization of);
  Jung's special interest in,
  4, 104, 107-9; psychic
  meaning of, 115, 117, 119,

doctrine (*Continued*)
  131, 134, 141, 142-44, 150,
  155; symbolic nature of, 7,
  12, 139, 143, 148, 155, 165;
  transforming power of, 124;
  universal meaning of, 114,
  115, 117, 123-24, 131.
  See also Trinity
doctrine--Jung's interpretation
  of, 3-4, 97, 106, 107, 134,
  136; as anthropologization,
  149, 150, 154 (*see also*
  Trinity, as portrayal of
  man); compared to Jung's
  interpretation of fantasy,
  132-37; as de-construction,
  107; as iconoclastic, 107,
  124; as psychologization,
  116-17, 122, 131, 134, 135,
  149; as re-construction,
  107, 122, 124, 126, 127-29,
  146-47; as re-interpretation, 107, 109, 146. *See
  also* interpretive work--
  Jung's; method(s) of inter-
  pretation--Jung's; psychology of doctrine, Jung's
dogma: and doctrine, 103-4,
  192 n.20; mystery of, 11-12
dream(s), 62, 77, 80, 128, 185
  n.6, 187 n.43; associations,
  77, 80; compensatory function of, 46, 67; Jung's
  interpretation of, 77-84.
  See also fantasy
ego, 44
empirical standpoint/method,
  11, 14-15, 17-18, 22
estrangement. *See* alienation
ethics. *See* interpretation,
  as ethical task
evil, 32, 124, 126, 193 n.35;
  Jung's critique of Christian
  view of, 21. *See also*
  demonic
experience, 155, 156-58, 159,
  160; dialectic between doctrine and, 21, 105-8, 122,
  130, 143, 145-48, 196 n.94;
  of fantasy, 66, 67, 70, 84;
  as inherently symbolic, 155;
  Jung's life- (*see* life-
  story--Jung's); psyche as
  ground of, 155; psychic, 21,
  98, 155; religious, 24-25,
  32, 105, 106, 158, 201 n.36;
  role symbols play in, 156-
  57; secular, 163, 164, 165;
  as source for theological
  reflection, 158, 201 n.36

interpretation (*Continued*)
88; 186 n.27; field of, 60-
62; of dreams, 77-84; of
fantasy (*see* fantasy, Jung's
interpretation of); role of,
in personal growth, 66-71;
of self, 91. *See also* her-
meneutic(s); interpretive
work--Jung's; method(s) of
interpretation; method(s)
of interpretation--Jung's
interpretive context, 59, 62-
63, 65, 86, 89, 110-11,
133-34
interpretive process, 71, 72,
84-88, 90, 93, 96, 110-11,
131, 132-37, 138, 187 n.39
interpretive work--Jung's, 5,
71, 136-37; methodological
underpinnings of, 5, 6, 36,
59, 131; three components
of, 84, 89, 92-93, 131, 132;
two domains of, 5, 132-37;
unity of, 5, 37, 97, 132,
133, 134-35, 136-37. *See
also* doctrine--Jung's interpretation of; fantasy,
Jung's interpretation of;
hermeneutic(s)--Jung's;
method(s) of interpretation
--Jung's
libido. *See* psychic energy
life-story, 31, 32-33, 94, 133,
134, 148, 158, 159-60, 162,
200-1 n.32-33; distinction
between personal and collective, 136; Dunne's reflections on, 31-33
life-story--Jung's, 31-32, 63,
69, 98-99, 108-9; role of
Church in, 108-9, 110; role
of clinical experience in,
63, 71
man: as *animal symbolicum*, 161,
201 n.34; archaic heritage
of (*see* collective, past;
collective, world of imagery); depth psychology's
view of, 29, 30; as *homo
religiosus*, 25, 161; images
of God as images of, 23,
151-52; modern (*see* modern
man/modernity); mystery of
God as mystery of, 121, 150-
53, 198 n.14; religious dimension of, 2, 25, 161-62,
163, 164, 201 n.36; Trinity
as portrayal of, 120-21, 150-
52; Western (*see* Western man).

man (*Continued*)
See also human becoming; human nature; human subject
materiality: depreciation of,
113, 127
meaning, 95, 115, 144, 156,
182 n.89; abundance of, 41,
92, 96, 121, 135, 138, 139,
147, 148; archaic/collec-
tive world of, 86, 134 (*see
also* collective, past; collective, world of imagery);
archetypal ground of, 115,
123, 131, 132; depth of
(*see* depth of meaning);
discovery of new, 135; distinction between personal
and collective worlds of,
87, 111, 136, 138 (*see also*
collective, distinction between personal and ___ contexts); expansion of, 84,
88, 91, 134; felt, 156;
fusion of worlds of, 136,
137-38; multivalent, 93,
94, 165, 166; personal
world of, 134; prospective,
53-54, 56, 93; psychic, 15,
117, 119, 134, 141, 142-43,
155, 165, 166 (*see also*
doctrine, psychic meaning
of); restoration of, 94;
symbolic, 5, 7, 29, 136,
138, 155-56, 163, 166, 167;
symbolic dimension(s) of,
in psychic life, 15, 41,
57, 59, 94, 135, 154-55,
160, 161, 162, 165, 166
(*see also* depth of meaning,
inherent in psychic life;
universal patterns of, 87,
114, 115, 116, 117, 123-24,
131
mediation. *See* religion, and
mediation; symbol(s), as
mediators between language
and experience; symbol(s),
as mediators between the unconscious and consciousness
metaphysics, 15, 119
metaphysical neutrality, 18,
194 n.59
method(s), 19-20, 35-36, 71-72,
89, 94, 139, 187 n.40;
Lonergan's notion of, 187
n.40; phenomenological, 18,
27 (*see also* phenomenology
of religion). *See also*

symbol(s) (*Continued*)
  archetypes and, 175 n.74;
  distinction between signifier and signified in, 39,
  40, 177 n.8; distinction
  between signs and, 28, 40-
  41, 53, 73-74, 75; distinction between symptoms and,
  74; existential value of,
  157; as expressive of a
  depth of meaning, 41, 92,
  156 (*see also* depth of
  meaning); formation of,
  55, 157, 182 n.90; as
  issue in contemporary
  theology, 7; Jung's notion
  of, 28-29, 37-40, 42, 60,
  61-62, 72, 74, 92-93, 156,
  182 n.89, 201 n.34; Jung's
  psychology of, 52, 56; as
  mediators between language
  and experience, 157; as
  mediators between the unconscious and consciousness, 41-42, 51-53, 55, 72,
  182 n.89-90; prospective
  meaning of, 53-54, 56, 93;
  as reconcilers of psychic
  conflicts, 50-52; role of,
  in personal development, 29,
  42, 50-56, 72, 74, 156, 157;
  tension built into structure
  of, 40, 178 n.15; as thema-
  tizations of felt experience,
  156-57; as transformers of
  psychic energy, 50, 53, 54,
  72; unconscious origin of,
  41, 72, 156, 178 n.25, 182
  n.90; as unifiers of psychic
  opposites, 51-52; the "as
  yet unknown" nature of that
  which is symbolized by, 37-
  38, 39-40, 52, 55-56, 73
symbolic, 94, 155, 158, 161,
  163, 166, 201 n.34; attitude,
  61, 72; dimension(s) of meaning inherent in psychic life,
  15, 41, 57, 59, 94, 135, 154-
  55, 160, 161, 162, 165, 166
  (*see also* depth of meaning,
  inherent in psychic life);
  human experience as inherently, 155; the ___, as interpretive principle, 23, 60, 62,
  72, 150, 154; ___ knowing as
  related to personal becoming,
  56-57, 95, 161; man, as ___
  animal, 161, 201 n.34; meaning, 5, 7, 29, 136, 138,

symbolic (*Continued*)
  155-56, 163, 166, 167 (*see
  also* depth of meaning; meaning, abundance of); method,
  18, 73, 75, 92, 160; nature
  of doctrine, 7, 12, 139,
  143, 148, 155, 165 (*see
  also* doctrine, depth of
  meaning of); nature of fantasy, 61, 72, 92-93, 94,
  138, 139 (*see also* fantasy,
  depth of meaning of); relation between the hermeneutical and the ___, 93-94,
  163, 166; relation between
  the psychic and the ___,
  154-55, 161, 188 n.48; religious phenomena as inherently ___, 7, 155-56, 161, 163,
  166, 199-200 n.25, 201 n.35;
  standpoint, 61, 73, 154
symbolics of fantasy, 72, 92,
  94
symbolism--religious, 28, 157,
  200 n.28
symptom(s), 74
synthetic method, 73, 74, 75,
  81
teleological/teleology, 159,
  161, 200 n.31
theism/theistic, 17, 162, 164
theological: appropriation of
  Jung, 10, 20, 23, 25, 26,
  27, 30, 31, 33-34, 35; col-
  laboration/dialogue with
  Jung, 2, 3, 4, 6, 7, 13,
  19, 20-21, 23-25, 26, 27,
  35; commentary on Jung, 1,
  7, 9-10, 19, 20, 23, 26,
  31, 34; Jung as ___ re-
  source, 7, 10, 21, 27, 28,
  30, 31, 32, 33-34, 139, 141-
  42, 148, 154, 158, 165-66;
  Jung's use of ___ categories, 120, 121; method (*see
  method(s)--theological;
  styles of reading Jung, 1,
  9, 10, 13-14, 16, 22, 23,
  25, 26, 27, 31, 33-36
theology: and biblical studies,
  164; of culture, 33; and
  doctrinal interpretation,
  142-48, 154, 163, 165; experience as source for, 158,
  201 n.36; and hermeneutics,
  36, 162-67; as inherently
  hermeneutical, 36, 163;
  Jung's infringement on terrain of, 11-13, 14-15, 16,

INDEX OF JUNG QUOTATIONS

(Page numbers on the left side of the column refer to works by Jung; those on the right side refer to the text above.)